Moments of Grace and Spiritual Warfare

in

The Lord of the Rings

Anne Marie Gazzolo

WestBow
PRESS
A DIVISION OF THOMAS NELSON

ISBN: 978-1-4497-6968-0 (sc)
ISBN: 978-1-4497-6967-3 (e)

Library of Congress Control Number: 2012918284

WestBow Press books may be ordered through booksellers or by contacting:

WestBow Press
A Division of Thomas Nelson
1663 Liberty Drive
Bloomington, IN 47403
www.westbowpress.com
1-(866) 928-1240

Printed in the United States of America

WestBow Press rev. date: 10/8/2012

To J. R. R. Tolkien,
Frodo Baggins, Sam Gamgee,
and Aragorn, son of Arathorn,
who have taught me so much by word and example.
Eglerio!

To my father,
who said the day I was published
would be the happiest day of his life.
Welcome to that day!

To C. S. Lewis,
without whose support
the tale of the War of the Ring
may never have been finished
to the great loss of all the world.

Most of all,
to the Writer of the Story.

"I'm glad you are here with me."

Finally, brothers, fill your minds with
everything that is true,
everything that is noble,
everything that is good and pure,
everything that we love and honor,
and everything that can be thought virtuous or worthy of praise.

- Phil. 4:8

Lord, God Almighty, I owe You,
as the chief duty of my life,
the devotion of all my words and thoughts.
I pray for the gift of Your help and compassion,
that the breath of Your Spirit may fill the sails of my faith,
and a favoring wind will be sent to forward
me on my voyage of instruction.
We shall bring an untiring energy
and we shall seek entrance at every gate of hidden knowledge,
but it is Yours to answer prayer,
to grant the thing we seek,
to open the door on which we knock.
Our minds are born with dull and clouded vision,
our feeble intellect is penned within the barriers
of an impassible ignorance concerning things divine.
We look to You that we may take words
in the sense in which they were written
and assign the right shade of meaning to every utterance.
Grant us therefore
precision of language,
soundness of argument,
grace of style
and loyalty to the truth.

- St. Hilary of Poitiers

Contents

Preface

J. R. R. Tolkien mentioned more than once that he felt he was not so much inventing *The Lord of the Rings* as he was discovering it (*Letters of J. R. R. Tolkien*, 104, 211-212, 230). To align with this recurring sense, my book speaks from inside the tales as those in it perceive God, the Writer of the Story (*Letters*, 253), guiding events, rather than from outside as an Oxford professor penned them. For the most part, it uses the latter end of the Third Age as the present, and so referenced Biblical and other events are set far in the future rather than millennia in the past. It assumes that the reader is already familiar with the Red Book. It would be helpful also to have read the first two portions of *The Silmarillion*, which speak of the Great Music of creation and describe the angelic Valar and Maiar.

Edmund Fuller remarked that *The Lord of the Rings* "gives joy, excitement, a lift of spirits, and it contains the kind of wisdom and insight which, if applied to the world we inhabit, might help our sore-beset race to hang on through the present shadows of modern Mordor into yet another age" ("Lord of the Hobbits," *Tolkien and the Critics*, 39).

It is my hope that you will find inspiration within these pages to apply to your life.

Acknowledgments

In a marvelous book called *Love Your Life*, Victoria Osteen started her acknowledgments page in a way that is my experience as well: "The experience of writing this book has stretched me and helped me to grow in so many ways. The truth is, though, it is only through God's grace and the people He put in my life that this book became a reality."

My most hearty cries of *Eglerio!* go to:

My mother, who wanted to know how I was growing spiritually. As I could not adequately express myself with the spoken word, I hope this will help speak for me. Thank you for celebrating my achievements!

Ashley Harrison, who taught me so much about grammar and helped with editing. *Le hannon, mellon nîn!* If Frodo would not have got far without his Sam, I certainly would not have got far without you! This book would not shine anywhere so bright, or I grow as much a writer, without you. I am sure that Gandalf would agree that it was meant to be. I send you many, many hobbity hugs and all the mushrooms that you will ever want! *Melinyel!*

Elisabeth Wolfe, who edited this book, gave me insights into the tale that I had not had before, and provided me with a second set of eyes. *Le hannon!*

Amber Cuadra, who I also send a huge share of hugs and mushrooms, in gratitude for all your prayers, friendship, excitement, and support through this whole endeavor. *Melinyel*, dearest!

Peter Jackson, Elijah Wood, Sean Astin, and everyone else, who changed my life. If it were not for you, I would have not met Mr. Underhill and his Sam or any of the other wonderful people from the Third Age or this present one. I would not be the person I am today, and I thank you from the bottom of my heart!

Jef Murray, who provided the lovely cover art and supported me in other ways as well. You are one of those Elrond spoke of when he said the Company would have friends unlooked for on their journey.

Margaret Watkins, who designed the cover so beautifully. Many hobbity hugs and much love, my dear!

My sisters, brother-in-law, and uncle, who I give thanks for loving me.

My nephews and nieces, Joseph, Margaret, Peter, Bernadette, John Paul (Merry), Dominic (Sam), Joan (Pippinsqueak), and Elizabeth (Rosie), who allow me to be the greatest thing in the world: their aunt. You are wonderful lights in my life and a joy to be around. Much hobbity love and hugs from your Frodo!

My fellow travelers down the Road, who I am indebted to having deepened my understanding of the marvelous world and peoples of Middle-earth. You will find some of their wisdom sprinkled through these pages. I hope this encourages you to seek them out and absorb much else.

Last, but certainly not least, my friends at the office and elsewhere, who have supported me and my writing so enthusiastically. Great thanks, hugs, and love. You guys rock!

Introduction

I offer You, Lord, . . . my sufferings:
to be endured for Your greater glory.
I want to do what You ask of me:
in the way You ask,
for as long as You ask,
because You ask it.
I pray, Lord, that You
enlighten my mind,
inflame my will,
purify my heart,
and sanctify my soul. (Pope Clement XI)

Teach me, good Lord,
to serve You as You deserve,
to give and not to count the cost,
to fight and not to heed the wounds,
to toil and not to seek for rest,
to labor and not to ask for any reward,
except that of knowing that I do Your will. (St. Ignatius of Loyola)

It may seem odd to open a book concerned mainly with the end of the Third Age of Middle-earth with two quotes closer to our own. But even though these words are from millennia after the War of the Ring, those who fight against Sauron could have also spoken them, and they actually do through their actions. The most important battles of that time and the years before do not occur on fields but in souls. Hobbits, Elves, Men, and Dwarves contend not just against the rising Shadow but also with their own fears and desires. The greatest lessons are of self-sacrificial love and docility to the will of God, or Ilúvatar as He is known in Middle-earth, "'that one ever-present Person who is never absent and never named'" (*Letters*, 253).

Joseph Pearce notes that even though those in Middle-earth "have a knowledge of God that is less complete than that which has been revealed to the Christian world, the God who is dimly discerned in Middle Earth is nonetheless the same God as the One worshipped by Tolkien himself. The God of Earth and the God of Middle Earth are One" (*Tolkien: Man and Myth*, 110). Gandalf, Aragorn, and the Elves are the most aware of His presence in their lives. The hobbits belong to a people, who, as St. Paul says, do not have the law but keep it as if by instinct, having it written in the heart (Rom. 2:14-15).

The more you read *The Lord of the Rings*, the more aware you become of the presence of God. At the most profound level, the tale is a love story between Him and His Children and how they accept and return this love in obedience, faith, and trust or how they spurn it and throw it back. God uses both choices to guide events. "To human beings God even gives the power of freely sharing in his providence by entrusting them with . . . responsibility. . . . Though often unconscious collaborators with God's will, they can also enter deliberately into the divine plan by their actions, their prayers and their sufferings" (*Catechism of the Catholic Church*, 81). It is not only the willing instruments that God uses during the War that give witness to this. Nothing happens without somehow advancing Sauron's defeat.

The conflict that engulfs Middle-earth is Sauron's continuation of the one that Melkor/Morgoth launched many thousands of years before against his Creator, his fellow angels, and the Children of God who followed. The tales that have come down to us tell of this struggle and how the Valar and Children fought against their adversaries.

Throughout *The Lord of the Rings*, there is an acknowledgment of this "graver sort of quest in which every human life is secretly engaged" (Kocher, *Master of Middle-earth*, 31). Aragorn speaks of this in his refusal to enter the City of Minas Tirith as king after the victory of the Pelennor Fields. He knows that his throne is not secure while Frodo continues to wage the more vital battle against Sauron. While the outcome of this fight hangs in the balance, everything else does as well. The Ring-bearer's battlefield is not a physical one, as for those at Helm's Deep and Minas Tirith. Rather it involves his mind, heart, and soul, which is where all those in the tale face the greatest weapons of the Enemy.

This spiritual struggle against evil and evil against us occurs even now within the soul of each person. As we cannot leave the field of battle until death takes us from it, we should learn as much as we can about how to fight from those who have labored before us. Certainly the Red Book of Westmarch is one source to draw from, as "there are few more moving portraits of humanity under stress than Frodo Baggins" ("Q & A with Verlyn Flieger," *More People's Guide to J. R. R. Tolkien*, 118). The hobbit guides us as he makes his torturous journey from Bag End to the Mountain of Fire and must endure the Ring's unceasing temptations in subtle whispers and coercive screams. Watching him contend with the demonic object, we see that sometimes we overcome our temptations and weaknesses, and at other times they overwhelm us. We also learn, as he and Boromir do, to get back up and start the struggle anew. We may not have to sacrifice ourselves as Gandalf does, but we can learn from him and his wise counsels and from the others who he taught. Sam leads us to the heights of devotion and obedience as well.

Tom Shippey notes, "If there is one moral . . . it is that you must do your duty regardless of what you think is going to happen" (*The Road to Middle-earth*, 183). Many show this throughout the story but none so touchingly as Frodo does on his way of sorrows toward Mordor, especially as each step and breath become harder to take. "Frodo is not intrepid, that is, fearlessly courageous," says Claudia Riiff Finseth. "He is fearfully courageous" ("Tolkien in Winter," *theonering.net*). The hobbit is hallowed for his terrible and grace-filled journey and hollowed out by it. His body seems too small for all that he endures but not so his heart. Fear, fatigue, cold, hunger, and thirst torment him, but he continues out of love. Frodo's struggle shows that there are, in fact, two quests going on: his to destroy the Ring and the Ring's to dominate and destroy him. Despite the despair that it causes, which both fills and empties him, the Ring-bearer remains as intent upon saving everyone as Denethor is not. Frodo's torn heart still beats, and it pushes past terror and hopelessness because of Sam's blessed aid and his own battered and bleeding will to do so. Both hobbits teach us the great value of redemptive suffering, which strips them down to naked will and endurance and clothes them in immortal grace that pours in as their mortal strength pours out.

Tolkien received inspiration from the Writer of the Story Himself to have his tales resound with such truth. He was "a little pencil in

God's hands," as Blessed Teresa of Calcutta described herself, or, to use the Professor's own words, he was one of God's "'chosen instruments'" (*Letters*, 413). The tale did not come from him but through him. Peter Kreeft expresses the gratitude of many by saying, "We thank both authors of *The Lord of the Rings*, the inspired one and the Inspiring One" ("Wartime Wisdom," *Celebrating Middle-earth*, 35).

Tolkien noted in a letter that the meaning of life was to seek all possible ways to know God as well as we could and to have this knowledge move us to give Him worship and thanksgiving (*Letters*, 400). *The Lord of the Rings* allowed the man to do this and gives us the same opportunity. More than one admiring critic has noted this fact.

> The history of Middle-earth in the novel and in the tales of *The Silmarillion* depicts a pre-Christian world before the flowering of humankind's dominance. As mythology, *The Lord of the Rings* promotes a specific moral and religious understanding, implying that the Christian principles of sacrifice, redemption, and forgiveness are central to the way the world is and has always worked – even before the appearance of Christianity as a religion. (Gardner et al., *SparkNotes: "The Lord of the Rings,"* 205)

> A more comprehensive mythological understanding of the universe is difficult to conceive. It issues in a profound Christian vision of the immensity of evil, the mystery of its grip on created beings, and the pernicious quality of its disintegrating and destructive nature. At the same time, he develops in his readers a fuller vision of the moral purity, or glory, of the Divine Power whose will will be realized, not at the expense of men, but for his greater good. (Hein, *Christian Mythmakers*, 213-214)

Joseph Pearce states, "This Catholic theology, explicitly present in *The Silmarillion* and implicitly present in *The Lord of the Rings*, is omnipresent in both, breathing life into the tales as invisibly but as surely as oxygen. . . . Tolkien . . . was so saturated with the Christian concept of reality that it permeates his myth profoundly" (*Man*, 94). "Ultimately, *The Lord of the Rings* is a sublimely mystical Passion Play. The carrying of the Ring – the emblem of Sin – is the Carrying of the Cross. The mythological Quest is a veritable Via Dolorosa. . . . At its deepest [the reader] might finally understand that the Quest is, in fact, a Pilgrimage" (Pearce, "True Myth," *Celebrating Middle-earth*, 92-93).

Edmund Fuller notes, "A theology contains the narrative rather than being contained by it. Grace is at work abundantly in the story" ("Lord of Hobbits," 29). The more you are aware of this, the more obvious it becomes. "The Gospel resounds in its depths," says Ralph C. Wood (*The Gospel According to Tolkien*, 5).

Pearce and Wood, among others, have also remarked that the Red Book is not an escape from reality but into it (*Man*, 152; *Gospel*, 1). In Tolkien's desire to create a mythology for his homeland, he actually made one for every person, every land, and every age. It is a catechism of spiritual warfare cleverly disguised as a fantasy. Sean McGrath observes, "This 'escapist' literature presents in vivid dramatic pictures what is otherwise intangible and inexpressible: our battle for salvation, for overcoming the all-pervasive, crippling legacy of sin" ("The Passion According to Tolkien," *Tolkien: A Celebration*, 177). Do you wonder, as does Théoden, what can be done against reckless hate? Read the story and find out. It does not hide from horror. It confronts it and tells us how to deal with it. It does not flinch from letting the reader know of the pain involved in the battle that engages each soul.

Verlyn Flieger writes beautifully of the men and hobbits in the story, who "illustrate, with the consequent pain and loss of all that seems most precious, the absolute necessity of letting go, of trusting in the unknown future, of having faith in God" (*A Question of Time*, 114). How difficult it is to achieve the level of self-surrender that Frodo, Aragorn, Gandalf, and Sam do, but the many saints who followed them give evidence that it is indeed possible. Blessed Pope John XXIII's description of such a person is also apt to the greatest heroes of the War of the Ring.

> To deny oneself at all times, to suppress, within oneself and in external show, all that the world would deem worthy of praise, to guard in one's own heart the flame

of a most pure love for God, far surpassing the frail affections of this world, to give all and sacrifice all for the good of others, and with humility and trust, in the love of God and of one's fellowmen, to obey the laws laid down by Providence and follow the way that leads chosen souls to the fulfillment of their mission – and everyone has his own mission – this is holiness, and all holiness is but this. (*A Joyful Soul*, 54)

May the light of the saints of Middle-earth be a beacon to draw strength and inspiration from while we make our own journeys to Mordor or confront the Shadow in other ways and places.

Chapter One

A Well-used Chance

One particularly important stroke in the war against Sauron takes place at the end of the Second Age as the Last Alliance of Elves and Men overthrows the Dark Lord on the slopes of Mount Doom. In the Enemy's lust to dominate all things, he had secretly forged the One Ring and filled it with much of his power. This was a grave mistake on his part, for if the Ring were ever destroyed, it would also ensure his own defeat. He does not consider this possible, but it is one of many examples of evil thwarting itself, as any material object can be unmade.

Sauron kills Elendil during the battle but receives no time to gloat over his triumph. Isildur uses his father's shattered sword to cut the Ring from the Enemy's hand and vanquishes him for a time. But this great victory gives way to great tragedy, or seemingly so, after the power of the Ring traps Isildur's will. The man refuses the counsel of Elrond and Círdan to destroy the fell thing in the Sammath Naur. Using this inability to make a right choice, God still brings good. As He does with all wrong, He has a plan in place that threads its way through history to contain or counter what evil has wrought and help mend the wounds.

"The Disaster of the Gladden Fields" contains the first good fruits that come from the Ring's seduction of Isildur (Tolkien, *Unfinished Tales of Númenor and Middle-earth*, 271-287). Set at the beginning of the Third Age, it concerns the king's death while he is on the way to Imladris to see his wife and youngest son and also to gain the counsel of Elrond. Before he and his men reach their destination, however, Orcs attack them and are repelled.

As the Orcs gather for a second assault, Isildur's son, Elendur, wonders about using the Ring. The king now recognizes the folly of such a move and refuses. He has grown in wisdom since he claimed the demonic object for his own, and he knows it is beyond his strength to wield. He dreads even to touch it because of the pain it brings him, and he is ready to surrender it to the Elves.

As Isildur has come to understand, sometimes only through errors and falls do we realize that previously given counsel may indeed be wiser than we first deemed. The king blames his pride for his mistake in judgment at Mount Doom. Such hubris was fed no doubt by the overwhelming power of the Ring at the time. Yet, as Gandalf tells Pippin much later concerning the hobbit's own brush with the power of temptation, "the burned hand teaches best" (*The Lord of the Rings*, 584). Isildur's hand literally was burnt by the fierce heat of the Ring. Now two years later, he is still not free of the torture.

The Orcs attack again with fresh fury, and with one of Isildur's sons already dead and another mortally wounded, all seems lost. Elendur commands his father to leave the battle with the Ring lest he be captured or killed as well. The king begs his son for forgiveness, again blaming his pride, before he flees and puts on the Ring. Elendur and the rest of the king's men fall in battle, save one squire and two others who were already sent away with the shards of Narsil.

Isildur plunges into the River Anduin close to midnight. "By chance, or chance well used," (*Unfinished Tales*, 275) the Ring slips from his finger. In the black night, the man knows that he will never find it. At first, he is so overcome by loss that he nearly gives into the temptation to drown himself. But this thought passes as quickly as it comes, and a release from pain replaces it. This freedom from torment and the 'chance' of the evil thing falling off his finger are two indications of God working through history to bring good out of Isildur's original evil choice to keep the Ring. The man makes it across the water but falls to the poisoned arrows of Orcs.

Another example of the good that comes from evil is that the Ring, which was still filled with Sauron's malice, was partly responsible for the extraordinary ferocity of the second attack. If the Orcs had not done so, Isildur, his sons, and many of his men would have survived, yet the Ring would not have been lost in the River. If it had made it to Rivendell, its power would have eventually overwhelmed Elrond and plunged him and Middle-earth into ruin. Instead, the Elf-lord remains safe to use his own Ring, free from Sauron's taint and out of the Dark Lord's control, and so maintain the haven of Imladris where faith, light, and beauty abide.

Almost 2,500 years later, the Ring snags Déagol while he and Sméagol fish in the River Anduin on the latter's birthday. After Déagol refuses his friend's demand that he give it as a present, Sméagol murders his companion. It seems strange that he falls so instantly to the destructive power of the Ring, especially as he is a hobbit. This particular branch, however, lived near the River, where the fell object had laid buried deep for so long. Sméagol's fall seems quick because this is the first that we see of him, but he may well have felt its pull before. It could have slowly dripped poison into his soul for years, and what appears so sudden may actually be the consummation of a long seduction.

After earning the name Gollum and suffering banishment from his family, Sméagol takes the Ring under the Misty Mountains for nearly 500 years. There it lies, a thing both loved and loathed, until it leaves him in response to its master's call. In the wrong hands, it could have cut a wide swath of destruction throughout Middle-earth, but instead, it remains underground and consumes the one creature that it can reach. Except for this unfortunate victim, it remains virtually impotent until Ring-bearer and Ring-destroyer meet at the end of the Third Age.

Several other important meetings, however, must take place first.

Chapter Two

One Lucky Hobbit:
Bilbo's Great Adventure

As Gandalf travels to Bree in the early spring of 1341 by the Shire Reckoning, the dragon Smaug is much on his mind. The growing threat of Sauron also looms ever larger over Middle-earth. How both could wreak the most grievous harm if not defeated concerns the wizard greatly. The hidden Maia had already decided to immerse himself in the peace of the Shire in the hope that it would settle his overburdened heart and help him to come to a solution to the perplexing question of how victory over both worm and Shadow could come.

Gandalf receives part of the answer in the grace-filled moment of another well-used chance as he meets Thorin Oakenshield on the road. Both are aware of the providential timing that brings them together at this particular moment and readily obey the will behind it. As Thorin says, he had been thinking about the wizard, "as if I were bidden to seek you" (*LOTR*, 1052). Gandalf marvels at such words and replies that the dwarf was in his thoughts as well, and he had felt a similar stirring in his heart. They agree to meet at Thorin's home, but what the wizard hears there does not completely please him. He leaves to seek out Bilbo.

"The Quest of Erebor" tells more about this period (Tolkien, *Unfinished Tales*, 321-336). At the time of Gandalf's last visit years before, Bilbo had not yet come of age and was then full of questions about the outside world. According to the news that the Maia receives after visiting Thorin, Bilbo still has the same curiosity. Various hobbits say their eccentric neighbor often travels, sometimes to talk to dwarves passing through or this time, as Holman the gardener reports, in the hope of seeing Elves at their New Year. This seems wonderful, and a plan begins to form in the wizard's mind. Though Bilbo belongs to the thoroughly conventional and practical Baggins family, Gandalf knows that he has a strong Tookish streak as well. These hobbits were infamous for their unrespectable taste for adventure. From the reports and Gandalf's own memories, Bilbo seems like the ideal candidate to help defeat Smaug. Convinced of this good fortune, the wizard leaves with a lighter heart to seek out seek out Thorin again.

Gandalf admits in his recollections of this time that he later thought it a mistake not to check with Bilbo personally first. But the fact that the hobbit just happens to be away at the time is another sign of grace, for it would have discouraged the wizard to know that Bilbo is not actually all that local gossip makes him. The Maia could have sought elsewhere if he had found out this out earlier, but fortunately he does not. Gandalf hints that another Power had already selected this particular hobbit: "I dare say he was 'chosen' and I was only chosen to choose him," he tells Frodo, Merry, Pippin, and Gimli (*Unfinished Tales*, 331). Grace shields Gandalf from the fact Bilbo has changed until after the wizard convinces Thorin to take the hobbit along and to come to Bag End with the other dwarves.

All Gandalf then has to do is convince Bilbo himself, which proves quite difficult. Though the hobbit makes it perfectly clear that he is not at all interested in any adventures, the wizard is not put off and returns later with the dwarves. As Bilbo listens to the songs about gold, his Tookish side begins to assert itself, and he starts to long once more for excitement. The Baggins part has kept this under strict control because all it wants to do is to stay comfy and cozy at home. The more it hears of the perils to come, the more frightened it feels. That Bilbo cries out and collapses in terror does not endear him to the dwarves, who are ever more unsure of Gandalf's choice as a companion for them.

Hobbits do appear unlikely heroes, but God uses improbable people at times to fulfill a role that He specially designed for them. Just from the Bible alone, there are many examples. David will appear an unlikely king because he is the youngest son and a shepherd boy, yet God will guide Samuel to anoint him (1 Sam. 16:11-13). The young man will be just as improbable a champion for the Israelites in the contest against the giant Goliath (1 Sam. 17:40-54), yet he will succeed admirably where no one else could. Amos will be a shepherd and caretaker of sycamore trees at the time God chooses him as one of His prophets (Amos 7:14-15). The world will see as nothing the group of fishermen, tax collectors, and others who become Jesus' closest followers. But to God, all these mean everything, for as is said of David, "the LORD does not see as mortals see; they look on the outward appearance, but the LORD looks on the heart" (1 Sam. 16:7, NRSV). This fits Bilbo and Frodo, who were also "chosen and selected," as Gandalf says of the elder Baggins (*The Hobbit*, 21).

Bilbo and Frodo overcome the objections of the Baggins side of themselves in order to embrace the Quests that await them. Sometimes we have the same struggles as they do. The Took in us wants to pursue dreams, and the Baggins part wants to stay safe and conventional. Too often we heed the negative thinking that convinces us that we do not have the time, money, energy, or opportunity to make our desires come true. We think we have too many other obligations blocking our way. Sometimes we also saddle ourselves with the false guilt that tells us it is not right to do anything for ourselves, especially if we have a family to take care of first. We must not abandon our true responsibilities, of course, but would it not be better if we could fulfill them in a way that fed our soul and not just our pocketbook and got us excited about going to work rather than dreading the drudgery?

We are not placed when and where we are by accident anymore than Bilbo or Frodo. We are given experiences, molded in a particular way, and set along specific roads, so that we may be in the right place at the right time to do what God wants of us. We can discern the unique way that He wishes us to live out our vocation by the interests, talents, and abilities that He gave us. He did not bestow these graces upon anyone else in exactly the same way. Rather than allow our fears to stifle them, we must find the courage to leave our comfortable and secure hobbit holes for an exhilarating and terrifying adventure that will bring us alive in a way that we have not been since childhood. For too many, our youth was the last time that we believed all things were possible. This does not need to be true.

Bilbo and Frodo learn much on their journeys about strengths they did not even know they had. Their growth and endurance bolsters our own. God already knows that we can be heroes if the right circumstances come. We have to find this out in the thick of things. Neither hobbit would have discovered the seeds of greatness that lay within them if they had continued their sheltered lives in the Shire. Neither can we. Though lost for the most part amid the cacophony that invades our daily life, we hear at times snatches of the particular notes in the Great Music that our soul especially hearkens to, and we long for the day we can truly sing our heart out. Unfortunately, we learn to stifle such things, just as Bilbo has whenever he heard the adventurous melodies that have stirred him since childhood. Nonetheless, we must still be ready for the special day that God calls us.

On some level, Bilbo is aware of this. In the "Erebor" narrative, Gandalf gives his hypothesis of why the hobbit chose the unusual path of remaining unmarried: "I guessed that he wanted to remain 'unattached' for some reason deep down which he did not understand himself – or would not acknowledge, for it alarmed him. He wanted, all the same, to be free to go when the chance came, or he had made up his courage" (*Unfinished Tales*, 331). This captures in a nutshell how Bilbo and Frodo were both prepared in advance for their vocations, which ultimately carry the heavy cost of leaving behind all that they love but each other.

Do we have such dual feelings of fear and anticipation ourselves? Are we listening for the time our calling comes calling? Do we answer? Do we even want to? Bilbo and the hobbits who follow decades later on their own Quest discover how perilous it is to step away from home, but we must do this if we are sing our part of the Music. What adventure and excitement awaits us! If we do not leave our hobbit hole, our piece will not be heard as it is meant. Perhaps it will never be heard at all. Let us not hide in seeming shelter from the harsh winds that blow in the world. Let us turn our face into them and follow where the Road takes us, as Bilbo, Frodo, Sam, Gandalf, Aragorn, and others do. Even if what God entrusts us to do seems impossible, He has given us a tremendous gift in sharing in the making of the world. We need to find out what unique shape He gave us and fit ourselves into the spot that suits us best. We should not try to force our square into a circle or allow someone else to squash our rectangle into a triangle. We also have the freedom to reject God's careful and deliberate planning. Such is our Father's gift to us. But should we say no, we will not perform what we were made to do.

Before the plan for Bilbo to discover his particular shape falls apart, Gandalf reveals two things that he has long kept secret. Thorin's father, Thráin, had borne one of the Seven Rings of Power that had been wrought for the dwarves. Sauron wished to use the Rings to enslave them, but the only thing the Dark Lord succeeded in doing was exciting their desire for gold and other precious things. They remained otherwise unaffected, for they were given from the first the ability to resist any outside domination of their will. The lust for material things, however, was fatal enough for them. Sauron captured and tormented Thráin and took his Ring from him. Yet good came from this through a mistake made by the Dark Lord. Once he regained the dwarf's Ring, he did not care for anything else. In the end, Thorin's father died in the dungeons of Dol Guldur, but not before he passed a map and key to Gandalf, who had come to seek the identity of the evil power that dwelt there. He discovered that it was Sauron, but he did not know who the prisoner was or who the son was that the wretched creature wished to have the items given. Still, Gandalf took them and heeded an intuition to keep them hidden for nearly a century. Musing in "Erebor" about the odd luck to still have the things, he says that he realized only in the Shire what Providence had put into his hands and why. It is a marvel to ponder how much the success of any venture is engineered behind the scenes, and only afterwards do we connect the dots. Thorin gains more hope for the journey. The dwarves still remain doubtful about Bilbo, but Gandalf is most adamant that they include the hobbit in their party. The wizard does not know the future, but, as a Maia, he has a deeper intuition than most. He senses that without Bilbo, other much more important events will not occur.

After Bilbo wakes in the morning, he finds the dwarves gone, which relieves his Baggins side but quite disappoints his Tookish part. Gandalf enters shortly afterward and practically forces him out the door, like a mother bird pushing her chick out of the nest so he can learn to fly. But it is still Bilbo's choice that allows for the success of this push. He could have refused. At last he finds his courage and allows himself to be drawn into that unique part of the Song only he can sing. He hurries down to *The Green Dragon* without even a handkerchief. We, too, must either be pushed out or somehow gain the strength to jump out ourselves. We are not truly alive until we do.

The reasons why Bilbo must go on his journey soon begin to manifest themselves. The hobbit imprudently decides to live up to his job title as burglar and picks the pocket of a troll. The trolls catch him in his folly and the accompanying noise attracts the dwarves, who the creatures capture as well. Gandalf had gone ahead but heeds an intuition he should return and turns this potentially fatal act of Bilbo's into a deadly one for the dim-witted trolls instead. The wizard shows how easy it is to defeat them by throwing his voice and taking advantage of the propensity of evil creatures to always fight among themselves. They do so until the sun rises and turns them to stone. Much later, Pippin is similarly clever with words to Grishnákh when the hobbit pretends to have the Ring. Perhaps a memory of hearing of Gandalf's successful trick inspires the tween, for it was the mission of the Istari to instruct those under their care to use the wits and skills that they already possessed to fight the Enemy. The hidden Maia could have used his own native power to defeat the trolls, but, as Bilbo and the dwarves cannot use such themselves, it would teach them nothing, akin to always fishing for someone rather than showing them how to fish.

Great good comes from Bilbo's foolish actions. Travelers can now safely pass through the area. Much more importantly, the hobbit providentially finds an Elven knife in the trolls' cave, which he uses as a sword and later passes on to Frodo. Gandalf and Thorin also discover ancient swords once used in battle against the goblins.

As Thorin and company travel on, they encounter Elves singing and teasing among the trees. Jim Ware provides insightful commentary as to why they are so silly in *The Hobbit* compared to their gravity in *The Lord of the Rings*. Let us take his words to heart.

> Like the Good People of Elrond's valley, we live in troubled times. Like them, we dwell under a shadow. We are exiles in enemy territory, hemmed in on every side by darkness and despair. . . . Can anyone laugh and sing in a world like ours?
>
> The elves of Rivendell say *yes*. And they say so out of a context of hard-earned practical experience. More than any other people in Middle-earth, the elves know what it means to fail. They have fallen from grace and

tasted the bitter cost of redemption. They realize what it will take to defeat the Shadow and heal the wounds of the world. And yet they are not above singing in the trees. Indeed, they understand that a certain amount of joyful abandon is *essential* to a life lived in harmony with the truth, however foolish it looks to small and serious-minded folk like Thorin. For to laugh in desperate circumstances and sing in the face of disaster is nothing less than an act of bold and daring faith. It's a sign of salvation to the watching world, evidence of the hope that lies just beyond the fringes of the darkness. (*Finding God in "The Hobbit,"* 29-30)

Bilbo longs to stay in the Last Homely House forever, where everything is perfect for anything you might wish to do. In addition to receiving care for their physical needs, the Elves also provide spiritual support to their guests. Another 'chance' happening takes place here, as Elrond translates the moon-letters on the map that the dwarves possess, which could only be read while the moon was in the same phase as it was on the day the runes were made. The timing of the discovery of this secret code is nothing but providential, for, as John D. Rateliff points out, "one particular phase of the moon would only coincide with a specific night of the year roughly once per century" (*The History of the Hobbit Part One: Mr Baggins*, 124). The dwarves, Bilbo, and Gandalf leave refreshed and ready once more to continue their journey. Let us hope to find such oases ourselves along the Road.

Another moment of grace occurs after Thorin's company finds shelter in a cave from the thunder-battle that rages around them. Restlessness afflicts Bilbo that does not affect anyone else. After rousing from an uneasy dream, he gives a loud cry upon seeing it is actually reality. He watches the last of their ponies disappear into a crack in the wall. That Bilbo stirs in time to raise the alarm is another hint of the Power watching over them. The hobbit's shout wakes Gandalf, who is the only one who remains free after goblins pour out of the crack and capture everyone else. The wizard kills the Great Goblin with the sword that he found in the trolls' cave. Many of the other evil creatures also lose their lives.

Gandalf rescues Bilbo and the dwarves, but the goblins nearly apprehend them again. In the confusion, the hobbit gets separated from his companions and trapped underground. In what appears to be merely a lucky chance, Bilbo blindly puts his hand upon a small ring. He puts it in his pocket without much thought and continues on, alone and terrified. He has no idea what he just picked up, what value it has, or what a profound impact this simple action will have on him, his yet unborn cousin Frodo, and indeed all Middle-earth.

This ring is, of course, none other than *the* Ring, which just shortly before Bilbo came heard its master's call and slipped away from its bearer to answer. However, it needs a host to travel, and God makes sure it has the right one. Gandalf's later comments to Frodo about this remarkable happening clearly state that it was neither Bilbo's nor Sauron's will that the hobbit find the Ring. No one foresaw this turn of events but the Writer of the Story, who has carefully placed everything and everyone exactly where needed for their parts in the Music. The wisdom of King Alfred the Great also applies here: "I say, as do all Christian men, that it is a divine purpose that rules, and not fate."

In the terrible dark, another fateful meeting takes place as Bilbo comes upon Gollum at an underground lake. The lost hobbit hopes the horrible creature will lead him out of the tunnels, but Gollum challenges him first to a riddle-game with two possible endings. If Bilbo wins, Gollum will show him the exit; if Gollum wins, he will eat Bilbo.

In the beginning the riddles are easy, but they grow increasingly difficult. While Bilbo desperately seeks to answer the one about fish, Gollum starts to get out of his boat in anticipation of the delicious meal that he soon expects to have. But the wicked creature's lustful haste gives his would-be prey the solution after Gollum puts his foot in the water and disturbs a fish that leaps out and lands right on Bilbo's feet. "Pure luck" (*Hobbit*, 74) provides the response to Gollum's next riddle. Bilbo wishes to blurt out a plea for more time to think, but all that comes out is "Time!" He did not mean this as an answer, but it is the correct one nonetheless.

"The plans of the mind belong to mortals, but the answer on the tongue is from the LORD" (Prov. 16:1, NRSV). Bilbo is unaware of this providential guidance, but it is easy to see God's continuing presence in the hobbit's life, for the Ring-finder receives the solutions he needs at the time that he needs them without consciously coming to them himself. Katharyn Crabbe notes, "Both God and man have a hand in shaping all that happens: God through the medium of grace, which Tolkien calls 'luck,' and man through his physical and rational excellences, bravery and sense, which, at their best, represent the God-like in man" ("The Nature of Heroism in a Comic World," *Readings on J. R. R. Tolkien*, 57).

Luck also allows Bilbo to win the game after he finally stumps Gollum by asking what is in the pocket that now holds the Ring. Bilbo did not actually intend his question to be a riddle, but he stands by what Providence gives him. Gollum protests vehemently against such a breach in the rules, but he attempts to answer. After he cannot, Bilbo holds the creature to his word that he will show Bilbo the way out. Gollum agrees, but says that he must gather some things before they set out. By this he means the Ring, which he plans to use to come upon his prey invisibly and have his meal after all. Grieved to discover that his hated and beloved treasure is missing and suspecting that it is the solution to the non-riddle, Gollum asks what Bilbo has in his pocket. The Ring-finder cannot think of a reason why he should not answer such a seemingly innocuous question, but out of irritation he refuses. How different things may have turned out if he had replied and given the Ring back or had it taken from him! Grace prevents either thing from happening.

Evil defeats itself again during Bilbo's desperate flight from Gollum. The hobbit puts his left hand in his pocket, and the Ring "quietly slip[s] on to his groping forefinger" (*Hobbit*, 78). Bilbo does not consciously will to put it on, but the Ring initiates it in its desire for Sauron to discover it. Yet such malevolent intent saves Bilbo's life at the precise moment most needful. The now invisible hobbit trips and falls, and Gollum goes right past him. If Bilbo were not wearing the Ring, Gollum could have easily overwhelmed him in his vulnerable position. But because of another well-used chance, the fleeing hobbit receives a great advantage instead. He pursues his pursuer in the hope of escape rather than blindly running away in the dark.

Richard Mathews notes that the Ring is "just the size to fit a hobbit finger" (*Lightning from a Clear Sky*, 13). Of course it was not made to do so, yet it does, just as the Elven knife Bilbo found in the troll's cave is also perfect for a hobbit to use, which Mathews observes as well. Much later, Frodo tells Gandalf about how Bilbo had remarked that the Ring seemed to grow and shrink on its own. It fit Isildur's much larger hand, but it still slipped off in the water. It left Gollum's hand, which is even smaller than Bilbo's because of the state of near starvation in which the wretched creature lives. It enlarged enough to fall from his finger in time for Bilbo's meatier hand to grab and use.

At the end of Bilbo's chase after Gollum, the Ring-finder fights within himself one of the most important battles ever waged in Middle-earth. He finds that his would-be murder has unintentionally brought him to the exit, or at least as far as the miserable being is willing to go without risking capture by the goblins. He then stops there, blocking Bilbo's way. Gollum detects by hearing and smell that the thief of his precious is near. In Bilbo's desperation to escape with his life, he faces the temptation that to do so, he must slay his adversary. Certainly this could be easily justified as self-defense. The world would know nothing of it. It would take a while for even the goblins to notice that their kind were no longer disappearing with the creature no longer around to eat them.

Luckily for Gollum and all Middle-earth, Bilbo still has the presence of mind to heed the presence of God. The impulse to kill Gollum disappears as fast as it comes. There is absolutely no reason to pity such a terrible thing, yet such springs up in the Ring-finder's heart and restrains his hand. Though not speaking specifically of the hobbit, Mathews notes, "Time and time again the spiritual decisions of the most consequence are faced by individuals alone" (*Lightning*, 32). Bilbo intuitively understands what it means to love an enemy, as he feels for an instant the agony of one so long trapped in darkness with no way out of it. This realization turns Gollum from a feared enemy into a fellow human being with a tormented heart and soul.

What also helps Bilbo to decide is the fact that although he knows Gollum wishes to kill him, the evil creature has not actually tried to do so. Bilbo bases his response, as Frodo does later, on what *has* happened, rather than give into fears of what *might* happen or even is *likely* to but has not occurred yet. The elder Baggins has once more laid some important groundwork for the destruction of the Ring and the salvation of his future cousin and heir. No foreknowledge of this moves his heart, however. Rather, he responds even more admirably, for he shows "mercy *for mercy's sake alone*" (Ware, *God in "Hobbit,"* 53; italics in original). The later Quest to destroy the Ring could not have succeeded without others giving this same seemingly imprudent pity. We need to be watchful for such moments in our own life and give mercy if possible. Just as Bilbo has no idea what impact his actions and choices will have on his world, neither do we. As such, we must move cautiously.

Bilbo's merciful act could have well turned out fatal for him, for Gollum remains intent on eating him. But new strength gives the Ring-finder the ability to spring forward and over his foe and leave him unharmed. Providence protects Bilbo from knowing how dangerous this jump is, or he might not have attempted it. If he had leapt any higher, he would have hit the ceiling, exposed himself, and likely been killed before he could recover. Instead, he gets away.

Bilbo sees a sliver of daylight at last but also the goblins surrounding the exit. Worse, he realizes that they can see him. Desire for the Ring and fear of losing it is already growing in him. As he searches for it in his pockets, it is once more clear that Bilbo does not decide to put it on, but it does this itself. Now invisible again, it saves the hobbit's life. He escapes at last, just as Frodo does later from Boromir.

Bilbo reveals his inherent decency after he decides that he must re-enter the tunnels and search for his missing companions. He has absolutely no desire to go back in, even with a magic Ring, but he conquers his fear and makes the decision to do so. Katharyn Crabbe notes in a parallel between Bilbo and Christ the great love that is ready to lay itself down to save its friends (*J. R. R. Tolkien*, 41-42). Bilbo receives his reward just for making this brave choice, rather than actually having to follow through after he hears voices and reunites with Gandalf and the dwarves.

As the company continues their journey, they come to a point where they must hide in trees to escape the Wargs. With these creatures hungry for their blood and no escape apparent, Gandalf aims some fireballs at them and sets some of the animals aflame. The commotion attracts the attention of the Lord of the Eagles and his companions. The goblins arrive and worsen the predicament of their treed enemies by feeding the flames. Gandalf's tree catches fire and the others soon follow, but the Eagles come and save the wizard, hobbit, and dwarves from a terrible fate.

In this tale and the one following, the Eagles make five more timely appearances, perhaps at the bidding of their master, the Vala Manwë, whom Gandalf also serves. Jim Ware observes, "deliverance from certain doom and defeat is always a matter of pure, unmerited grace – the same grace that seeks us . . . goes before us at every moment of our lives, prepares paths for our footsteps without our knowing it, and draws us irresistibly toward the loving heart that beats at the center of all things" (*God in "Hobbit,"* 62). God's timing is perfect, even if help comes at the last minute. This will echo in the Eagles' rescue of Frodo and Sam in Mordor.

Beorn is the next to give aid to Thorin's company. The shape-changer tells them not to leave the path once they go into Mirkwood. He also tells them to enter the forest through a way that the goblins will not go near. Bilbo and the dwarves would not have chosen this on their own, and indeed, it is nearer to the enemy. Nevertheless, Beorn deems it safer for being unexpected, as the goblins are likely to search farther afield for them rather than looking closer. Frodo and Sam will use such tactics to great advantage as they inch their way toward Mount Doom.

Several days after parting with Beorn, Gandalf distresses Bilbo and the dwarves by announcing that he must leave to deal with some other urgent business. The wizard tells them to think of what the successful end of the Quest will mean rather than the perils they must pass through first. He encourages the travelers at least not to think of such dangers during the night. Galadriel gives similar advice much later after Frodo and his companions arrive in Lothlórien while grieving their own loss of Gandalf. At the edge of Mirkwood, the hidden Maia repeats Beorn's counsel not to depart from the path and then leaves the company.

The "Erebor" tale reveals that Gandalf is anxious to leave for a meeting of the White Council, during which he urges them to drive Sauron out of Dol Guldur. Saruman has been successful in keeping the Council from acting against the Enemy until Gandalf convinces them to do so at last. Sauron abandons his first plan of attacking Lothlórien and Rivendell and chooses instead to flee back to Mordor and re-establish his power there. Gandalf notes that the original idea would have worked out much better for their adversary to the great detriment of those who fought against him. Indeed as events prove, it would have made his defeat impossible by the means carried out later, but the Dark Lord's own choice prevents this from happening. He is far away shortly after the Ring emerges from where it has lain hidden for centuries. Gandalf calls this "a strange chance, if chance it was" (*LOTR*, 244). In truth, it is another of the many threads held in the hands of Providence.

Need we ever worry that, although we cannot see all ends ourselves, if we only trust in the One who can, all will happen at the time and in the manner that it should? We have trouble doing this while enmeshed in our troubles, as even Gandalf admits to in "Erebor." But he also says all turned out well, which is something he and we see only in hindsight.

Thorin's company trudges on for days in Mirkwood with nothing to see but trees and more trees. They long to see the sun, just as Frodo and Sam will yearn for the same while they struggle through Mordor. What we need to remember as we walk our own dark paths is the Chinese proverb that says you can only go half way into a dark forest; after that you are on your way out.

Ever-dwindling rations concern Bilbo and the dwarves. The day after they run out of food, they decide to veer off the path and follow some mysterious lights. They hope to find something to eat, as they can see that the lights belong to a company of feasting Elves. Each time, however, the lights disappear at their approach, only to spring up elsewhere. After the third unsuccessful attempt to reach them, another danger ensnares the wandering company as myriad webs spun by giant spiders bind them. Shelob, mother of these monstrous creatures, will do the same to Frodo in her lair on the border of Mordor.

Bilbo cuts himself free with his Elvish knife, which he christens Sting after he kills a spider. In his efforts to rescue his companions, he uses the grace that abundantly blesses him and also takes advantage of the lust of evil to devour its prey. In its hurry, it defeats itself. The hobbit puts on the Ring, and the multitude of spiders spin web after web in an effort to trap their invisible and mocking foe. They nearly succeed, but "luckily" Sting destroys one web that was woven too hastily. Bilbo leads the spiders on a merry chase before quietly hurrying back to the dwarves. He reaches them because "luckily" one of the spiders left a thick rope, which the hobbit uses as a ladder. He kills the guard and frees Fili. Bilbo, and later Frodo and Sam in their own battle, show that love and courage can accomplish great things.

After releasing the other dwarves, they discover that Thorin is missing. The next day, the Wood-elves, who had already captured Thorin, take the rest of the dwarves prisoner. Bilbo follows invisibly to the gates of the Elvenking's palace. Here the hobbit once more battles with his fear of continuing, just as he had in the goblin tunnels. In the nick of time, he decides to go forward. After some days, he finds the cells of his companions spread throughout the palace and works to figure out how to free them. Providence guides him much here and guards him from discovery by both the Elves and Sauron, as he wears the Ring to avoid capture.

In Bilbo's investigations, he learns of a grand feast, which the king's butler and chief of guards decide to start early on their own. A particularly potent wine puts them to sleep and allows the hobbit to steal the keys to his companions' cells and free them.

Bilbo has already made the fortunate discovery of barrels that regularly left the Elvenking's palace on their way to Lake-town, and it is into these that the hobbit stuffs the dwarves. His luck is particularly evident here because he forgot to plan for his own escape. Unable to close himself into a barrel, he invisibly clings for dear life to the outside of one. He struggles to get on top but cannot. His failure is actually a blessing, for it saves him from being crushed between the barrel and the steeply sloping roof. Even if we think we could be in a better spot, God knows exactly where we need to be and keeps us there until it is safe to be elsewhere. We have to trust in this, even if the place is as miserable as Bilbo's.

There are two more moments of grace during the trip to Lake-town. Because the stowaways arrive at the tie-up point at night, the Elves do not inspect the barrels, which they probably would have if they had come during the day. Upon overhearing the raftmen talk the next morning, Bilbo realizes to his amazement that forsaking the strict warnings not to leave the path, a decision that has caused so much misery, is actually the best thing he and his companions could have done. Gandalf and Beorn did not know the road had changed since their last knowledge of it, or they would have provided different counsel. With the river the only way to get to the town, and with the water guarded by Elves, the only way Bilbo and company could have come is the way they actually did. They could not have done this if they had not strayed from the path and been captured. Another seeming disaster turns out to be a good in disguise.

After more than two weeks of the most indulgent treatment by the people of Lake-town as they celebrate the return of the King under the Mountain, Thorin and company leave and approach the Desolation of the Dragon. They know that their long journey is nearly over, and it could possibly end in a terrible way. The same fears will plague Frodo as he and Sam approach the Mountain of Fire. They all struggle through dangerous wastelands without any hope of aid. They show that we, too, must simply keep going through all our tribulations and terror. Though the way may be dark, if we are on the right path, turning back is not an option.

Another moment of grace comes after Bilbo and the dwarves reach the dragon's Mountain. After days of trying to find a way in without success, the hobbit has a strange feeling that something important is about to happen. A ray of sunlight streams through the clouds and shines upon the keyhole of the door. Thorin turns the key, and they all push against the door. Once the door opens, Bilbo gets another chance to prove his unique worth to the party. Throughout the journey, the hobbit has grown steadily into a brave hero, but fear paralyzes the dwarves. All but Balin stay outside as Bilbo enters the darkness, and Balin soon returns to his companions.

Bilbo presses beyond his own terror until he hears the sound of Smaug snoring. "Going on from there was the bravest thing he ever did. The tremendous things that happened afterwards were as nothing compared to it. He fought the real battle in the tunnel alone, before he ever saw the vast danger that lay in wait" (*Hobbit*, 197). The hobbit fought and won this same spiritual battle while trapped in the goblin tunnels before he met Gollum. Indeed, Bilbo has grown so much that he enters into Smaug's dreams as a small but mighty warrior. The hobbit makes his way into the dragon's treasure room while wearing the Ring and steals a cup.

Smaug demonstrates the ugliness of materialistic greed, as he guards his treasure but does not enjoy it, cannot possibly use it, and does not even know what has true value and what is just a trinket. Even so, he does not wish to share his amassed wealth with anyone. His overreaction after discovering that the cup Bilbo stole is missing is almost as bad as Gollum's regarding the Ring, and it will grow much worse.

The benefits accompanying ignorance of danger are evident as Bilbo approaches Smaug the second time. He knows, or thinks he knows, what is ahead because of what he has endured already, but in actuality, he does not. This is a good thing, as the truth could have paralyzed his will. After the dragon wakes, the invisible hobbit confronts Smaug's incredible presence and is not overcome by it. Rather, the Luck-wearer fills the room with riddles and is confident in his ability to evade the worm. In their conversation, Smaug attempts to drive a wedge between Bilbo and his companions and cause the hobbit to doubt the sincerity of the dwarven promise to share an equal part of the treasure or to share at all. The serpent in the Garden of Eden tried – and succeeded – to do the same between Adam and Eve and God and made them doubt God's wisdom and love for them. Bilbo tries not to let Smaug's lies bother him and instead tricks the dragon into revealing his vulnerable spot.

After Bilbo barely escapes with his life, he returns to the dwarves and convinces them that they must all hide, which they do by blocking themselves in the Mountain. Smaug makes a terrible racket outside in his efforts to find them, and then there is even more horrible silence. The dwarves reach their lowest point and think they will die in the tunnel, but Bilbo feels an odd lift to his heart. Not for nothing did a Power above guide Gandalf to enlist the hobbit as the dwarves' companion and, more than once, their savior. Bilbo quotes his father and says, "While there's life there's hope" (*Hobbit*, 214). Sam will repeat this decades later, quoting his own Gaffer. Bilbo leads the dwarves deeper into the Mountain and toward Smaug's treasure room to see whether the giant worm has left or not.

Bilbo's calling out for Smaug to come out and so end the terrible suspense and silence of the place will echo in Sam's cry to his enemies at the Tower of Cirith Ungol. Both hobbits learn to conquer their fears by becoming emboldened by the horrifying experiences they will themselves to survive.

This time Smaug is not at home, but the dwarves still hesitate to enter the treasury for some time while Bilbo goes on ahead. The dragon-sickness inflames the hobbit's heart the moment he sees the

Arkenstone. He takes it and keeps it secret, though rather guiltily. He has a feeling that it is not really his to claim, that it would not count as part of his share of the hoard, and that ill would result from having it. He is right on all counts, but God uses this slight intoxication with greed to bring good, for Bilbo was meant to find not only the Ring but also the Arkenstone. Grace enables him to hold these great and perilous treasures and to release them at need as well.

The dwarves eventually gather their courage to enter and reclaim what stolen wealth they can. During this time one of the greatest moments of grace in the tale occurs. Thorin finds and gives Bilbo a coat made of priceless *mithril* as partial payment for all his services. Not only is everything which helps destroy the Ring put into place for Bilbo to possess but also for him to pass along to Frodo. If the Ring-bearer did not receive this coat, it could not have saved his life in Moria. Who then would have become Bearer? Would the Quest have even succeeded without the one who was born to help fulfill it?

After the people of Lake-town see strange lights in the sky, they speculate that the King under the Mountain is at work making gold, but Bard recognizes what is truly happening. The townspeople scoff at him, but he is right. He raises the alarm, and only because of him are the people ready to fight when Smaug comes. The Master's only interest, however, is in saving himself. He prepares to flee but does not do so until later. Though there are courageous fighters during the dragon's assault, Bard is the only one at the end who stands against the great worm. The man throws down his adversary because of what he hears from a thrush who tells him of Smaug's one vulnerability.

Thorin now faces a much greater foe, as Smaug's vast treasury remains to be plundered by whoever can. The dwarf does not know that Bilbo already possesses the greatest prize of all. The demonic Balrog that woke in Khazad-dûm is aptly called Durin's Bane, but this title could also describe the greed that roused the hidden enemy there. Such avarice inflames Thorin's heart. He claims Smaug's holdings for the dwarves and refuses to share any of it. Bard reminds him of the care given to him and his companions in their need and says those who succored them now require his aid. Thorin responds that he will repay the people of Lake-town, but he has no intention of sharing anything at all under the threat of the gathered force of Men and Elves. The dwarf considers the wealth solely the property of his people. Bard leaves, but another representative comes to claim a portion of the treasury for him and reports that the man will share some with those newly homeless. The speaker encourages Thorin to do the same, but lust for the dragon's purloined wealth so overwhelms the dwarf that he shoots an arrow at his foe instead.

Bilbo retains a clear head. His fall into dragon-sickness was a passing thing and was used for good. The hobbit has served the dwarves well and faithfully, and his theft of the Arkenstone is part of this. Indeed, he does what he thinks is best for both sides as he enters the 'enemy' camp alone and surrenders the Arkenstone to an astonished Elvenking and Bard. Though it is a wrench to give it away, his ability to detach himself from the jewel for the greater good prepares him to later part with the Ring and allows Frodo to come into his own vocation.

Bilbo knows that Thorin will not be pleased after finding out what happened, but the hobbit returns out of loyalty to his friends. This takes great courage because doing the right thing is not always the easy thing. Perhaps it will even bring us grief, but it also gives peace. Bilbo sleeps soundly after he comes back.

Bilbo's contented rest also shows the difference between the materially rich and poor. The rich man may have physical wealth, but if this is all he has, a greater poverty fills him than does the poorest man or hobbit. Peace of soul is true wealth, which is precisely the thing lacking in one constantly fretting about losing his goods and plotting to gain more. The poor man may not have much materially, but he can sleep easier because his possessions do not control him. If his faith is strong, he knows that God will provide all that he needs. The rich man, if he does not have the same focus and understanding of where his wealth comes from, will not even put God in the equation. The poor man may still go to bed hungry but not in the same way the rich man does. Bilbo loses his peace only after the Ring begins to gain control, which causes him to fear losing it and to continually check whether it is safe. It also later increasingly possesses Frodo, which is an extra torment because he has already dedicated himself to destroying the object he lusts after.

The lowest point in Thorin's life comes after desire for the Arkenstone so bewitches him that he nearly murders Bilbo after the burglar bravely confesses what he did. Like an addict, the dwarf has eyes only for what is destroying him and is blind to the beauty around him, including friends who try to help. Gollum, Smaug, and Thorin are disturbingly similar in what their avarice drives them to desire. "For where your treasure is, there will your heart be also" (Matt. 6:19-21). Thorin's heart is with the priceless artifact that Bilbo has willingly given away. St. Paul's words to Timothy about the perils of pursuing wealth are also applicable to this dwarf and the general dwarven lust for material things: "People who long to be rich are a prey to temptation; they get trapped into all sorts of foolish and dangerous ambitions which eventually plunge them into ruin and destruction. 'The love of money is the root of all evils' and there are some who, pursuing it, have wandered away from the faith, and so given their souls any number of fatal wounds" (1 Tim. 6:9-10).

Despite the terrible threat to Thorin's soul, good still comes. The arguing over who will get Smaug's hoarded wealth delays the start of battle, and rather than destroying each other to gain it, the Dwarves, Men, and Elves unite instead against their true enemies. The goblins come out of rage and hate caused by the death of the Great Goblin, and they seek to destroy any and all. But such evil will is used against them, and many are slain who would have otherwise lived. Janet Brennan Croft observes that if the Dwarves, Men, and Elves "had not been ready to fight, or had already fought their own battle, the Goblins and Wargs would have overwhelmed them, captured the Lonely Mountain, and used it as a base to conquer Laketown, northern Mirkwood, and much of Wilderland" (*War and the Works of J. R. R. Tolkien*, 96).

Thorin reaches the high point of his life on his deathbed after the battle is won. He realizes that he cannot take with him any of the treasure that had so consumed him shortly before. He acquires instead true wealth after he comes to understand that the uncomplicated, cheerful, and peaceful life of a hobbit detached from greed is the way to achieve contentment. It would indeed be a better world if we could each let go of what we think we must have and simply enjoy God's bounty as He bestows it upon us. He will always make sure that we never lack anything that we truly need.

Another moment of grace is Thorin's belief in the afterlife. He says that he will pass "to the halls of waiting to sit beside my fathers, until the world is renewed" (*Hobbit*, 262). He dies repentant of his harshness toward Bilbo and cleansed of the dragon-sickness. This comes too late to save his body but in time to save his soul. The grief-stricken hobbit recognizes how blessed he was to hear the dwarf's last words to him and that they parted as friends. Thorin acquires the Arkenstone at last but only after death.

After Bilbo and Gandalf return to the Shire, the hobbit stops to recite a poem. The wizard responds by saying Bilbo is not the same person he was before and implies that he has become who he was always meant to be.

Bilbo comes home with his worldly treasures in time to stop the remaining auction of his more homely ones. In the aftermath, he discovers that not only are his silver spoons beyond recovery, but so is his reputation as a conventional hobbit. The latter does not matter to him because through such loss, he has gained so much more. He has taken advantage of the slow-kindled courage of his kind and given full rein to his Tookish side without abandoning his Baggins side. As a result, the Baggins part has decided that it is not so bad to be a Took, and the Tookish part has discovered that it is not so bad to be a Baggins. Each can enjoy the good things of the other, and Bilbo can indulge them both as he pleases without worry of conflict.

This integration of both sides of Bilbo is something we should strive to achieve in our own life. How wonderful it feels to pursue and achieve our dreams with the different parts of ourselves happy and willing to live in peace with each other rather than always in a state of tension. This new, unrespectable, 'mad' Baggins is the one who Frodo will love and who will also deeply influence Sam.

Just as Bilbo's tale is at its end, Gandalf makes one of the clearest statements about the role of providential guidance in the hobbit's life: "You don't really suppose, do you, that all your adventures and escapes were managed by mere luck, just for your sole benefit?" (*Hobbit*, 276). These veiled words become evident after it is understood Who preserved Bilbo through his trials, so that the hobbit could play his part in the Great Music and later help Frodo to do so as well. It is also nice to know Elrond is wrong in his fear that the Necromancer's final downfall will not happen for many ages to come. In less than a century, a blink of an eye for an Elf, it will occur. All of this is a part of it, though for now, only the Writer of the Story knows it.

Chapter Three

Chosen

*M*any years after Bilbo returns home, he becomes increasingly restless. He wants to go on another adventure and also to return to Rivendell, the one place he knew true peace. He decides to leave on his eleventy-first birthday, which is the same day Frodo comes of age at thirty-three.

Bilbo plans to leave the Ring with Frodo and hopes that hosting an elaborate party and leaving gifts for others will make parting with this particular treasure a little easier. But it is even more of a wrench to surrender than the Arkenstone. His possession so possesses him that he tries to justify keeping it by saying that because he found it, it is his. We should be aware that if we start rationalizing something, it is likely not a proper thing to do or to have done.

As Gandalf attempts to persuade Bilbo to go through with the original plan, the hobbit becomes afraid that the wizard wants to steal it and nearly draws his sword on his friend. But he soon realizes the truth. "The ear attentive to wholesome correction finds itself at home in the company of the wise. He who rejects discipline despises his own self; he who listens to correction wins discernment" (Prov. 15:31-32). In the end, Bilbo's ear is indeed attentive. Although hobbits have little or no knowledge of their Creator, they still show faith in those that He sends as guides and guardians. Bilbo's own will is almost not strong enough to surrender the Ring, but with angelic assistance, he corresponds with the grace that he receives to release himself from it. He trusts Gandalf's word that giving up the Ring is the right thing to do because he trusts Gandalf. The wizard does not force this choice upon his dear friend, but he bolsters Bilbo's own decision, which allows the Ring to pass to the one ordained to carry it to the Fire.

After Bilbo lets go of the Ring, he is angry for a moment but then laughs. He no longer needs to worry about losing it. He has generously given away the physical treasure that he acquired on his great adventure and kept only his spiritual growth and a few other invaluable things. He knows that all his needs will now be met by the Elves, so he takes nothing with him but the book he is writing, the clothes on his back, and a small pack that providentially includes Sting and his *mithril* coat. As Bilbo sets out, he declares to Gandalf that he has never been happier. Such joy can accompany any new venture or after gaining freedom from a harmful addiction, whether it be drugs, gambling, pornography, alcohol, or anything else.

Seventeen years pass before Gandalf returns to tell Frodo exactly what Bilbo had bequeathed to him. "The Hunt for the Ring" gives more details of the events leading up to this and beyond (Tolkien, *Unfinished Tales*, 337-354). It starts with a mention of the grace that protects Gollum after the Nazgûl capture him in Mordor in 1417 by the Shire Reckoning. Though the Ring consumed him for centuries, there is still enough hobbit nature, as well as something else, left in him to withstand the hideous torture of Sauron. The Dark Lord perceives the unbreakable strength in his prisoner, but he does not understand the source of it. His own abandonment of the Light blinds him to the deeply hidden and corrupted good in the ruined hobbit.

What Sauron does clearly see is Gollum's hatred for the thief who had robbed him of his treasure. The Dark Lord releases his captive and sends spies to follow the wretched creature in the hope that this will lead to the Ring. But what the Enemy fails to realize is that Gollum hates him more than Bilbo and so lied about what he knows of the Shire's location.

Sauron learns of Gollum's capture by Aragorn, who brings his prisoner to the Elves in Mirkwood. The Dark Lord gains little other information because of the watchfulness of Saruman and also the Rangers. These men double their guard on the Shire after Gandalf suspects that Bilbo's surrendered treasure is more than it seems. Sauron decides none but his most enslaved and fell servants can bring him further news. The Nazgûl are both his greatest weapons and worst liabilities. The terror that they use to debilitate their enemies is so powerful that it cannot be hidden even when Sauron would desire it, as he would now. In an attempt to obscure the true purpose of his slaves, Sauron has Orcs attack Gondor and take

Osgiliath and assault Mirkwood and recapture Gollum. In these small strokes some later historians saw the beginning of the War of the Ring.

The Nazgûl later learn that Gollum escaped from both the Orcs and the Elves who followed. As the wraiths have no knowledge of the Shire after the exposure of Gollum's lie, the Witch-king leads his men North in the hope of finding it and the hobbit but to no avail.

An alternate version of "Hunt" states that Sauron has no idea Gollum knows where Baggins lives. The Dark Lord incorrectly assumes that it is near where Gollum himself lived long ago. This mistake costs Sauron dearly, as the Nazgûl waste precious time searching the area around the Anduin. This is, however, all part of the providential timing of events.

This different version continues that after Gollum's release from Mordor, he enters the Dead Marshes, where Sauron's spies cannot or choose not to follow the creature. The men had to have been aware that their master's wrath would fall upon them if they failed in their task, yet fail they do, whether willingly or not. This allows Aragorn to capture Gollum.

Gandalf learns of Gollum's capture before returning to the Shire. The fortunate timing of this event gives the wizard an opportunity to question the wretched hobbit and learn enough to strongly suspect that Bilbo's magic treasure is none other than Sauron's.

Armed with this alarming information, Gandalf comes to Bag End to warn Frodo. He gives the hobbit a catechism lesson about the history and horror of the Ring and how it comes to dominate and destroy those who bear it. The wizard also tells his friend that he had thought of consulting Saruman about it, even before he knew what it truly was, but something always prevented him. He did not know then the reason that he held back, but he trusted in the "still small voice" (1 Kings 19:12, NKJV) that he heard in his heart. We should also listen to such warnings, for there is wisdom there, even though we may not understand it at the time.

Gandalf has only one last test to perform to confirm that Bilbo's prize is indeed Sauron's. He uses Frodo's humble fire to set alight the script the Dark Lord inscribed on it, which brings the hobbit's vocation to light as well. Frodo reacts fearfully and wishes that the rise of evil was not taking place while he was alive. Gandalf agrees, but he says that it is not up to any of us to choose what happens when. Rather he counsels, "All we have to decide is what to do with the time that is given us"

(*LOTR*, 50). In a book chock full of wisdom, this is one of the best and truest guides in how to live our life and one that Frodo takes deeply to heart throughout his ordeal.

Gandalf's statement that not only was Bilbo meant to find the Ring by a power other than Sauron, but Frodo was just as clearly meant to possess it, demonstrates the fascinating interplay of fate and free will that is woven throughout the tale. The emphasis the wizard deliberately places on 'meant' is a clear indication that Providence continues to guide everything along. But even so, the ensuing events also depend on Frodo's free choice to accept the role ordained for him.

Gandalf desires for his words to comfort and encourage Frodo, but the hobbit does not feel either. He definitely wants the Ring destroyed and the danger removed, but he does not want to be the one to do it. Nonetheless, even though he wonders why in the world he was chosen, he still realizes that he was. In some way, he hears in his heart, 'Before I formed you in the womb I knew you; before you came to birth I consecrated you' (Jer. 1:5). This knowledge frightens Frodo, but God has spent decades preparing His beloved child for this sacred task and allows even tragedies into the Song to help shape who the hobbit is and what he is meant to do. If Frodo's parents had not drowned in a boating accident when he was twelve, there would have been no need for Bilbo to later adopt him and bring him to live with him, close to Sam. It is no coincidence that Sam was born the same year Drogo and Primula died, or that he followed in his father's footsteps and became the gardener at Bag End. During the years before the Quest, the Writer of the Story planted the deep roots of love for Frodo in Sam's fertile heart that are so vital to the coming journey. Even Bilbo's bachelorhood, so rare among hobbits, is meant to be, for it allows him to make Frodo his heir and heir to the Ring.

Frodo protests that he does not have what is needed for the terrible task that looms over him. This assumption that we know ourselves and our limitations is quite common. We must realize, however, that God knows us far better and chooses us for the strengths that He sees in us, even those that have not yet manifested themselves. An observation Jentezen Franklin makes about why Jesus chose twelve particular men as His disciples also fits the hobbits who venture out beyond their land: "He did not choose them because of what they were to start with. He chose them because of what He knew they could become through His mighty power infused with their passion" (*Believe That You Can*, 85-86). God knows that Frodo has a great store of courage within. He allows the Quest to play out as it does so that the hobbit can discover this himself.

Frodo's objection about not having the strength required to fulfill a perilous vocation will echo through the ages. To name just a few Biblical examples, Jeremiah will say that he is too young (Jer. 1:6), Isaiah will protest that he is too unclean (Isa. 6:5), and Gideon will think himself too weak (Judg. 6:15). Many of us naturally resist what seems impossible or incredibly dangerous. Fear can seize us after we learn that we must leave our comfortable life behind and become a needed instrument of God's will to destroy some dread evil. Even Jesus will be afraid of His coming trials, so God perfectly understands the times we feel that we are not up to facing our tribulations. As we cry "Why me?" and quail before the wave ready to drown us, we must understand what Frodo comes to know during his ordeal: God does not call the equipped; He equips the called. Few of us think that we are superheroes out to save the world, and we should not necessarily trust those who believe that they are. Better to be like Frodo and all those who are terrified and want nothing to do with what is asked but still submit themselves to the fact they were indeed chosen. They shoulder their crosses not out of ambition or a quest for glory but out of love and service, and through blood, sweat, and tears accomplish what they are meant to do. Let us say with them, "Here I am; send me!" (Isa. 6:9, NRSV) and "Nevertheless, let your will be done, not mine" (Luke 22:42).

The more we surrender control over ourselves to God, the more wonders He will work in our life as we discover our own unique vocation. We must trust that if we take the first steps, God will remain with us. Though the path may become dark, His Light will always be there, even if we do not perceive it. "I know God will not give me anything I can't handle," Blessed Teresa of Calcutta will say. "I just wish He didn't trust me so much." But what is so beautiful, humbling, and awe-inspiring is that He *does* trust us. He, who is Power itself and could do all things far more perfectly than we ever could, chooses instead to use us frail, mortal, quivering, imperfect creatures. He will not give us a task that is beyond us, even if we think that He has. If we cooperate with His grace, we will discover the strength that He has given us, which sometimes can be refined only by passing through fire.

This is a lesson Frodo learns and teaches on his terrible journey. But at the moment he is still too afraid to go and asks Gandalf to take the burden of the Ring. The wizard's sharp reaction offers an interesting contrast to the hobbit, who protests about how ill equipped he is for dangerous adventures, yet will prove a much better Ring-bearer than his far more powerful friend.

> We might expect the great figure of good in the novel to be able to rise above the wicked power emanating from the Ring, transcending its ability to seduce its Bearer into selfishness and greed. If anyone is superior to the Ring's evil, it seems, it should be the morally unimpeachable Gandalf. But, in fact, when Frodo offers the Ring to Gandalf, the wizard pulls back sharply. . . . His explanation is candid and revealing. He says that his power makes him too susceptible, and that his great moral goodness could turn to equally great evil under the Ring's influence. The Ring's power is greater, he admits, than his own moral strength. (Gardner et al., *SparkNotes*, 36)

Gandalf is well aware and respectful of the dreadful power of the Ring and its ability to perceive and corrupt the deepest desires of any heart. For the wizard, this is pity towards those he has stewardship over and his desire to better their lot. He knows, however, that to use such a fell object for good is a fatal lie and would put the immense strength locked within him at the Ring's disposal. This and recognition of his own potential for weakness allows him to reject the temptation. If he wielded it, he would no longer be a servant of God and the Valar but the Lord of the Rings himself. He would betray his Creator and the mission entrusted to the Istari, which had the prohibition of using their powers to dominate others. Saruman falls prey to this temptation, but Gandalf understands the mandate quite well. In his rejection of the Ring, he is the only wizard who remains true to his calling. He is content as a servant and does not wish to rise above his station. He has no desire to impose his will but to guide others to make their own decisions and to aid them in carrying their burdens. This includes helping a small hobbit carry around his neck the terrible weight of the sins of a fallen angel.

After Gandalf refuses Frodo's plea, he says that the hobbit must decide for himself what to do. In the long and thoughtful silence that follows, Frodo's active imagination sees the volcanic Cracks of Doom within his own small fire. He finally accepts that he must take custody of the Ring no matter what the peril to his life and soul in order to draw the danger away from the Shire and from the possibility that Sauron will recover his lost treasure. This choice echoes in the words of the great Bishop, spiritual director, and Doctor of the Church, St. Francis de Sales.

> The Everlasting God has in His wisdom foreseen from eternity the cross He now presents to you as a gift from His inmost Heart. This cross He now sends you He has considered with His all-knowing eyes, understood with His divine mind, tested with His wise justice, warmed with His loving arms and weighed with His own Hands, to see that it be not one inch too large and not one ounce too heavy for you. He has blessed it with His Holy Name, anointed it with His grace, perfumed it with His consolation, taken one last glance at you and your courage, and then sent it to you from heaven, a special greeting from God to you, an alms of the all-merciful love of God.

Even with Frodo's newfound determination, he still hopes that another custodian will be found quickly. He admits that he has toyed with the idea of leaving on an adventurous journey like Bilbo's, but he wants to return to his peaceful life afterwards. The Quest that comes calling instead is quite a bit outside his comfort level, and its full terror has not yet revealed itself to him. His endurance of it will push him to his uttermost limits, which are far beyond the ones he currently thinks that he has. Even before he sets out, he is already sure that he will not return. Here again, St. Francis de Sales provides counsel for the times we fear that a burden will crush our fragile spirits.

> Do not look forward in fear to the changes of life. Rather look to them with full hope that as they arise, God,

whose very own you are, will lead you safely through all things; and when you cannot stand, God will carry you in His arms. Do not look forward to what may happen tomorrow. The same Everlasting Father who takes care of you today, will take care of you tomorrow, and every day. He will either shield you from suffering or will give you unfailing strength to bear it. Be at peace, then, and put aside all anxious thoughts and imaginations.

This wisdom is what Frodo comes to understand. Even in his ignorance, he learns to trust and speaks openly about this later in the Emyn Muil. There is so much to learn from his inspirational example!

To help Frodo to carry his cross, many grace-filled moments bless him throughout the ordeal. Some occur even before he leaves the Shire behind. The first is that Gandalf catches Sam eavesdropping on their conversation. The wizard thrills the humble gardener with the punishment of requiring him to accompany Frodo on his dangerous errand. If one moment could be singled out as more important than any other, this would be it, as the success of the Quest would have been impossible to achieve without Sam.

Preparations for the Ring-bearer's departure are made as secretly as possible. As far as anyone knows, Frodo is moving back to Buckland where he spent part of his youth. He is not yet aware that several of his cousins and Sam have formed a conspiracy to keep him and the Ring safe. He thinks that only he, Sam, and Gandalf know that he actually intends to leave the Shire altogether. After helping Frodo to celebrate one last birthday at Bag End, Merry sets off in the morning to get his cousin's new home ready while Pippin and Sam stay behind. That Gandalf does not return as promised distresses the Ring-bearer, but even the evil delaying the wizard is made good because it forces the hobbit to make his own decisions and grow more into his vocation. God does not waste anything. He uses every opportunity to help us mature, even though sometimes it is painful. "We know that by turning everything to their good God co-operates with all those who love him, with all those that he has called according to his purpose" (Rom. 8:28).

The "Hunt" tale gives the background of another moment of grace. The Nazgûl capture two spies of Saruman, one of whom has maps of the Shire. The wraiths use them to come upon the southernmost borders the night of Frodo's birthday. After a valiant but futile resistance by the Rangers, the Black Riders enter the Shire before dawn the next day and separate to search it. One of them reaches Hobbiton in the evening just as the Ring-bearer and his companions set out. The timing of this is incredibly close and all because Saruman lusted after pipeweed and so employed the spies. Gandalf found out but kept his superior's secret. He did not know that the White wizard's knowledge of the land would bring great peril and the victory of Sauron within grasp. But the Dark Lord does not achieve such triumph. Even though the Riders learn where Baggins lives and do indeed come dangerously close to him, it is the least dangerous Nazgûl, Khamûl, who questions the Gaffer about Frodo's whereabouts. Though the wraith is second only to the Witch-king himself in sensitivity to the Ring's presence, he is also the one whose power is weakest in daylight, which is when he later comes near the hobbits on the way to Buckland. Hunter and hunted are more than once within hearing distance of each other, but neither know it.

Frodo overhears the conversation that Khamûl has with Sam's father, but he does not know who the visitor is and why relief fills him after the stranger goes down the hill rather than up to where he stands. He thinks of asking the Gaffer about the event but decides for the "better (or worse) of it" (*LOTR*, 68) against doing so. Comments such as this are another thing that brings reality to this tale. Even as Frodo is not sure whether his decision to stay away is the right one, we do not always know if our choices are correct or not. This particular instance shows he has indeed made the right decision because the Ring would have betrayed him, or attempted to do so, and the Quest would have been over before it even began.

Frodo sleeps easily his first night on the Road. His heart is sad with the burden that he will soon leave his beloved Shire and friends behind, but he remains for the moment innocent and unharmed. The fear of pursuit that will soon hound him for months has not yet taken hold, though it will begin the next day. But evil is not the only Power watching out for him.

Chapter Four

The Grace of Friends

On the way to Buckland, Frodo repeats to Sam and Pippin the warning of Bilbo to use caution on the Road because there was always a risk of being swept off one's feet. Tom Shippey notes that not only can the Road symbolize life, but it could also be

> an image of Providence. After all, Bilbo is right about the road outside Bag End leading all the way to Mordor. On the other hand there are on that road, which Frodo takes, thousands of intersections, as also thousands of choices to be made or rejected. The traveller can always stop or turn aside. Only will-power makes the road seem straight. Accordingly, when Bilbo and Frodo say they will pursue it, eagerly or wearily, till it is intersected by other roads, lives, wishes, and *will then continue into the unknown, if they can,* they are expressing a mixture of doubt and determination – exactly the qualities that Gandalf so often recommends. This has become much stronger and clearer with Frodo. (*Road*, 188; italics in original)

The spiritual warfare that Frodo engages in on the Quest started with his decision to leave with the Ring. It becomes much more earnest as he walks toward Crickhollow. Though he has kept to Gandalf's cautions to leave the Ring untouched in the years since Bilbo left, the temptation to use it hounds Frodo throughout his journey. But grace fills him as well.

One such instance of this potent combination is after Sam's sharp ears pick up the sound of a pony or horse coming behind them. This gives the hobbits time to hide, but Frodo does not do so as quickly as his companions. He wants to, but this wish battles with "curiosity or some other feeling" (*LOTR*, 73) about whoever is near. This is another example of how true this tale is to life. We do not always know what motivates us to do something anymore than the Ring-bearer does here. In this case, the Ring recognizes the proximity of the Black Rider and tries to get the wraith's attention by delaying Frodo from hiding. Only in the nick of time does the hobbit hide as the Rider comes sniffing for him.

Though physically hidden, Frodo is still not safe from the call of the Ring. His heart and mind fill with terror that the Rider will discover him and also with the thought that if he puts on the Ring, he will escape notice. It nearly seduces him into thinking Gandalf's warnings are nonsense and its own promise of deliverance is what he should hearken to.

The enemy of our soul works this same way. The delusory powers of our foe are great, and sometimes they are so subtle that our easily confused will finds it difficult to know right away that it deals with deception. How often we fall prey to fell whispers that put truth on its head and make it appear a lie and a lie truth. What appears to be a way out is in reality not a path to escape the net but to fall deeper into it. We may resist a temptation at first because we know that we should and because wiser souls have told us what could happen if we do not. But then it begins to look attractive, and we start to want it. Sense and nonsense switch places in our mind, and we begin to think the opposite of what we were taught. It may be a while before we realize who told the truth and who the lie, and what we thought was solely an act of our own will was actually the press of another upon ours. Rose Zimbardo notes that "the power of darkness cannot see into the heart of light. It must depend for its power upon a failure of the will to good. Yet the vulnerability of each creature to such a failure is built into his very nature" ("Moral Vision in *The Lord of the Rings*," *Tolkien and the Critics*, 105). Frodo increasingly comes to understand this.

Let us guard ourselves against the siren songs that constantly vie for our attention and keep our heart, mind, and soul out of the traps that are set to ensnare us. As the tactics of our adversary have not changed from the beginning, we can counter them as we perceive them. The foe tempted Eve, and she fell for the attractive lie of becoming powerful and immortal if she only ate a forbidden apple. Only after she and Adam bit into it did they discover the worm. How much better to avoid a proscribed path, no matter how enticing it seems, rather than to have the light fail and the door close behind us. Let us recognize such traps before we must gnaw off our own foot to escape them. Our foe outmatches us in will and strength, but just as God guards Frodo and protects him from discovery, He also watches over us.

The Black Rider does not know how close he is to his prey, and his departure dissipates the compulsion that almost engulfed the Ring-bearer completely. Evil defeats evil on the cusp of its victory.

Frodo wishes that he had waited for Gandalf, as this adventure is already a bit too much for him. But he wonders whether this would have only worsened the situation, which is indeed true. He left just in time. Sometimes we know only after the fact whether or not a particular decision was right. However, if we trust the Writer of the Story who sees the whole book, as we walk from page to page and see only letters and sentences, then we can travel more confidently amidst our doubts.

The next temptation to put on the Ring is much stronger and again nearly overcomes Frodo, but the Vala Elbereth intercedes on his behalf. The hobbits encounter the rarity of a company of High Elves singing hymns to the revered Lady of the Stars, which breaks the coercive force of the Ring and frightens the Rider off. Many, but not all, of the times the Ring assaults its Bearer demonstrate that "You can trust God not to let you be tried beyond your strength, and with any trial he will give you a way out of it and the strength to bear it" (1 Cor. 10:13).

Frodo has talked with Elves before and uses a little of their own language. Cami Agan notes that this meeting is a "sacred moment" ("Song as Mythic Conduit in *The Fellowship of the Ring*," *Mythlore* 26, 50). Joy, awe, and even a little fear overwhelm Sam after his dream of seeing Elves comes true so soon. It is no wonder that this night lives forever in his heart and mind as a treasure beyond price, though he retains little clear memory of it. Such a marvel would be beyond the ability of mortal words to express.

After Frodo asks Gildor for counsel, the Elf does not wish to give much. He does not clearly discern the hobbit's path, and he does not want to say anything that would inadvertently deflect the Ring-bearer and companions from the Road that they are to follow. Gildor is right to suspect, however, that this is not just a chance meeting. Throughout the story, he and others come to the aid of the hobbits during the times that they are most at risk of their enemies devouring them. The Elf invokes Elbereth's protection against the threat of the Black Riders and says that he will pass word along to more of the Wandering Companies and others of good will to watch out for Frodo and his friends.

Frodo asks Sam the next morning whether he still wants to continue and bluntly tells him that it is unlikely that either of them will return. The younger hobbit does not hesitate to say that he intends to go on, and if Frodo is not going to come back, then neither is he. The humble gardener receives the gift of seeing the path ahead clearer than perhaps anyone. This is not to frighten him but to strengthen him. He realizes that the Road will lead into great darkness, but this knowledge does not deter him. He reports that he told the Elves the night before that he will follow his beloved master to the moon if need be. In fact, it will be to hell on earth. The sacrifice of his own life in service to Frodo is one that Sam is willing to make, just as Frodo is willing to die for all Middle-earth if necessary. The devotion that Sam gives in such exemplary fashion throughout the Quest echoes in Dag Hammarskjöld's words about medieval mystics: "Love – that much misused and misinterpreted word – for them meant simply an overflowing of the strength with which they felt themselves filled when living in true self-oblivion. And this love found natural expression in an unhesitant fulfillment of duty and an unreserved acceptance of life, whether it brought them person-ally of toil, suffering – or happiness" (*Markings*, viii).

The short cut that takes the hobbits out of their way is another grace-filled moment because it leads to Farmer Maggot's homestead, where they otherwise would not have come. The farmer recounts the strange visitor who came looking for Baggins shortly before. Both Maggot and Gaffer Gamgee demonstrated little fear in the presence of the Black Rider and even talked back to him. In contrast, even the bravest of the soldiers of Gondor are afraid as they hear the cries of the Nazgûl flying above Minas Tirith. The terror that the wraiths inspire apparently needs to have something already in place to feed upon and magnify. The hobbits have not received the schooling in fear that those who live in the shadow of Mordor's mountains have, so they could perhaps simply not know they should be badly affected.

Maggot is indeed right that it is not accidental that Frodo, Sam, and Pippin arrive at his farm this particular afternoon so shortly after the Rider left. Even those who are not intellectually aware of their Creator still recognize a pattern to events and thus dimly recognize the Pattern-Maker. As the Nazgûl are most powerful at night, Maggot provides another moment of grace by giving the hobbits a lift by cart, which gets them safely to the point where Merry meets them near the Bucklebury Ferry. Rather than becoming caught in a dense fog on the same side of the Brandywine as the pursuing wraith, they cross the River just in time.

Powers above continue to keep close watch over each step of the Quest and to provide help at the precise moment most needed. Water, under the guardianship of the Vala Ulmo, provides the necessary barrier this time between the Nazgûl and his prey. We must realize that we are just as guarded and guided. Let us never believe that one instant of our life is outside God's providential care.

Sam receives little nudges that help him to fulfill his calling to take care of Frodo. Just as the gardener had earlier looked behind as he, Frodo, and Pippin paused to decide what to do after encountering a stream that cut across their path, Sam does so again after reaching the other side of the River. He saves the Quest both times by heeding whatever instinct or inner voice that told him to alert the others about the Rider.

The time at Crickhollow proves Aristotle's words that friendship is "most indispensable for life." The revelation of the conspiracy formed to ensure that Frodo did not leave on his own stuns the Ring-bearer. Merry tells his cousin of the fear that he, Pippin, and Sam have of what is ahead but also of their determination to follow and face the peril of the Ring with Frodo because of their bond with him. If Sauron had heard these words and understood the power wrapped up in them, "Barad-dûr would have been shaken to its foundations" (Wood, *Gospel*, 127).

Sauron would also find incomprehensible the innocent excitement of his mighty enemies, as the young hobbits dance around Frodo in celebration that their company is indeed welcome. Their fear has not left them, but the joy of being with the one they love overwhelms it.

Implacable malice such as Sauron's cannot understand such happiness; unwavering hate cannot fathom unconditional, sacrificial love; selfishness cannot penetrate the wisdom of selflessness. Love allows us to do amazing, even otherwise impossible, things, and these hobbits excel at love. "You are worth what your heart is worth," Blessed Pope John Paul II said. This makes Frodo, Sam, Merry, and Pippin priceless. As the Quest unfolds, the hobbits prove that "a friend is a friend at all times, it is for adversity that a brother is born" (Prov. 17:17).

Frodo dreams that night of the Sea, a sound he has heard many times while sleeping. Erica Challis notes, "If Frodo was born hearing the voice of Ulmo, he must surely be singled out for some special fate" ("Secret Messengers," *More People's Guide to J. R. R. Tolkien*, 34).

The next morning, as Frodo, Sam, Merry, and Pippin enter the Old Forest, the tale reminds us that even though we are always under the watchful care of God and His angels, there are other powers that keep an eye on us as well. Wicked wills determine part of the path the hobbits travel, though again, great good comes from it, as the four travelers are now close enough for Tom Bombadil to rescue them.

After an unnatural sleepiness overcomes everyone else, Sam's vocation to protect his Frodo reveals itself once more. The gardener realizes that there is something not quite right about this urge to nap and receives the strength to resist the compulsion of the song-spell woven about them. He rescues his unconscious master after the evil willow-tree tips Frodo into the River.

Old Man Willow also brings Merry and Pippin into mortal peril by drawing them into himself. After Frodo and Sam's efforts to rescue them are in vain, the Ring-bearer runs away and frantically yells for help, though he does not know why. As far as he knows, there is no reason for him to think anyone who can aid him will hear. Some situations leave us as desperate as Frodo, but just as he receives inspiration to call out for assistance, we can also. Let us never believe that there is no help for us or that we must rely on our own strength. God will reveal what we are to do at the time that is best for us and the ones we are to help. We need only to respond to what He speaks in our heart and soul, even if our mind do not understand. Of course, our enemy reaches us in the same way, but if we are open to the grace God gives, we will recognize the difference.

One of the more unusual people in Middle-earth answers Frodo's panicked cry. We do not need to know where Tom falls in the Entish list of races to know that he is as much a child of God as anyone and a servant of His. It is not quite clear where Goldberry belongs either, but certainly she is a being of power and grace, who fills Frodo's heart with a joy that he does not entirely comprehend. Taryne Jade Taylor observes, "Upon seeing Goldberry and witnessing her power, Frodo has noticed her resonances of the Great Music of the Ainur, although he may not recognize it as such" ("Investigating the Role and Origin of Goldberry in Tolkien's Mythology," *Mythlore* 27, 153).

Taylor continues, "Goldberry's task . . . is not simply to represent goodness and joy, but to cleanse the hobbits" (ibid.). She notes that Tom and his lady bring back the hobbits' love of nature, which was damaged by the malice in the Old Forest. They are no longer as naive as they were before leaving the Shire, but they have not lost their "love and innate joy in the world" (ibid., 154).

After a hearty meal, Frodo asks if Tom heard his cries for help. Tom says no, but his hints to the hobbits make it clear that someone called him to be nearby at that particular moment: "Just chance brought me then, if chance you call it. It was no plan of mine, though I was waiting for you" (*LOTR*, 123-124). This is, of course, not a chance meeting at all, any more than coming upon Gildor was or any of the other fateful encounters to come. They are all part of the Music composed before the dawn of time. When speakers refer to such as fortunate coincidences, and especially when they qualify them as Tom does to imply that the opposite is true, it is because they suspect or know that Providence is instead at work. Words like seemed, chance, or meant all give veiled hints of the Invisible working in and through the visible. In writing about this, Frodo leaves the door open that some happenings are not pure luck, but instead there is a thought and purpose behind them that he only sees "in a mirror, dimly" (1 Cor. 13:12, NKJV). Events often seem murky to us as well, even with the light of faith. The grace that fills the Ring-bearer allows him to see as clearly as he does.

In a dream, Frodo witnesses the rescue of Gandalf from Orthanc, though the hobbit does not realize what he has seen until he reaches Rivendell. In the morning, he looks out the window and half expects to see the marks of the Black Rider's horse, but he does not. He is glad that rain prevents his departure because he dreads to leave such a place of safety.

While the hobbits wait for the storm to pass, Tom entertains them with many tales. After dinner, he asks to see the Ring and shows that he is the only one apparently immune to its corruption. To the great shock of his guests, he does not even disappear after while wearing it. He has no ambition it can latch onto because he does not seek to be anyone other than himself. He is his own master and completely at home and at peace with his own little corner of Middle-earth. He has no desire to travel beyond its borders. He has power over others, like his ability to sing Old Man Willow back to sleep or later to banish the wight from the barrow, but he does not seek to use his will to enslave others. He knows that the Ring is evil, but it does not concern him overly much.

Even if the Ring poses no threat to Tom, it still does to Frodo. It makes another attack on the hobbit's will and soul, as he watches his host treat the Ring as a mere trifle and not the great danger Gandalf said it was. After Frodo receives it back, he wonders whether it is even his anymore or if Tom is fooling him. To test this, he reacts to the subtlest of the Ring's temptations without even realizing it and takes another step down the slippery slope that he finds himself on while he bears it. He pretends to delight in Merry's surprise at his sudden disappearance, but he rightly feels guilty instead. We should as well after we do something we know we should not.

Before Frodo, Sam, Merry, and Pippin leave Tom and Goldberry, a vision of the West blesses the Ring-bearer. Goldberry spiritually fortifies the hobbits for the arduous road ahead by telling them to remain determined to carry on with what they have set out to do. As Taylor notes, she "instills in the hobbits the wisdom, love and hope of Ilúvatar as they were passed to her in the Original Music" ("Investigating," 155).

The Ring-bearer and his companions have need of such blessings throughout their terrible trials. One of the more frightening times for Frodo occurs after he becomes separated from his friends in a terrible fog not long after they leave Tom's house. Frodo hears their cries for help, but he is unable to aid them until a barrow-wight captures him as well. After he rouses from an induced sleep, he thinks that his journey has already come to a horrible end, but he does not despair. Rather, Ralph C. Wood notes the use of the "passive voice to indicate that Frodo is being graciously acted upon, even as he himself courageously acts: 'He found himself stiffening' (1.151)" (*Gospel*, 122).

As Frodo watches the terrible arm of the wight move toward Sam and the sword that lies across the necks of his friends, the Ring-bearer struggles again with the temptation to put on the Ring in order to save himself. Part of the attempted seduction this time is the rationalization that even Gandalf would agree flight is the only option, even though it means sacrificing Sam, Merry, and Pippin. Such lies bewilder us at times as well, as the thought of self-preservation has mighty appeal, and we begin to waver like Frodo. Just as Bilbo did in the tunnel, and just as we must, Frodo has to struggle against his own self to win this battle.

> Sauron's power . . . afflicts the mind and heart of its wearer, working its insidious effects from the inside out. . . . The struggle Frodo undergoes in this episode is therefore not just between himself and a wicked demon, but between two parts of himself. . . . We see again that Tolkien's tale is not just about external happenings, but about inward development. (Gardner et al., *SparkNotes*, 49)

In what may be the moment most fraught with peril so far, the Ring-bearer's will stands poised on the knife edge between flight or fight, ruin or rescue. His courage then kindles and, after battling himself once more, he makes the fateful choice to stay and fight to save his friends. He sees through the lie the Ring offers, and Gandalf later confirms his wisdom. Frodo has no idea how vital his cooperation with grace is at this moment. Such grace will fill us too, if we are strong enough to use it as the hobbit does. That he overcomes temptation and terror here shows him what he is capable of and stands in contrast to his earlier protest that he had little of what was necessary to deal with deadly danger. This knowledge grows throughout the Quest, as the assaults on him increase. It allows him to resist the wound inflicted at Weathertop, to answer the call that he receives at the Council of Elrond, to fight the terrible battle on Amon Hen, to make the decision to leave the Company at Parth Galen, and to struggle against the siren song of the Ring on the terrible Road to Mount Doom. Each success strengthens him for the next contest. We should use any opportunity to bolster our own will against the attacks of our enemy.

Tom Bombadil comes to the rescue again after Frodo responds to the inspiration to sing the verse that Tom taught the hobbits to use if in peril. Their innocent joy as they run on the grass and bask in the sun as though nothing happened shows their remarkable ability to quickly spring back from horrific events.

Before leaving the area, Tom gives the hobbits swords from the barrow that were wrought many centuries before. During the hunt for the Ring, the Lord of the Nazgûl roused the wights to watch for the Ring-bearer, but God used this malicious will and that of Old Man Willow for good. Without encountering the Willow, perhaps the hobbits would have never met Tom, and without becoming lost in the fog and captured by the wight, they could not have found blades made especially with spells against the Witch-king. The wraith's desire to harm others helps defeat him in the end. How intricately woven is this story!

After the hobbits reach *The Prancing Pony* at Bree, Frodo faces another temptation to put on the Ring, as he tries to distract the inn's customers from Pippin's story about Bilbo's birthday party. At first, the Ring-bearer strongly resists the compelling desire, but the Ring slides on as he slips and falls while singing. The hobbit's sudden disappearance shocks everyone in the room and alerts those of evil will, who were watching for anything out of the ordinary. After Frodo reappears, he wonders how the Ring got on his hand. He does not remember willing to put it on and insists to Barliman that it was an accident. It is actually more, as the Ring responded to the wickedness present in the room and overcame its Bearer without the hobbit's conscious awareness.

Such is the way with temptation. We resist with no problem one moment and give in the next. Our enemy does not always shout and bang on the door and give us time to raise our defenses. He knows that a howling wolf at the front gate will have the door barred against it, but if the back door is ajar, it can slip in quietly. Sometimes he does not even whisper but glides in through a crack, and we are overcome and wonder what in the Four Farthings just happened. The demonic powers that constantly lay traps at our feet know that it is much easier to seduce us into evil rather than to coerce us. The subtle attacks are the ones that we must be most watchful for. Our adversary is then at his most dangerous, and we are most at peril of becoming swept off the Road and into darkness. Throughout the Quest, Frodo endures both types of tests.

Other times God Himself leads us into darkness, as He does during Frodo and Sam's torturous journey to Mordor. We must be careful that we follow the right Person and do not rely on our own wisdom as to who leads us because our perspective could be tainted. Rather we should seek the guidance of others to confirm or deny our insights. Anywhere we walk, we need to hold onto God's hand and go where He leads. Frodo does not go alone to the Fire. He would have never made it on his own. Our Creator will not bring us into danger without protecting us through His own presence and those He sends to protect us.

One of Frodo's guardians is the unkempt Ranger who paid special attention to the tales Sam and Pippin told of the Shire. It was at this man's instigation that the Ring-bearer interrupted Pippin. As Strider's appearance in the tale surprised even Tolkien, no one knows right away if he is friend or foe. The man does not look like the king he is destined to be but someone possibly sinister. Soon enough, though, Aragorn appears as he truly is. He has spent his adult life providing unappreciated aid to those he and his kin have sworn themselves to protect. This life of humble service has required great sacrifice, including going without the comfort of being trusted, but it is also the path he has chosen to walk.

Aragorn has an opportunity to claim the Ring for himself, but it does not pose a serious temptation to him, even less than it later does to Faramir. Their humility and wisdom shield them from the allure of the demonic object. These virtues also help protect Sam during the hobbit's own trial in Mordor. Instead, Aragorn pledges himself to aid Frodo, whether it be by living or dying. The man is well aware that by placing the Ring-bearer's needs above his own, he may have to sacrifice his desire to wed his beloved Arwen. He knows, however, that his dreams cannot come true without sustaining others in their part of the Music.

The grace that continues to grow in Frodo once more reveals itself in his admission that he wanted to trust Strider, even before Gandalf's letter confirms this intuitive belief. The hobbit remarks the man frightened him but not in a way he thinks someone evil would. He shows his ability to see beneath the Ranger's scruffy looks and into Aragorn's kingly soul.

This discernment, which Frodo later demonstrates with Gollum and Saruman, is another gift that he receives to help him on his journey. His observations are astute, for our foe can indeed choose a fair form in order to entice us, as Sauron did with the Elves who made the Rings of Power. However, if the soul is awake and not dazzled by the seeming beauty, it still perceives the stench of evil underneath, or conversely, if not repelled by unattractive surface appearances, it sees inner goodness.

Merry regrets missing Frodo's song, but he had providentially decided instead to go out for a breath of fresh air. Aragorn already knows that the Nazgúl are looking for Baggins, but it is Merry's alarming brush with the wraiths that alerts the man not to let the hobbits go to their rooms and to remain with them in the parlor. The Quest could well have ended at the *Pony*, but instead, Aragorn leads his charges away from Bree the next morning. As unpleasant as traveling through the Midgewater Marshes is, it is certainly better than being murdered in bed, as the hobbits would have been if Merry had not been drawn to make his discovery.

Chapter Five

Wounded and Blessed

At Weathertop, the thought of the Ring attracting the Riders terrifies Frodo. Aragorn tries to comfort the hobbit by assuring him that he is not alone. The Ranger refers not only to his own protection but to the other unseen Powers who watch over the Ring-bearer. Not only do we always have our guardian angel in our own struggles, but there are others with us as well. The heavenly host surrounds us, and they go with us into battle.

The Nazgûl are not far away, but Cami Agan notes that Aragorn's telling of the love story of Beren and Lúthien "surrounds the cave at Weathertop, albeit momentarily, with the power of sacred song that somehow holds back the evil that lurks just beyond" ("Song," 52). After the song ends, Sam and Merry walk away, but soon the gardener runs back and alerts his companions to the approaching wraiths.

The temptation to put on the Ring again assaults Frodo's will. He remembers Gandalf's warnings and also the victory in the barrow, but after a period of valiant struggle, the hobbit collapses under the weight of the attack. He puts the Ring on his left forefinger, which is a sign that his own will did not choose this but acted from coercion of the enemies who surround him. "Not all evil is chosen. For while evil can subtly seduce, it can also brutally enforce its will" (Wood, *Gospel*, 70).

We all have moments in our life like Frodo does here, as we are all Ring-bearers' of one kind or another in our struggle with whatever is our principal temptation. We withstand up to a point then, at times, succumb to the assault. Sin weakens us all, and we must guard against what we are most prone to fall into and not presume that we will always have the strength to resist. On our own, we cannot overcome the demonic forces that wish to lure us to our destruction, but there is no need. Making the Sign of the Cross and invoking the name of Jesus stops them in their tracks. So does this prayer: "St. Michael the Archangel, defend us in battle. Be our protection against the wickedness and snares of the devil. May God rebuke him, we humbly pray, and do thou, O Prince of the heavenly hosts, by the power of God, cast into hell Satan, and all the evil spirits, who prowl about the world seeking the ruin of souls. Amen."

In Frodo's case, aid comes after he responds to the inspiration to cry to Elbereth. "Rather than deciding to pray, Frodo discovers himself praying" (Wood, *Gospel*, 123). Agan also observes, "Calling out a holy name against an unholy foe, Frodo seems to understand that sacred forces are at work. Has he learned this through his encounter with Gildor, through his teaching from Bilbo, or through some prenatural link to the divine? It is not clear, but it is certain from this point on in *LotR*, Frodo calls on Varda in moments of the greatest darkness" ("Song," 53). We must do the same and cry out to God, His Mother, or any of the saints for help.

After the Ring-bearer realizes that he had not chosen to put on the Ring, but that the Nazgûl had influenced and usurped his will, he berates himself for not having the strength to resist. Nonetheless, even the evil wound he received brings good. In his long struggle against the Morgul-shard loosed within him, Frodo discovers some of the fortitude that he will need to endure the long months of increasing torment during the Quest. Tom Shippey remarks, "The knife works by subduing the will, and if the will does not cooperate, it works less well – though it does not lose its power entirely and altogether, as it would if evil were entirely a matter of inner temptations" (*J. R. R. Tolkien: Author of the Century*, 137).

What helps Frodo from yielding to the increasingly deadly power bound up in the shard is not just the *athelas* plant itself but whose hand holds it. After one king tried to maim him, another tries to heal him. Humble assistance to another is beyond evil's understanding. Neither Aragorn nor Frodo can do much physically to resist the movement of the shard toward the heart, but instead they launch a spiritual assault upon it. This includes not just the kingsfoil, but also the hobbit's laughter after seeing the trolls that turned to stone during Bilbo's adventure. Such a sound is another thing that evil does not comprehend. This and the Ring-bearer's determined will and courage enable him to survive a bitter seventeen-day battle during which he is slowly drawn into the shadow world of the Nazgûl. After Glorfindel finds Frodo and his companions, the Elf-lord joins in the attack and provides the hobbit with not only some physical relief from pain but a clearing of the veil that he felt over his eyes and a return of hope.

Glorfindel tells Frodo to ride Asfaloth, and that if the need arises, the horse can outrun even the Riders who wait for the Ring-bearer to succumb to his wound. At first, the hobbit refuses because he does not want to leave his friends behind to face the wraiths. His wish to sacrifice himself rather than place those he loves in greater jeopardy is the opposite of the desire to save himself that he faced in the barrow.

Near the Ford of Bruinen, the Nazgûl come upon them and command Frodo to stop. The hobbit feels both fear and hatred as powers stronger than his own will constrain him, but the Elvish tongue, spoken by Glorfindel to Asfaloth, breaks the might of the Black Riders. They cannot bear to hear such words, just as exorcists use Latin in our time to expel demons, who cannot endure the language of the Church.

As Frodo crosses into Ulmo's domain, the Vala again provides the barrier against the closely pursing evil. "He will put you in his angels' charge to guard you wherever you go" (Ps. 91:11).

Baptism also uses water, and Frodo receives his as he crosses the River. "Should you pass through the sea, I will be with you; or through rivers, they will not swallow you up" (Isa. 43:2). Gracia Fay Ellwood makes note of this important time in the hobbit's life.

> Frodo's successful crossing of the Ford of the Bruinen, followed by the overwhelming of the Ringwraiths in the flood created by Elrond and Gandalf, is almost identical to Israel's dryshod crossing of the Red Sea and Moses' destruction of Pharoah and his hosts by the releasing (with his staff) the dammed-up waters upon them. For the [Church] Fathers this became the basic symbol of Christ's bringing the soul safely through the baptismal waters . . . and destroying its demonic foes. (*Good News from Tolkien's Middle Earth*, 112)

Sam receives his baptism at Parth Galen as he almost drowns in his great determination to follow his beloved master. Both hobbits receive the graces this sacrament bestows, which are "the supernatural powers to do what is impossible to human nature alone" (John A. Hardon, S. J., "Baptism, the Sacrament of Regeneration and the Supernatural Life," *therealpresence.org*). At first Frodo needs this extra strength just to survive his wound, as he is but hours away from it engulfing him by the time he reaches Rivendell. He requires it afterward to fully respond to his vocation at the Council, to show charity toward Gollum, and to continue to carry his increasingly terrible burden. Sam needs it to have enough strength to carry his master emotionally and spiritually throughout their ordeal and physically at the end. He also needs it for protection from the demonic attacks that he endures, though they are nowhere near as severe as those that Frodo suffers.

After Frodo makes it to the other side, the Nazgûl again command him to stop. He gathers his last strength to invoke Elbereth and Lúthien. Just as the Ring-bearer sees the white riders in the flood that Elrond sends to overcome the Black Riders' horses, the servant of the prophet Elisha will see invisible guardians nearby while in a town surrounded by enemies (2 Kings 6:17).

Without the blessed aid of Elbereth, Ulmo, and Glorfindel, Frodo would have never reached Rivendell alive. He wakes to find Gandalf at his bedside and learns that his friend was held captive. The wizard says that his delay in returning to Bag End as promised was almost disastrous for the Quest, but he also notes that it may have been a good thing. Both statements are true, as is also the case regarding the other seeming calamities throughout the tale.

Gandalf recounts how Elrond brought Frodo back from the threshold of the wraith world. The wizard commends the Ring-bearer on the remarkable achievement of surviving his wound and notes that the shard failed to reach Frodo's heart in part because the hobbit never ceased his valiant resistance against it. The cloaked Maia also makes a veiled mention of the providential aid that kept Frodo from succumbing. The Bearer says that he is glad that he did not know the mortal danger his body and soul were in, or he would have been too frightened to move.

Frodo had already told Gandalf that he has had quite enough of adventure, but the wizard intuits that the hobbit may be asked to go further. In his observation of the light that softly glows from the Ring-bearer, the Maia wonders where the Road will lead his dear friend. He does not think that it will turn Frodo to darkness, but that by the end, the hobbit will become "like a glass filled with a clear light for eyes to see that can" (*LOTR*, 217). This light, which reveals "his innate spiritual kinship" with the Elves (Kocher, *Master*, 112), continues to increase throughout the Quest.

Judith Klinger makes some interesting observations about the effects of the Morgul-wound.

> The wizard's subsequent musings reveal that the transformation triggered by the Morgul-blade cannot be undone, yet the ultimate result may subvert all evil intentions. . . . Frodo's wounds are ruptures in a twofold sense: their immediately debilitating effects are complemented by a far-reaching process of transformation . . . . While this process may be equally unsettling for Frodo, it is also set apart from destructive intents and effects. ("Hidden Paths of Time," *Tolkien and Modernity 2*, 148)

Sam blesses Frodo with a glad reunion and receives his own reward by the sight of his master healed. Reunions with Merry, Pippin, and Bilbo follow. The ancient hobbit's lingering desire for the Ring, however, mars the joy of this longed-for meeting. It transforms him into a veritable Gollum that Frodo feels an urge to hit. The shadow soon passes from between them, but it opens the eyes of the younger Baggins to the corruptive power of the Ring more than anything has yet. Bilbo quit 'cold turkey' from bearing the Ring, but his heart, soul, and mind have still not completely healed from the long years of possessing it. After Frodo told Gandalf at Bag End that he would take custody of the Ring no matter what it did to him, he had no idea in a personal sense what it could do. Now having seen how "the poison of the Enemy" still twists his beloved uncle, Fleming Rutledge notes how much Frodo longs for a world beyond evil (*The Battle for Middle-earth*, 91). The good that comes from this unnerving vision, however, is that it helps to prepare the heart of the younger Baggins to pity Sméagol, who suffers from the same lust and loss to a much greater degree.

While listening to songs in the Hall of Fire, Frodo receives, just as he had at Tom's house, the gift of another vision of the Undying Lands he will one day travel to, though he knows it not.

Chapter Six

God's Council

The Quest to destroy the Ring was conceived at Bag End but is born in Rivendell. Toward the beginning of the Council that Elrond convenes to determine the fate of Sauron's treasure, the Elf-lord makes one of the clearest indications of the Providence that guides all events.

> "What shall we do with the Ring. . . ?
> . . . That is the purpose for which you are called hither. Called, I say, though I have not called you to me. . . . You have come and are here met, in this very nick of time, by chance as it may seem." (*LOTR*, 236)

Glóin and Gimli think that they are there only to get advice about how to answer a dark messenger, who came looking for information about a hobbit thief. Boromir thinks that he has come just to seek the answer to a troubling dream. Legolas believes that he is present to report the escape of Gollum. Sam, Merry, and Pippin are not aware of any other reason being there beside their friendship with Frodo. "Yet it is not so," Elrond says. "Believe rather that it is so ordered that we, who sit here, and none others, must now find counsel for the peril of the world" (ibid.).

The first to speak is Glóin. We should be as wary of honey-covered demands as the dwarves are and ask for counsel among the wise for discernment when we are not sure how to respond.

After Legolas reports Gollum's escape, Aragorn considers it terrible news, but Gandalf repeats his intuition that the wretched creature may have an unforeseen part to play. This vital role would not be possible if the ruined hobbit had remained captive, which is another instance of a seeming disaster that is in reality a good.

Gandalf bears the grievous news of Saruman's fall. He reveals that their former ally has not only betrayed his Creator and them, but he also plans to deceive his new master in his desire to become the Lord of the Rings himself. Just as the Vala Melkor fell from the Light in his lust to obtain the Flame Imperishable, the Maiar Saruman and Sauron also gave their souls over in the pursuit of power that is God's alone. Their tragic falls demonstrate that, although created for the good, anyone can become evil as a result of the choices they make and the temptations to which they surrender. They prove Lord Acton's maxim that "Power tends to corrupt, and absolute power corrupts absolutely." The only One who can handle ultimate power without becoming enslaved by it is the One who *is* ultimate Power. Though Sauron and Saruman are among the most powerful in Middle-earth, they are no freer than their slaves.

The sorry state of Saruman's soul clearly demonstrates the effects on those who do not resist temptation. Gandalf relates that the White wizard now calls himself Saruman of Many Colours. He abandoned his purity and chose instead to become whatever color fit the current situation. He is now an amoral being rather than one with the highest morals and sees white only as a starting point. It is clear from the ranks of the Istari that Gandalf the Grey is lower than Saruman the White and higher than Radagast the Brown. White is not meant as the beginning of service but its pinnacle. That Saruman considers multi-colored better than white is a sign of how far he has fallen into darkness. He no longer desires to serve but to rule. He does not want to be just one color but all colors. Hayden Head observes, "In his delusion, Saruman believes that he is becoming greater while in reality he sacrifices the very greatness he possessed" ("Imitative Desire in Tolkien's Mythology," *Mythlore* 26, 144).

We must not make the same mistake. Our enemy wishes to present his side as exciting and vibrant and show righteousness as dull and gray. Why choose boring monochrome if we can choose from all the colors of the rainbow? If only we could just get past the repressiveness of the good. Such are the lies that he whispers to us. Gandalf is right to prefer white. We do indeed have the choice of all colors, but we must make the voluntary, moral decision to restrict ourselves to those of the Light. Do not be tricked by the flashy glitz of the other side, for these false beacons will fizzle out and leave you in darkness. Instead, remain in the Light that surrounds and nourishes you, so that even if you do walk in the black night, as do Gandalf, Aragorn, Frodo, and Sam, it will not be because you have forsaken the Light but because it led you there and is beside you.

Gandalf tells of how Saruman tried to convince him that they should either join forces with Sauron or rule the world through the Ring themselves. Even though they may detest the evil things that they do, it would be all right because it would allow them to achieve their aims. In the Grey wizard's utter rejection of the folly of the ends justifying the means, he shows that he did not abandon the enlightenment his multi-colored superior did. Gandalf knows that evil cannot be used for good, though good can be brought out of evil. We must be just as careful in what we choose to do and how we pursue a goal. Evil stops at nothing, but good holds itself back from doing things it knows it should not, lest it become its own enemy. Tolkien lamented in a wartime letter to his son, Christopher, that Gandalf's wisdom apparently vanished with him (*Letters*, 94).

"The Hunt for the Ring" tale reveals a little more about this perilous time for both Saruman and Gandalf. After the news of the prophecy that sent Boromir to Rivendell reaches Sauron, increasing terror fills him that the Wise will discover the Ring before he does. He orders the Nazgûl to interrogate Saruman at Isengard. The wizard is now in a precarious position, for he has betrayed not only God and the Valar but also the Dark Lord. A traitor to both sides, Saruman is utterly alone, but he still has the power of his voice and convinces the Witch-king that Gandalf, just lately escaped, may have the information that the wraiths seek.

The Nazgûl leave and come upon Wormtongue, who is on his way to tell his true master that Gandalf had told Théoden of Saruman's treachery. The terrified man betrays Saruman and states that the wizard does indeed know where the Shire lies, though the fallen Maia had not said so. After Gríma gives the Witch-king the necessary information, the wraith spares the man's life, partly from the intuition that the evil creature will later bring harm to Saruman.

An alternate version of Saruman's meeting with the Nazgûl has him suddenly realize the magnitude of what he has done in pledging himself to darkness. He resolves to go to the imprisoned Gandalf and to beg for forgiveness and aid. But after seeing an Eagle in the distance bearing the captive away, the multi-colored wizard returns to his fallen state in a rage of pride and jealousy of the grace that accompanies the Grey Istari. The traitor Maia then pretends to the Ringwraiths to still be a servant of Sauron. One wonders what Saruman's fate would have been if he had remained firmer in his determination to return to the Light.

That Gandalf makes his escape from Orthanc to inform the Council of his superior's treachery is the good contained within the evil of his imprisonment. As Saruman did not tell Radagast of his true intentions behind his call of Gandalf to Isengard, the Brown wizard had no reason to warn his brother Istari or to disregard the Grey's instructions to send any news learnt of the Black Riders. Radagast tells all his animal friends to watch out, and so Gwaihir comes with news to Saruman's stronghold where and when he otherwise would not have.

Gandalf makes the interesting statement that Sauron's power, while mighty, is not as great as fear makes it appear. Our doubts and worries rob us of so much. They make the small shadows on the wall into huge phantasms about to swallow us whole. But the truth is that much of what we fear are either illusions or are realities that are not as terrible as we imagine.

In the midst of the discussion about the Ring's fate, Tom Bombadil's name enters. Because of his immunity to its power, he seems the ideal one to keep the fell object safe, but Gandalf says that Tom would actually be the worst guardian. He would forget about it or toss it away. Either of these would be disastrous for Middle-earth. Glorfindel points out that even if Tom were a worthy keeper, it would only delay doomsday, for the Ring would still be in existence. In the end, Sauron would defeat even Tom after laying waste to all else. The Elf offers two other alternatives: to send the Ring into the West where its maker cannot reach it or to destroy it. After Elrond rejects the first, Glorfindel suggests drowning it in the Sea, but Gandalf says that would not be the permanent solution that the Council seeks. The only viable choice is the one their Enemy could never imagine.

Gandalf acknowledges that the effort to bring about the Ring's destruction may not succeed, but the attempt is to be made nonetheless. Our outlook must be the same, so that the magnitude of what is before us does not daunt us. The only way to eat an elephant is one bite at a time. The only way Sauron's defeat comes is through the heroes' overcoming the fear of continuing along deadly paths and the taking of many steps over hundreds of miles, even while tormented by exhaustion, hunger, thirst, and choking on foul air. We need to bring this same devotion and dedication to our own tasks, even if we cannot see them to the end ourselves.

Edmund Fuller speaks of what confronts the Council: "The power of evil is formidable and ruthless. The initial decision . . . is whether or not to attempt to resist it at all. So great and discouraging are the odds involved in resistance that the possibility of surrender . . . seems only in degrees more terrible than the fight – unless the deciding element is the moral choice of rejecting evil regardless of consequences" ("Lord of Hobbits," 24-25).

After the Council makes their decision, it seems utter folly to the military-minded Boromir to deny themselves the power of the Ring and to seek to destroy it instead. But what seems foolish to this man is the wisdom of God. The Wise would be more attuned to this than any, as they have learned from harsh experience what happens if they are not.

Boromir calls for the use of the Ring to gain victory. Elrond refuses for the same reason that Gandalf did at Bag End and does so again here. Because of the grave peril bound up in the evil object, the Elf-lord says that he will not wield it or even take it into his custody to hide it. He and Gandalf both know it would burn away their mind, will, and resistance, and they would eventually fall to the temptation to use it, even with all their knowledge and wisdom. The wizard later warns Denethor of the same thing.

Elrond shares the two theories of what would happen to the three Elven Rings if the master Ring was destroyed. Either they would gain freedom from it and mend the damage Sauron wreaked upon the world, or, as the Elf-lord believes, the power within them would wither away and with them the Elven lands that they built and sustain.

With the choice made to take the Road to the Fire, the next decision concerns who will bear this terrible burden. Bilbo volunteers even though he complains that it will take time away from his book and ruin the happy ending that he plans for it. Gandalf, however, refuses him. In the silence that follows, the ancient hobbit's reason for being nears fulfillment. He was made to be Ring-finder and to keep it safe until its next Bearer was chosen. In giving Frodo love and security, Bilbo has shown his beloved heir what is worth fighting and even dying for. This gives the younger Baggins the strength to fight and win one of the most important battles in the War of the Ring. Frodo could have said no after the Holy Spirit presents him with his full vocation. He could have chosen to remain silent, but he does not. In speaking of this and the decisions that confront us all, Cheryl Forbes wrote, "we choose to be chosen" ("Frodo Decides - Or Does He?," *Christianity Today*, December 19, 1975, 12).

The Biblical stories of Esther and the Virgin Mary also demonstrate this fearful and fateful moment of choice. Esther will have a chance to save the Jewish people after she becomes Queen. She will hesitate to do anything because revealing that she is a Jew could prove fatal. But a message from her kinsman Mordecai will convince her to act: "Do not suppose that, because you are in the king's palace, you are going to be the one Jew to escape. No; if you persist in remaining silent at such a time, relief and deliverance will come to the Jews from another place, but both you and the House of your father will perish. Who knows? Perhaps you have come to the throne for just such a time as this" (Esther 4:13-14). Jim Ware and Kurt Bruner observe, "She had been called to play a part in the story, one she could not fulfill by remaining silent" (*Finding God in "The Lord of the Rings,"* 58). Mary will have an opportunity to say no at the Annunciation. She will be alone when the angel visits her, and she knows that death by stoning is the penalty if her pregnancy is discovered. God, however, set Frodo, Esther, and Mary aside from the beginning of the Music and formed them for their special tasks. "For we are His workmanship, created in Christ Jesus for good works, which God prepared beforehand that we should walk in them" (Eph. 2:10, NKJV).

Even though it is true that "what you are to say will be given to you when the time comes; because it is not you who will be speaking; the Spirit of your Father will be speaking in you" (Matt. 10:19-20), this does not mean that the Holy Spirit coerces a decision from Frodo after stirring the hobbit's heart to accept his calling. Although God knows our answer before we do, He still gives us the free will to choose it. Our vocation is His gift to us, and He wants us to unwrap it. Nevertheless, He has such great respect for the decision-making powers that He gave us that He does not force us to do anything even though He knows it will benefit us or others. Frodo knows what it is like for an outside power to usurp his freedom. Though he does indeed feel that another will speaks through his voice, it is not the terrible violation of the Ring, which bludgeons if it cannot seduce. The hobbit longs to stay in Rivendell with Bilbo, but instead, to his own astonishment, he allows his fiat (Let it be done) to be spoken by him and through him.

None of the Wise say "I will take the Ring" (*LOTR*, 264). Rather a frightened, mortal hobbit freely speaks "the sacramental, operative words that set in motion the only power that can conquer Sauron" (Kreeft, "Wisdom," 39). It is an amazing thing to hear from such a small being, who has already nearly suffered a fate worse than death. But it is precisely because Frodo is literally and figuratively little that he was chosen for this task. Gandalf and others of the Wise recognize in their strength how terribly weak they truly are and dare not touch the Ring. Frodo, in his humility and knowledge of his weakness, discovers his strength. His fiat takes him on a harrowing journey that his heart already quails to contemplate. Enabled by his cooperation with the grace that continually fills him, he receives the strength to hold to it.

Frodo demonstrates that it takes great courage and sacrifice to say yes as we scream no inside and to give up control and totally surrender ourselves to Someone else. Yet in this crucible, we discover the person God has already seen us becoming. An Australian professor, Barry Gordon, noted Frodo is "the Lamb whose only real strength is his capacity to make an offering of himself" ("Kingship, Priesthood and Prophecy in *The Lord of the Rings*," *uoncc.wordpress.com*). As he, Aragorn, and Gandalf respond to their callings, Clyde Kilby observes that each "grows in power and grace" (*Tolkien and "The Silmarillion,"* 56).

The Virgin Mary will give her fiat to the angel and many other times, even at the Cross as she watches her Son die in agony. The saints and martyrs will say it over and over while their enemy and his fell servants torture them. Surrender is not a one-time event that needs no repeating but an ongoing embrace every day and every moment. Under the coercive pressure of the Ring, Frodo says no several times, but with almost every breath and step he takes, he says yes, even as those breaths and steps become harder to take.

Words of Giacomo Cardinal Buffi concerning the choices we make also apply to the Ring-bearer.

> But the Spirit sent by the crucified and risen Christ also empowers the invisible world inside – the minds, hearts, and consciences. This is the sanctifying effect.
>
> Therefore, man senses the gift of illumination. It gives him an understanding of the divine truth. Even when it seems difficult and remote, the gift of inspiration moves him to resist temptation, give up old vices, or perform a good deed that taxes his abilities. (*The Man Christ Jesus*, 106-107)

Not only later from Faramir's loving heart does Frodo receive honor but also now from those at the Council. Elrond tells the newly confirmed Ring-bearer that he will have a place with the other great heroes of history. What makes this statement all the more impressive is that the Elf-lord says it before Frodo does what will indeed earn him such a seat, which he will share with Sam. Elrond and Aragorn before him both recognize that the Providence which guided the Council "appointed" and "ordained" Frodo to have custody of the Ring.

After Sam announces his hidden presence at the end, all he says of the horrible danger that awaits them is that it is a "nice pickle" (*LOTR*, 264). Nothing like hobbity understatement to brighten the day and lighten its load! If only we could have such a response to all that is thrown at us. The natural cheer of hobbits and their profound love for each other see them through their terrible trials and keep the Quest from collapsing into ruin.

After the Council of Elrond ends, a 'Council of Hobbits' begins with two contrasting views about going on the Quest. Pippin objects that the Elf-lord rewarded Sam by saying that the eavesdropping gardener would accompany Frodo. The Ring-bearer replies that he cannot think of a worse penalty, but his cousins and Sam feel that the punishment would be to be left behind. Indeed, Sam later tells his beloved master that he would die if he could not accompany him. Pippin is right to say that they should remain together, which they do as far as they are meant. Gandalf thrills Frodo with the possibility of coming with him, but soon the Ring re-infects the hobbit with pessimism. After Bilbo asks about an end for his book, the younger Baggins replies that he has thought of a few, and none of them are good. He is not at all confident that the happy ending Bilbo wishes will come to pass.

Yet, as time passes in the Elven haven, both physical and spiritual strength return to the Ring-bearer and his companions. Part of Frodo's enjoyment is long-missed, glad companionship with Bilbo. Everyone enjoys the present moment without fear of the morrow overwhelming their contentment. Of all the great lessons throughout the Red Book, this is one of the best, though perhaps one of the hardest to learn and implement ourselves.

As the time nears for the Ring to set out, Elrond asks Frodo if he still wishes to continue. The hobbit confirms that he does and that Sam will accompany him. The Elf-lord then announces those who will make up the reminder of the Company. Pippin protests after Elrond leaves him and Merry out, but the Elf is against their going and claims that they cannot conceive of the perils before them. Gandalf speaks up in their defense and says that no one is sure what lies ahead, and the hobbits would still want to go even if did know or would at least wish that they had the courage to do so. The wisdom that it is good not to know the future proves true each time it is mentioned. If we knew what was ahead of us, we might lack the strength to do what we must. Gandalf knows well what is held within the heart of hobbits. He advocates for Elrond to include Merry and Pippin because of their love for Frodo. After Pippin insists that he will follow unless forcibly restrained, Elrond surrenders to Gandalf's suggestion, even though the Elf-lord does not clearly discern the wisdom of it. May we have the same courage and strength as these hobbits, so small in body and so great in heart!

"You did not choose me," Jesus will tell His disciples, "no, I chose you; and I commissioned you to go out and to bear fruit, fruit that will last" (John 15:16). The Writer of the Story has nurtured Sam's love for Frodo over decades, so it will remain ever faithful on their dark road. God knows that Boromir will fall to the lure of the Ring and place the Bearer in peril, but He also knows how vitally important this fall is for the success of what else is to come. Though the warrior is not aware of it, the true reason behind his coming was so that he would be there in time to be chosen as one of Frodo's companions. Even the delays en route are part of God's impeccable timing to ensure this. He also places Merry and Pippin beside Boromir to allow for the man's redemption. Their insistence at Crickhollow that they were going to accompany Frodo makes all this possible. How deep are the roots which God plants; how far back His plans go to bring four hobbits to this moment of service to all Middle-earth. In their support of Frodo in his vocation, they fulfill their own.

Shortly before the Company's departure on a day that a later age will call Christmas, Bilbo gives Frodo the invaluable gifts of Sting and the *mithril* coat.

Though Bill the pony is the beast of burden, each of the Nine Walkers carry heavy loads that press upon them. No one wants to go, but they know that they must. We can grow too in our tribulations, for this is the reason they are put before us. We can fight them like a bucking horse, or we can stop and ponder, what does God want me to learn from this?

Elrond makes it clear that only upon Frodo is there any obligation to continue. The others need only travel with him as long as they freely choose to do so or as luck makes possible. The Elf-lord tells the Company that there has not yet been any test of their devotion to the cause, so they are unaware of what could make them waver or fall away. After Gimli protests that only a disloyal heart would abandon one in need as the Road grows hard, Elrond correctly responds that one should not speak so boldly and confidently of one's strength until trials find it true or in want. How easy to say in sunshine and peace that, of course, we will remain faithful and never run away. Until the darkness comes, however, such a pledge remains only words, no matter how sincere. The brave deeds done or not done while surrounded by the night prove whether our vow is deeply rooted in hard rock or in shifting sand. The Elf already knows of the Ring's ability to corrupt and weaken the will. He has seen more than enough of failures in the hard fight against Sauron and victories that did not last. He genuinely fears what lies ahead for the Walkers, but he also recognizes Who brought them together. Gimli replies with hope for the dark hour during which loyalty receives its test, as he says that a promise already given may give strength to a fearful heart.

Nothing binds the Company to Frodo except love, the strongest force in the world. "Their friendship is the one thing that unites them at the beginning, sustains them throughout their long ordeal, and enables the success of their Quest at the end. Friendship is surely the chief virtue of the Company. . . . [Their] real bond lies in their forgiving faith and enduring trust in each other" (Wood, _Gospel_, 125-126).

Frodo's decision to leave the light-filled refuge of Rivendell for darkness is similar to Abraham's, who will also agree to step into a new experience and to leave the comfort of home to venture out into the frightening unknown. Peter Kreeft makes a note of that man's road, but his words could just as easily apply to the Ring-bearer.

> "O.K., time to go," says God to Abraham. . . . "Time to leave your comfort, security and happiness there in Ur in Chaldea, that civilized and cultured city. Out into the wilderness, to a land I shall show you. Out into suffering and insecurity and darkness and blind faith. You will fall flat on your face many times because you will be looking at the darkness I'm sending you into rather than at the light of my face and my words to you. But I will not give up on you, ever." (_Making Sense Out of Suffering_, 110)

Chapter Seven

Gandalf's Fiat

*M*ore than a fortnight away from Rivendell, Sam and Aragorn see *crebain* fly overhead. The man suspects that they are spying for Saruman. The Walkers become more cautious, which leaves Pippin put out that they will not have the hot meal he hoped for. Gandalf tells him to keep anticipating others, for they could still come, even if he cannot have the immediate one he wants. We all need this encouragement. As we cannot see far along the Road, we automatically assume things will only go from bad to worse with no possibility of betterment. We must firmly tell ourselves that there is another direction other than down because we do not know the many joys that lie ahead either.

After the frozen terror of Caradhras, Merry, Pippin, and Sam perk up at the thought of returning to Rivendell. Frodo would love to go back too. He and Aragorn both know that it is not easy to walk in the opposite direction from what the heart wishes. But one of the reasons the Ring-bearer and Ranger are such good models for us is because they also realize that their paths lie ahead of them and not behind.

In the debate over which way to take, Gandalf strongly advocates entering the Mines of Moria, which everyone else but Gimli is against. Aragorn speaks of his premonition that the wizard's life will be in danger if they go to the Black Pit. The howls of wolves decide for them. They will go under the earth.

Once the Company reaches the doors, Sam weeps to know that he must either part with his beloved Bill or his even dearer master. The choice is obvious, but this does not make it easy. Even giving up his cooking pans in Mordor breaks the gardener's gentle heart. Nothing, however, stops him from making the necessary sacrifices.

After Frodo's capture and narrow escape from the Watcher in the Water, he shows once more the marvelous power that hobbits possess to recovery quickly from terrifying experiences. Once the Company flees into Moria, all the Ring-bearer wants to do is sit down and have something to eat. What incredible insulation from hardship does a cheerful heart provide!

As the Walkers make their way through the ruined kingdom, Frodo exhibits some of the after-effects of his Morgul-blade wound. He sees better in the dark than anyone except perhaps Gandalf. He is more aware of the evil that surrounds them, but he keeps this to himself and continues on. He also hears, or fancies that he does, the sound of bare feet behind them.

On the Bridge of Khazad-dûm, Gandalf willingly responds to the need for greater sacrifice to counter the double peril of Sauron and Saruman. The original plan of the Valar for the Istari could go no further. Michael Martinez remarks about the Grey wizard's free will offering of himself: "Gandalf . . . was being asked to make a hard choice. And Gandalf made the correct choice, but in doing so he had to abandon the Valar's plan. It was the Valar's plan which was flawed, not Gandalf, and Ilúvatar needed to make some changes. Gandalf therefore went willingly to the sacrifice, as he had been forewarned" (*Understanding Middle-earth*, 439). Richard Purtill notes, "Gandalf . . . is a free creature who freely answers the call to imitate Christ. He and Frodo, who walks his own Way of the Cross, are thus closest to Tolkien's deepest moral ideals" (*J. R. R. Tolkien: Myth, Morality, and Religion*, 118). Either or both could have refused the sacrifices asked of them with ensuing catastrophic consequences, but instead they opened their heart and arms to embrace the necessary self-abnegation.

Have we this much courage, trust, love, and faith, especially when we might not comprehend how what God asks for could possibly have a good outcome? Abraham will struggle with this after God tells him to sacrifice his son Isaac, the one through whom was promised many descendants. The man will not understand, but his belief that somehow God will still make good on His vow will give him the strength to prepare the offering. Such faith will save both son and father. The same faith lends Gandalf the power to surrender his life.

It seems to mortal eyes that Gandalf's death is a disaster for the

Company, but the wizard's survival at this point is not necessary. In fact, it is essential that he *not* survive, so the Valar can return him with greater powers in order to defeat Saruman.

Other good also springs from the decision to enter the Mines, including the stroke of fortune that "The Hunt for the Ring" reveals. Frodo is right to think that he heard the sound of bare feet behind them, for they belong to Gollum, who is lost in the darkness and terribly hungry. Even though endowed with the strange good fortune to survive in near-starvation condition, he still could have perished or been captured by Orcs had the Walkers not come when they did. They unknowingly aid him and all Middle-earth by enabling his escape when they themselves leave. Aragorn's words after Gandalf's fall perhaps help give Frodo the strength to complete his journey to the Fire despite his hopelessness during much of it, for, as the man says in the wake of their grievous loss, they must continue on without hope.

Chapter Eight

The Lady of the Golden Wood

*B*oromir fears to enter Lothlórien, for he has heard that few visitors escape and none emerge unscathed. Aragorn corrects him by saying that it would be more proper to say none remain unchanged. He speaks from his own life, as this is where he and Arwen plighted their troth. Have we not experienced a life-altering experience ourselves by reading this tale, those of us who have entered with an open and unguarded heart? I certainly have.

Frodo once more receives the aid of Ulmo as the fatigue and marks of travel fall from the hobbit while the Company crosses the stream Nimrodel. Shortly afterward, the Ring-bearer and his companions encounter Elves keeping watch over the borders of the Wood. During the night, both Orcs and Gollum come near and fortunately at the same time. Haldir could have shot the latter intruder, but he tells Frodo that he did not because there were so many Orcs. Though the Elf is not aware of it, and certainly the soldiers of the Enemy are not, they both protect the success of the Quest.

In the morning, Haldir insists upon a blindfold for Gimli, so that the dwarf cannot see the secret ways through the forest. The Elf gives permission for the others to see a while longer, but Aragorn says that in fairness the eyes of them all should be bound. This offends Legolas, who is just as insulted to be included as Gimli was to be singled-out. How right is Haldir to say that Sauron's power is most apparent in the separation of those who should be allies against him. If the Dark Lord succeeded in dividing his enemies, he could then pick them off one by one. But his own armies are the ones disunited, as shown later by the rivalries between the various factions of Orcs. Their violent hate aids the Quest at several key points and helps cause Sauron's towering ambition to come crashing down.

Merry says that if he knew how terrible the world outside the Shire was, he would have never left. Again Haldir speaks wisdom by replying that there is also much that is beautiful. We would never behold such places if we stayed at home.

Frodo looks upon the land of Lothlórien, which appears to him as if sprung into being the moment he sees again but at the same time as ancient as though it has always been. What a marvelous place it is: so clean, clear, and pure. The Shadow that ever lurks beyond its borders constantly seeks a way to penetrate its protected bounds, but it has no power yet to do so.

At Cerin Amroth Sam says that he feels like he stands within a song. Just as Frodo was unaware of what moved him so in Goldberry's singing, the same blessing reaches Sam here. They are not within just *a* song but *the* Song, though they do not know it as such.

The wondrous land of Lórien holds captured within its timelessness the cry of extinct birds and the crash of the Sea against beaches that no longer exist. Frodo's sight of Aragorn lost in memory movingly shows the existence of past and present side by side. The man does more than simply remember the day that he and Arwen pledged themselves to each other; he actually relives it.

Elves then escort the Company to see Celeborn and Galadriel. As one of the Noldor who had befriended the dwarves in ages past, the Lady of the Wood reaches out to Gimli with her kind words about Khadzad-dûm. Galadriel amazes the dwarf, as he perceives love and understanding within the heart of a leader of a people long estranged from his own. Our own enemies should see this unexpected love from us as well. The marvel of the encounter transforms Gimli's heart, and Galadriel has his fervent and pure devotion forever after.

What a great lesson for us all. If such grace is given to us, we must be ready to receive it. Gimli is, though he is not aware of this until it happens. One of the greatest lessons from the Red Book is that even if our attempts to reach others find little or no way in, this does not mean that we should refrain from extending care to all in need. We must do so for our own sake, as well as for those we try to reach, and hope that the soil of the soul is receptive. Or perhaps we will water and cultivate in preparation for someone else's success. If the soil is still not right, through will or weakness, this is not our fault if we have given our best. Galadriel's compassion cleanses Gimli of a deeply infected wound, and we hope others of his race received healing through him. It also prepares him for the great love and friendship that he and Legolas will share.

Galadriel knows how close to the edge of disaster the Quest stands. She probes the heart of each of her guests and presents them with the possibility of achieving their deepest desires if they only forsake fear for safety and abandon the fight against Sauron. This test is akin to Frodo's terrible temptation in the barrow to flee from terror and to save himself.

After the tests are over, Gimli remarks that it appeared that his choice would be unknown to anyone else. We all face this trap from the adversary of our soul, who attempts to seduce us with fell whispers, 'Come on, why don't you do it? Who is going to find out? No one is going to ever know.' The cloak of secrecy and promise of anonymity adds to the attractiveness of the temptation. Such a thing must seem fair at first, for otherwise how could it ensnare us? This does not, of course, equate Galadriel with our enemy, but it exposes one of his easiest and most beloved ways to ensnare us. We cannot give into his lies. We must conquer them by telling him, 'I will know. God will know.' The Walkers all elect to stand firm, but Gandalf says later that Galadriel perceived the cracks in Boromir's heart and soul.

Sam again confronts the temptation to turn back after he looks into Galadriel's Mirror. He is the only one who receives a second test, as his fidelity and love are the two things the Enemy would most want to destroy and the two which must hold firm even if all else falls away. The humble gardener wishes to go home after what he sees in the Mirror, but luckily his heart remains firmly in his master's keeping. It stays him from choosing any other Road than the one that Frodo must travel. So much more than the Shire would have been ruined if Sam had chosen to turn aside to prevent one evil and not been there to strengthen the Ring-bearer's will against a much greater one.

We must also refuse to surrender to the enticing idea of turning back, even for an apparent good, as we do not know every consequence if we abandon the right path. We should constantly discern which is the true Road to follow and continue on it without fail.

As Frodo looks in the Mirror, he sees many things, including the Sea and the ship that will take him West. God continues to send him consolations and hints of the blessed reward that awaits him, but the hobbit does not recognize them as such until he reaches the Undying Lands. We can hope that they aided him in his grief if he wondered whether he made the right decision to leave and then saw everything already arranged for him and just waiting for his willing acceptance.

The Mirror also reveals to the Ring-bearer the Eye looking for him, but he realizes that unless he wills it himself, Sauron will not find him. This shows how much power we have over our own enemy. He holds no sway over us except what we give him through our sins and what God allows him to have. He is an immortal being of far greater strength and intelligence than us, but God has given us the tremendous gift of our free will to use against our foe. We must not squander this advantage! We make many decisions every day, and we should consider each one in the light of how much power it will give our adversary. We must give him no entrance, as Galadriel does not. The Elven-lady tells Frodo of the door that she keeps closed against Sauron's questing mind. She knows his thoughts, but he does not know hers. Our enemy does not know our mind, but he can influence it and introduce temptations into our heart and will. He will not, however, know how successful his attempts to seduce us are until we demonstrate such by our outward actions. With each of the myriad enticements that we experience, we have a choice as to whether we will give in or not. Each time that we surrender, our strength lessens, as we give our foe greater dominion over our will. Each time that we resist, our strength grows and his power to ruin us weakens.

By guiding Frodo and Sam to her Mirror, Galadriel empowers them so that they will not falter, or at the least in the hope that they will not. Amy L. Timco observes, "Galadriel's Mirror arms both Frodo and Sam with knowledge they will need as the Quest becomes harder. Frodo is able to leave the Fellowship at Parth Galen and strike out on his own with only Sam to help him. Sam is able to remain faithful long after hope is gone. The trails they face later on their road have already been met in the quiet glade of Lórien" ("Weavers, Witches, and Warriors," *Silver Leaves* 1, 42).

Galaldriel speaks of the terrible crossroad at which the Elves now stand. Whether the Quest succeeds or not, their lands will not survive. Either a triumphant Sauron will lay waste to Lothlórien, Rivendell, and Mirkwood, or the power of the Three Rings will fail in the aftermath of the One Ring's destruction and Time will sweep away all that they accomplished. One way or another, the Elves' way of life in Middle-earth will end. The Lady does not desire this, but after Frodo asks what she wishes, she says, "That what should be shall be" (*LOTR*, 356). Not even the fiercest storms can disturb the peace of the completely surrendered will, as it holds within itself the trust that all will work out the way that it should. Galadriel tells the troubled Ring-bearer that he is not responsible for what will happen to her kind. He is accountable only for fulfilling the task that he received. 'Do what you must do,' she tells him in essence, 'and do not fear to do it because of what will happen as a consequence to the land that we both love.'

Frodo soon tests Galadriel's state of mind and soul, as the responsibility bound up in his vocation so frightens him that he freely offers the Ring to her. She admits that she has long fantasized what she would do if it ever came to her. The temptation to claim it fills her, but she discovers the strength to withstand her trial. Janet Brennan Croft speaks of the two-edged sword the Lady well knows the Ring represents: "It is the weapon by which either side could totally destroy the other – and in it are also the seeds of the spiritual destruction (at the very least) of the victor" (*War and Works*, 104). After fully recognizing that the heights of power would actually plunge her into the depths, Galadriel shrinks back to her true self rather than the dark queen that Frodo beheld in a vision. Such perception removes the allure of the Ring from her and enables her to unite her will once more to her Creator's. She will remain His child, not the terrible being the Ring would have made of her.

Linda Greenwood notes, "Goodness, which is motivated by love, is the ability to step outside oneself, to have a vision of what will benefit the world to come, and to seek after it without any thought of the self. The Elves, who have the most to lose in the outcome of this war, reject the temptation to change the course of events in order to elevate themselves" ("Love: The 'Gift of Death'," *Tolkien Studies* 2, 184). Aragorn has practiced this ability for decades; Gandalf brought it to its pinnacle in Moria; and Sam and Frodo increasingly demonstrate it as well.

Galadriel, Aragorn, Gandalf, and the hobbits share the humility that Saruman has long forsaken. He never even saw the Ring, but he was overcome by lust for it and abandoned his true self in search for it. His grasp for it destroys him. Galadriel's refusal to grasp redeems her. His prideful choices close the path West to him. Her humble choice reopens the Road that her rebellion and pride closed to her long ago. 'Let my will be done, not yours,' he says to his Creator. 'Let your will be done, not mine,' she says. God knew what her decision would be, but He allowed the test so that she would discover it. We should pray for the same strength to pass our own trials and say 'I am yours. Do with me as you will.' Galadriel's words to Frodo about the choices they both made underscores the involvement of free will. They resist the temptation to turn back or become someone that they should not.

The Elven-lady acknowledges Frodo's developing spiritual discernment, which Saruman later also observes. It could well be that the hobbit was guided to Lórien to cure Galadriel of her Ring-lust. Through the grace of his presence, the venomous desire drains from her heart and soul and humility gains in strength.

Celeborn gives hope to the Walkers after he tells them that he will provide boats for the next stage of their journey. The Elf-lord's gift soothes Aragorn, as it delays the decision that he knows they all need to make about what path to take. Galadriel advises the Company to remember that the Roads they will walk may already be before them, even if they cannot see the way.

What a wonderful consolation Galadriel's words are! God has laid the path. We need only to seek for it and walk upon it in the trust that everything will come out right in the end. We do not have every answer, but we do have recourse to faith and prayer. Guidance will come, however hard it is to see through the murk. "Now your word is a lamp to my feet, a light on my path" (Ps. 119:105). God will ever be this, but, as the Psalmist says, He provides illumination only for the area around our feet, not for the whole Road. All we truly need is this little space, though it frustrates our longing to see farther and clearer.

Aragorn does not feel that he has enough light yet to see his Road clearly. He thought that he heard a personal call to travel with Boromir to Gondor after the young man spoke of the dream that brought him to Rivendell. The Ranger's original plan was to stay with the Company until their Roads parted and he and Boromir went to Minas Tirith while the Ring-bearer continued to Mordor. But now the man knows that it would not be right to abandon Frodo, though he wonders what help he can offer besides standing by him in the growing dark. As God always intended, this role will fall to Sam. The humble gardener would not think this support anything worthy of praise, but let us never underestimate the power of simply being with the ones we love in time of terrible trial and the comfort our presence gives them.

Aragorn's struggle is much the same as ours. We want to do God's will, but we are not always sure what this involves. Sometimes we make a decision that we feel is right but then circumstances change after we come upon an unexpected fork in the road, and we do not know what to choose. Should we go where it branches off or continue as before? Which way is the right way? We stand paralyzed and unable to decide, but we should not fear to make a choice simply because we do not know for sure. God knows that we do not know everything. He designed it this way, so that we would have more faith in Him rather than relying only on ourselves. When we cannot choose, we should pray for inspiration to St. Ignatius of Loyola. After coming to a division in his Road, he will let go of the reins of his donkey and surrender control over the direction he goes in the rightful trust that God will show him the way by wherever the animal went.

As the Company readies to leave, the Elves load them with gifts. The greatest is *lembas*, the life-sustaining, and more importantly soul-sustaining, bread that will help make the difference between the success and failure of the Quest. As much as Sam's love strengthens Frodo, if they were not both fed by this Eucharistic gift, they likely would have perished. The Walkers also receive Elven cloaks to help them blend in with their surroundings, no matter where they go. Sam also receives Elven rope, which will prove to be a greater boon than it might appear to be at first.

At the end of a farewell feast, Galadriel gives more gifts. Among these, she bestows upon Sam a small of box of earth from her garden, and she blesses Gimli with three strands of her hair. The reason behind these particular presents is that even though the Elves have suffered many defeats, and seen victories that did not bear the fruit they should have, Galadriel still shares in the hopeful vision of light beyond the darkness that Gandalf, Aragorn, Arwen, Sam, and Faramir have. Of the gift Gimli receives, Fleming Rutledge observes that "even in the midst of irreparable loss and inevitable suffering, a *hope* for a divinely ordained future is established" (*Battle*, 135; italics in original). This embrace of hope is even more inspiring after we remember the age in which it happens. Tom Shippey speaks of this when he says that the 'theory of courage' Tolkien spoke of in his famous lecture on Beowulf is something that "asks more of people than Christianity does, for it offers them no heaven, no salvation, no reward for virtue except for sombre satisfaction of having done right" (*Author*, 150). All those who fight for the Light in Middle-earth embody this courage.

Galdadriel gives her final gifts to Frodo. He receives a phial filled with water from her Mirror and which also contains light from the Silmaril that Eärendil wears on his brow as he sails the skies. The song that Frodo hears as the boats leave concludes with a prayer that he be granted the grace of a stay in Tol Eressëa, the Lonely Isle in the Undying Lands. The Lady already sees that the Ring-bearer will desperately need this, even though the rents in his heart and soul are not yet anywhere as terrible as they will become. She saw such tears in her daughter and knows that they cannot be healed in Middle-earth. This hint of his future is something that Frodo understands only later.

As Gimli laments his loss of his fair Lady, Legolas tries to comfort him by saying because the dwarf suffers it of his own will, the memory of his love will bless him. In deciding upon the difficult path of leaving rather than the easy way of staying, Gimli selflessly chose others over himself. Anyone suffering such a grief will sympathize with his desire to have more than just memories. But whenever we have loved deeply, we are never truly parted from those we hold dear.

Chapter Nine

Pierced

After the Company leaves the Golden Wood, they are content to drift with the current. Danger is before them no matter which way they choose, whether they go to Mirith Tirith to rest before attempting the dark road to Mordor or go straight to the Black Land. How easy it is to understand why they are in no hurry to decide. Who would not wish to delay peril if they could? These people are among the greatest heroes of Middle-earth, but they do not know it yet. They continue on, just as we must, for Aragorn is quite right about the Enemy not being idle.

During the eighth night since departing Lórien, an Orc arrow strikes Frodo from behind, but the *mithril* coat deflects it. Soon afterward, the hobbit feels a terrible cold around his heart and shoulder. Legolas brings down a flying creature with a well-aimed arrow, but none of them know exactly what he hit. Frodo suspects from the way his Morgul-wound responds, but like Gandalf who felt restrained from divulging his suspicions about the Ring to Saruman, something about Boromir's manner stops the Bearer from saying what he thinks.

The fall of the Ringwraith's fell beast is another good that comes from the rise of the Balrog in Moria. The demon's appearance had filled even Legolas with fear, but, as Michael Martinez notes, "the encounter may have better prepared him for confronting the Nazgûl over Anduin. . . . Now he had greater courage" ("Legolas Greenleaf," *Understanding Middle-earth*, 124).

Even after this unsettling incident, the Company still remains unsure of where to go, but the time for decision is fast approaching. Boromir remains set upon going to Minas Tirith, but Aragorn wishes to sit upon the seat on Amon Hen, where he hopes to gain some sign about how to proceed. The younger man bows to the Ranger's choice to continue down the River as long as possible after seeing Frodo's determination to go wherever Aragorn leads.

As Aragorn and Legolas leave the Company to seek the portage-way past the rapids of Sarn Gebir, Frodo watches without knowing if he will see them again. He soon discovers that he worried over nothing. What time we waste in worry! The Ring-bearer has legitimate reason for concern, and we think we do also. But rather than fretting, let us blunt our anxiety by the greater power of prayer. If we do this, we gain the dominion over worry that it formerly had over us. What peace this gives, as we come to understand that we are well taken care of, all our true needs are met, and we have the strength to endure whatever comes. Frodo slowly comprehends this fact as his Quest continues.

Awe and fear so overcome Frodo at the sight of the Argonath that he hides. Poor Sam is so afraid of the roaring waters that one wonders if he even saw the statues. Let us not have our fears blind us to the beauty and majesty around us. As Aragorn looks upon the mammoth statues of his forefathers of long ago, the Ring-bearer sees the man transformed for a moment into the king that he will become.

Upon reaching Parth Galen, the Company comes as far as they can without making a decision. After Aragorn tells Frodo that the choice is the hobbit's alone to make, the beleaguered Ring-bearer begs for some time by himself. Sam knows what must be, but he is willing to wait until his master conquers his terror enough to come to this point on his own.

While Frodo struggles to decide, Boromir comes upon him and tries to convince him to go to Minas Tirith. With the exception of the hobbit's greater torment, the Ring works its wiles best on Denethor's elder son. As a warrior, he still does not understand or agree with the choice to destroy the fell object when the use of it would give the foes of Sauron a desperately needed victory. After Frodo refuses Boromir's pleas to give the Ring to him, the man jumps at the hobbit in an effort to force it from him. Stricken by great fear and sorrow, Frodo puts it on to escape. After sense returns to Boromir, he at last understands the peril of the terrible thing that he coveted and realizes that the control of another will had induced a temporary insanity in him.

In Frodo's flight from Boromir, the Ring-bearer comes to Amon Hen. The struggle he has there shows in a painfully focused and amplified way the reality of the spiritual warfare inside every soul. "For it is not against human enemies that we have to struggle, but against the Sovereignties and the Powers who originate the darkness in this world, the spiritual army of evil in the heavens" (Eph. 6:12). As Frodo wears the Ring, he senses Sauron looking for him. Conflict fills the hobbit's response to this horrible threat, as he is not sure whether he is completely set against his Enemy or ready to come before him.

We cannot always tell either as the myriad temptations that assail us toss us about like a boat on a stormy sea. God will see us through and never abandon us. Even if we sometimes abandon Him, lured by the adversary who seeks to dash us against the rocks and sink us beneath the waves, our Father will still be there.

God continues to protect Frodo with angelic aid, as He has all along. This time it comes in the form of a voice, later revealed as Gandalf's, that commands the hobbit to take off the Ring. The Ring-bearer writhes in torment as he is pierced by this power, and its opposite, which seeks to compel him to keep the Ring on, so that Sauron will discover his location. He then comes to a point where he is merely himself. Free for an instant from both terrible pressures, Frodo makes his own choice. Neither power coerces him into anything. Gandalf aids him but does not decide for him. After Frodo removes the Ring at the last possible moment, Sauron's searching Eye misses him.

We need to remember that there is help for us during our times of trial. God provides many ways to aid us for our redemption, but He also respects our free will as to whom we follow. The Ring-bearer listens many times to God and His angels. He also hears and at times hearkens to the incessant whispers and shouts of the Ring. Divine, angelic, and demonic voices contend for our attention as well. Like Frodo, we feel the pressure of two diametrically opposed forces far stronger than we who vie for possession of our soul. Let us be fully aware exactly who we attend to, for we cannot afford to lose this fight. We may pray not to face such an intense test as the hobbit's. But if we must endure one, it will be for the same reason, which is to continue to learn how to bolster our will against the dark power that seeks to devour us and to realize we can indeed resist it. There is pain involved in such a trial but also illumination.

Anne C. Petty notes how Gandalf knew to aid Frodo, which is the latest example of how evil defeats itself.

> The final impetus Frodo needs to make the decision to
> leave the company comes from the Ring itself. . . . In
> attempting to reveals its presence to the Eye of Sauron,
> the Ring compels Frodo to put it on as he gazes across
> the River towards Mordor. However, in addition to the
> calling the Dark Lord to attention, the Ring also puts
> Frodo in touch with other powers equally strong and
> receptive to its message. (*One Ring to Bind Them All*,
> 50-51)

Boromir's fall to the lure of the Ring made Frodo more aware than ever of the horrible power of the Enemy. But instead of frightening the hobbit into inaction, this bald exposure reawakens his courage and hardens his resolve. The burden on his heart lessens, and he makes the decision to continue alone to Mordor. Peter Kreeft remarks, "Jesus was like Frodo!" in that both overcome terror to fulfill their vocations (*The Philosophy of Tolkien*, 199).

As Aragorn and the others wait for Frodo to return, Merry and Pippin stand by their word to remain ever by their cousin's side. Merry admits, however, that they were not aware at the time of their original promise exactly what this vow would involve. Neither of them want Frodo to go to Mordor, but Pippin says that if they cannot stop him, they will not part with him. Sam replies that Frodo knows perfectly well what he must do, but he has to first defeat his fear of actually doing it. The gardener is certain that his master will do so and will also insist on going alone.

As we watch someone we love travel a path of suffering, the temptation may be strong to cry for him or her to stop. But it would be well to remember Aragorn's words that it is not our place to try to stop our dear one or, alternatively, to force him or her to continue. No one should do this for another person. As with a child frightened to go down a slide, jump into a pool, or ride a bike alone, we should encourage but not force a decision, just as Sam knows not to push Frodo. After we witness our beloved ones struggle with weightier matters than a child has to contend with, we should support them and not interfere with their choice once they have determined that, as far as they can tell, it is God's will for them, even if it is not our desire. As Aragorn speaks of the futility of choosing for someone else, he alludes to the powers who watch over Frodo and protect him and his vocation.

The fear of Merry and Pippin will echo in Peter's wish to stop the Passion of Jesus. "This must not happen to you" (Matt. 16:22). Jesus will respond, "Get behind me, Satan! You are an obstacle in my path, because the way you think is not God's way but man's" (Matt. 16:23).

After Boromir returns, but Frodo does not, the Company scatters in a panic to search for the Ring-bearer. But as Wayne G. Hammond and Christina Scull wonder, is it truly "madness, or fate sending them on their appointed paths?" (*"The Lord of the Rings": A Reader's Companion*, 352). It is more the latter than the former. Frodo no longer needs a Company to protect him but one heart only. This leaves the others free to pursue the diverging Roads set out for them, so that they can sing their own parts in the Great Music.

Frodo tries to escape by boat, but Sam figures this out and refuses to be left behind. After the Ring-bearer rescues his loyal servant from drowning, he expresses annoyance at the delay but then laughs after Sam says that he will destroy all the boats if not allowed to come with his master. Fleming Rutledge notes such lightheartedness "almost always signifies an incursion of divine grace" (*Battle*, 146). The concern of everyone else is in saving Middle-earth as a whole, but Sam focuses on the one person dearest to him. In succoring Frodo by whatever loving means that he can, the humble gardener shows his kinship with the Virgin Mary. She will be there while her Son carries His cross, just as Sam is there while Frodo carries his. The Ring-bearer happily recognizes that having his faithful guardian with him is another thing meant to happen.

The burden of the Ring is Frodo's, but he was never meant to bear it alone. Three hobbits – Frodo, Sam, and Sméagol – are necessary for the Quest to succeed. We all need someone. God has spent decades knitting the souls of Frodo and Sam together, so that they are inseparable for this one task. They would rather be back home in the sun-filled, idyllic Shire, but they walk, stagger, and crawl to the heart of darkness instead. As the journey continues, the Ring-bearer learns more and more that "a faithful friend is a sure shelter, whoever finds one has found a rare treasure" (Ecclus./Sir. 6:14). They are only two small beings, but they are part of a much larger Story.

Chapter Ten

Three Hunters, Two Hobbits, and One White Rider

*W*hile Aragorn searches for Frodo, the man comes upon the mortally wounded Boromir, who confesses that he tried to take the Ring. The Ranger shows once more what a wonderful king he will become, as he does not immediately ask after Frodo's whereabouts but cares more to take the time to comfort his dying companion. He takes Boromir's hand, kisses his brow, and reassures him that he did not fail but instead attained a great and rare victory. Aragorn does not at all judge or blame the warrior for his transgression, for the Ranger knows it could happen to anyone. Lynn Forest-Hill notes that Boromir's death is "not merely heroic, but redemptive in its sacrifice" ("Boromir, Byrhtnoth, and Bayard," *Tolkien Studies* 5, 81). The pride that caused the man's fall "can be forgiven because it initiates self-awareness, contrition and confession. These are, of course, the required steps in the sacrament of Confession in the Roman Catholic faith to which Tolkien remained devoted throughout his life" (ibid.). In giving Boromir absolution, Aragorn shows another side of his pre-figuring of Christ, who is the One who forgives through the priest. Faramir later tells Frodo about the sight of Boromir in the funeral boat. He knows that his beloved brother died in a state of grace rather than disgrace.

Boromir received his reward. We must fight on to obtain ours despite our own failures. We have all been created for and by Light, but darkness can still overcome us as we seek to glorify ourselves. We should all strive to end as this son of Gondor with our fall confessed, amended, and forgiven; our peace achieved; and our escape made from the battlefield upon which we are born. We could not depart from this world in a better way.

The capture of Merry and Pippin is not the disaster it seems but occurs in order to bring good. The impeccable timing of this, which is right for Aragorn to come and absolve Boromir and learn of the hobbits' seizure but too late to rescue them, is all part of the tempo of the Music set from the beginning. We must never let seemingly terrible events dismay us, for God allows them for some purpose beyond our immediate sight. The Orcs will bring the two hobbits to the eves of Fangorn Forest, where they are meant to go to fulfill another part of their vocations and would not have come there any other way.

After sending off Boromir's funeral boat, Aragorn, Legolas, and Gimli try to figure out whether Frodo and Sam were captured as well. From the clues left behind, the man solves the puzzle by saying the Ring-bearer and his faithful servant escaped. After the Elf guesses that Frodo fled from Orcs, the Ranger agrees that the hobbit ran away, but he does not think it was from the enemy soldiers. He respects Boromir too much to reveal the younger man's temporary weakness and so leaves the memories that Legolas and Gimli have of their companion unstained by a fall already redressed.

Aragorn searches his heart whether to try to catch up with Frodo and Sam or to pursue Merry and Pippin. Fr. Jacques Philippe has a wonderful prayer for the critical times that we all face, as we seek to discern God's will about what path to take.

> Lord, I have thought about it and prayed to know Your will. I do not see it clearly, but I am not going to trouble myself any further. I am not going to spend hours racking my brain. I have decided such and such a thing because, all things carefully considered, it seems to me the best thing to do. And I leave everything in Your hands. I know well that, even if I am mistaken, You will not be displeased with me, for I have acted with good intentions. And if I have made a mistake, I know that You are able to draw good from this error. It will be for

me a source of humility and I will learn something from
it! (*Searching for and Maintaining Inner Peace,* 74)

Aragorn is ever a servant of God and a listener for the Spirit. The
indecision and uncertainty that plagues him clears for a moment and
allows him to make his choice. This happens continually throughout
the tale and helps lend to its incredible sense of reality. God reveals of
our long Road only what we need to know in order to take the next
step but not all that will happen in the thousands of steps that follow.
Aragorn knows who guides the Company when he speaks once more
of his awareness of the invisible world and the guardians placed over
Frodo. He realizes that his responsibility to look after the Ring-bearer
has ended. "He implies, though he does not say, that Frodo and Sam
have passed out of his hands, into other hands" (Rutledge, *Battle,* 149;
italics in original). The Valar, especially Elbereth and Ulmo, are near to
provide stronger protection than the man himself could. If one does not
believe in such guardians, it seems folly to abandon Frodo and Sam and
better to sacrifice Merry and Pippin. Aragorn, however, does believe and
understands that his task now is to go after the younger hobbits.

Who gives Aragorn, Legolas, and Gimli the incredible strength to
run for many leagues during their long chase after the Orcs? "Those
who wait for the LORD shall renew their strength, they shall mount
up with wings like eagles, they shall run and not be weary, they shall
walk and not faint" (Isa. 40:31, NRSV).

After the Three Hunters come across five brutally murdered Orcs,
Aragorn solves the mystery by referring to the hatred and malice be-
tween the various factions of their enemy. The same thing will work to
Frodo and Sam's great fortune in the Tower of Cirith Ungol.

Aragorn, Legolas, and Gimli must again decide how best to proceed
a day after Boromir's death with the Orcs still far ahead. Should they
continue the chase in hope of lessening the great lead of their adversaries, or should they stop to rest for the night and not chance missing
clues like the brooch Pippin dropped that Aragorn found earlier? We
face this ourselves. We see more than one alternative and none seem
completely clear. We must weigh all of them and choose what seems
the most correct.

Aragorn is right to say that the real Quest belongs to Frodo. The man does not know whether the choice to follow after Merry and Pippin was in vain even before he made it, but he does not go back on it. "Frequently, the will of the Lord is that we do decide for ourselves, even if we are not absolutely sure that this decision would be the best" (Philippe, *Searching*, 74). Sam also wrestles with this in Shelob's lair after Frodo's apparent death. None of us can see all the twists, turns, and switchbacks on the Road ahead, but our lack of knowledge should not paralyze us into doing nothing. Let us instead trust in the One who knows everything and use Him as our Compass. We all have parts to play in the greater Story, and what is seemingly small or wrong can prove in the end not so.

By the end of the third day, Legolas fears that the enemy host has reached Fangorn Forest. Gimli laments that all their hope and strenuous effort was for naught. Aragorn counters him by saying that their hope may be at an end but their labors will continue. They all feel the press of the dark power of Saruman, but they refuse to bow to it. How much heavier does Frodo feel the increasing spiritual and physical weight of the Ring, but he goes on as well.

We must do the same. After our adversary sees what direction we travel in, he will either throw his might against us in an attempt to stop us, or he will seek to entrap us and persuade us to follow his guidance rather than anyone else. Our foe will keep us in the dark that his true aim is the destruction of our soul. We must not give into despair under his attacks but run all the more toward God, which is the last thing our enemy wants. Once he sees such a result, he will switch tactics. The assaults will not cease but will grow less violent and obvious. We must proceed carefully, as the subtler ones are far more dangerous. But even they will lose the power to hurt us if we recognize them and remain firmly fixed to God's side. It would be well to bear in mind the words of Legolas after it seems that the heroic chase of Merry and Pippin is in vain. The Elf counsels his friends not to give up hope because they do not know what will happen in the future.

During the long chase, Aragorn, Legolas, and Gimli come upon the Rohirrim. As the Ranger reveals Andúril and his true name to Éomer, the Elf and Dwarf have a vision of the king Aragorn will become. We need such sights to provide us glimpses of a brighter future. Grace also grants one to Sam in Shelob's lair when he sees Frodo's inner light continue to shine, even after the Ring-bearer's apparent death.

Aragorn stuns Éomer by his words and the sight of the reforged Sword. Surprising also is Gimli's news that hobbits, thought only creatures in story and song, are actually living, breathing beings. Éomer begs Aragorn to come to Edoras, which the older man admits he wants to do, but he knows that he must find Merry and Pippin first. All his life he has placed the needs of others ahead of his own, and in doing so, he indirectly but actively advances his own cause. Such is how it must be.

After confronting so many legends coming true at once, Éomer asks an important question.

> "How shall a man judge what to do in such times?"
> "As he ever has judged," said Aragorn. "Good and ill
> have not changed since yesteryear . . ." (*LOTR*, 427-428)

Aragorn points out that moral judgements are not open to personal, subjective interpretation. There are such things as absolute truths, and they do not change, no matter to which race you belong. His wisdom is more proof of the grace that fills him. In every age, evil things, such as the murder of the born and unborn, are always evil even if viewed by some as desirable. Good things, such as self-sacrifice, are always good even if our selfish society does not recognize it.

Éomer goes against the laws of his king and releases the Three Hunters and even supplies them with horses. The young man knows that this could cost him his life, but he trusts that Aragorn will not betray him and will instead return his good faith.

Aragorn again corrects Gimli's discouragement after the dwarf laments that Gandalf's foresight allowed the wizard to know that Merry and Pippin were needed on the Quest but not far enough to prevent his own death. The man says that Gandalf did not make decisions based on the knowledge of whether they were safe or not, but because he knew that there were things that must be started even if death prevented their completion. The truth of this is woven throughout the tale, from Frodo's agreement to guard the Ring even after learning of the grave danger that it posed to his body and soul, through to the Council's decision to take up the seemingly impossible Quest, the march of the Ents, Théoden leading the Rohirrim into battle, Merry's quest to aid Dernhelm, and Frodo and Sam's tortuous journey to reach the Mountain of Fire. They are all shining lights for us to follow on our Roads, as the darkness presses close, and we are most vulnerable to our enemy's temptations to give up.

The heart aches to read of the terror and abuse Merry and Pippin suffer at the hands of the Orcs, but Michael W. Perry makes note of one more good that comes from Saruman's evil.

> As unfortunate as the capture of Merry and Pippin may have seemed, it had an often unnoticed good effect. Both Sauron and Saruman's Orcs were in a position to intercept the Ring-bearer. When Merry and Pippin were captured, Orcs that Sauron had placed just east of Nen Hithoel were drawn westward across Rohan, leaving the Dead Marshes approach to Mordor temporarily un-guarded (or lightly guarded) at the very time Frodo and Sam use it. It is unlikely that Sauron was bothered by this brief gap in his defenses, since as Gandalf will note when he meets Aragorn, Gimli and Legolas on March 1, Sauron assumes that his foes are going to Minas Tirith to use the Ring against him. (*Untangling Tolkien*, 144)

Grace remains with Merry and Pippin and gifts the latter with visions of Aragorn following them. It also inspires the tween to run away from his captors for a few moments to leave clear footprints and drop the Elven brooch from his cloak. Pippin does not know who prompted him to do this, but he immediately obeys.

After the Orcs continue on with their prisoners, Pippin fights to keep the tide of despair from completely overwhelming him. Help is not far away, though neither he nor Merry know this. Sarurman's lust for the Ring, which caused him to send out his Orcs to capture hobbits, combines with his hatred of Rohan at the moment it can bring the most good. To counter his fear of the Ring coming into Théoden's hands, the wizard increased his assaults against the land in the hope of defeating his enemy before he was overcome himself. The Writer of the Story, however, has other uses for this malice. The Rohirrim arrive precisely at the right time to destroy the Orc host while Fangorn Forest looms nearby.

The warriors of Rohan aid Merry and Pippin, who the men do not even know are there. Evidence of the supernatural and human protection that guards the hobbits is the death of Grishnákh, who had begun to carry off the two in the confusion after the attack. He draws his sword to kill them, but firelight reflects off the weapon and alerts one of the Rohirrim. The Orc shrieks after an arrow "aimed with skill, or guided by fate" (*LOTR*, 446) penetrates his hand. The warrior who kills him does not see Merry and Pippin, who are wrapped in their Elven cloaks and nigh to invisible in the night. The horse of one of his companions does, however, either by particularly sharp sight or "some other sense" (ibid.) and jumps over them. These events clearly hint at the invisible spiritual world that fills our own and shows that those in it are actively at work.

Another indication of this watchful care is that Merry and Pippin take the time to snack on some lembas rather than immediately escape the battle. At first, they only crawl away, but the bread's tremendous virtue soon strengthens them enough to walk. They talk lightly of their horrible ordeal, which gives more evidence of the great power the Little Folk have to recover quickly from trauma.

After Merry and Pippin enter Fangorn Forest, they come upon clean water. They barely notice the healing of their wounds and the restoration of their energy. They come then to Treebeard's favorite place to think. Saruman's obsession with gaining power brings about this fateful meeting between Ent and hobbits and causes his plans for domination to come crashing down. The hatred and anger of the Ents was already smoldering because of the fallen Maia's wanton destruction of the trees around Isengard, but such kindles into flame not long after Merry and Pippin's arrival.

What comes out of Saruman's maliciousness contains more signs that God does not allow evil without cause for good also to bear fruit, for even our wicked choices serve Him in some way. As Joseph tells his brothers in the book of Genesis, "The evil you planned to do me has by God's design been turned to good" (50:20). Or as Ilúvatar told Melkor long before, "And thou, Melkor, shalt see that no theme may be played that hath not its uttermost source in me, nor can any alter the music in my despite. For he that attempteth this shall prove but mine instrument in the devising of things more wonderful, which he himself hath not imagined" (Tolkien, *The Silmarillion*, 5). The Song continues to play out as foreseen by God from all eternity despite efforts to throw it off key.

The Ents show great wisdom in taking several days to resolve to destroy Isengard. We should not rush into deciding something as terrible as going to war. Nonetheless, there are instances when reckless hate must be countered with all the force that we can bring, lest it destroy us. The lessons of history show the folly of pretending that the danger is not there or thinking that if we play nice, it will ignore us and go away. As the march to Saruman's stronghold begins, Treebeard acknowledges to Merry and Pippin that there is a good chance that the Ents go now to their own deaths, but, as doom would fall upon them in any case, they decide to die fighting.

While Aragorn, Legolas, and Gimli search for Merry and Pippin in Fangorn, they watch an old man they had seen before. Gimli is sure it is Saruman. Legolas begins to ready his bow to shoot, but he feels another will fighting him. The dwarf grows impatient because he does not want the man to use magic against them, but Aragorn counsels caution. We must follow this worthy advice whenever there is time to ascertain the truth about any strangers we meet before we give into fear. We may be only imagining a peril or enlarging it beyond its reality. If we wait, we may avoid a disaster.

Rather than Saruman, the Three Hunters make a glad reunion beyond all hope with Gandalf. The returned Maia reveals that no weapon can harm him now. "He who has undergone the worst that the Abyss can do, and has conquered, is no longer subject to fear or to death. 'What is sown is perishable; what is raised is imperishable.' (I Cor. 15:42)" (Ellwood, *Good News*, 117). We see in the wizard's unsullied white the tragedy of his brother Maiar to forsake the Light and embrace evil.

Gandalf reveals that he was the voice Frodo heard on Amon Hen and how he battled Sauron to help save the Ring-bearer. Even though the hobbit escaped the Enemy then, the wizard says many more dangers are ahead. These are spread like webs before the Ring-bearer's feet, and we wonder how he could pass safely through all their snares. The wizard is right to be happy that the others assume that Sam went with Frodo because to help him to navigate around these traps is one of the reasons Sam is there.

The news that Boromir escaped gladdens Gandalf. The wizard makes clear the immense value of Merry and Pippin's inclusion in the Company, for it was through them that the warrior received the opportunity to redress his fall. But the Maia says this was only part of their vocations. "They were brought to Fangorn" (*LOTR*, 485) in perfect timing for their next roles. The word 'brought' shows the hand of Providence again guiding events along by using Saruman and Orcs as unwitting instruments.

Gandalf also states what he perceives of the mind of Sauron. The Dark Lord's greatest fear is that someone will use the power of the Ring against him. In his inability to conceive that his adversaries would do anything else with it, he reveals a great deficiency. W. H. Auden notes that "Evil . . . has every advantage but one—it is inferior in imagination. Good can imagine the possibility of becoming evil—hence the refusal of Gandalf and Aragorn to use the Ring—but Evil, defiantly chosen, can no longer imagine anything but itself" ("At the End of the Quest, Victory," *nytimes.com*). This lack fuels Sauron's strategy to make a preemptive strike against the one that he believes will come to challenge him. He has no idea that the greatest threat to his power will not come from Gondor but from the heart of his own realm. By the time the Dark Lord will realize his colossal error, it will be far too late.

Gandalf recognizes the good fortune blessing those who fight against Sauron in that the Enemy mistakenly assumes that his opponents think the same way he does. If he had instead solely focused on hunting for the Ring-bearer, as he should have and believes that he is, the White wizard says that the hope of the West would have faded away. Note that Gandalf does not say that the hope which already hangs by a thin thread would immediately fail but fade. His words contain the image of those on the side of Light continuing to battle valiantly against the doom that would fall if this thread snapped altogether.

Gandalf also speaks of how dangerous all beings are who serve the Light. As powerful as the adversary of our soul is, he still greatly fears us and the good that he knows we can do. He strikes hardest against those whom he considers his mightiest foes, just as Saruman and Sauron do. Let us have the same confidence in ourselves that our enemy does. We should rejoice that we are a peril to him and strive to become an ever-greater one! Let us be flaming arrows that God launches into the world to strike at the heart of evil, just as the heroes in Middle-earth are.

Gandalf is glad that the Ring is out of reach. As Fleming Rutledge points out, the fact that the White wizard considers Black more powerful than he shows that we all face temptation and the possibility of it devouring us (*Battle*, 162). The weakness of a body of flesh does not tell him this, for Melkor fell in his pursuit of ultimate power while a pure spirit. Rather, Gandalf's understanding of the heart and will of created beings, including his own, reveals it. Even as the White he fears the Ring, perhaps even more so because his power is greater. Good as he is, he also knows he is weak. His healthy fear of and respect for his limits are signs of humility and self-realization that evildoers do not have.

We must have this same awareness about the strength of our own will. If Gandalf does not trust himself to resist the Ring, then we, who are so much weaker, should not entertain the arrogant folly of thinking we are strong enough solely in ourselves to withstand evil in whatever form it comes. We are overcome in little and big ways all the time. We serve one master one day and another the next. Sometimes we do not even realize it until the damage is done. However, though Black is mightier than we in terrible, crushing power, God is mightier than Black, and He does not rest any more than His and our adversary.

Aragorn had said earlier that the valiant chase of Merry and Pippin was without purpose, but Gandalf assures him now of its fruits. He says that the man made the best choice he could, which has reaped the reward of their own meeting at the precise time necessary for other events to happen. Not only were the hobbits meant to come to Fangorn, but Aragorn, Legolas, and Gimli were also brought there. This allows the Ranger the freedom to choose to travel with the others to the hall of Théoden and prove that Éomer's faith in him was not in vain. He could not have made this choice without making the others first.

Gandalf tells of his terrible battle with the Balrog and how darkness and then new life came to him. Gwaihir rescued him and remarked on his incredible lightness. This foreshadows Sam finding Frodo unexpectedly the same at Mount Doom. Just as Gandalf's old self was burned away in battle with the demonic, so is Frodo's.

Gimli fears that his beloved Galadriel gave Gandalf no words to relay to him, as she had the others. He tells Legolas that he would even welcome words of his death if she had nothing else to impart. The dwarf dances with joy after he hears that his Lady is thinking of him. This love story is among the sweetest of the many in the tale.

Chapter Eleven

Counter-measures
to Reckless Hate

"The Battles of the Fords of Isen," speaks of Saruman's terrible obsession to destroy Rohan (Tolkien, *Unfinished Tales*, 355-373). Whether Théoden slipped into illness several years before the War of the Ring from natural causes or from poisons administered by Wormtongue is unknown. Whatever the means, the traitorous counselor gained control over his king and even began to dupe him into thinking that Éomer had become an adversary.

Such manipulation is nothing, however, compared to Saruman ordering the death of Théoden's son and heir, Théodred. The murder takes place in the midst of battle, after which the enemy withdraws from the field. The cost of this 'victory' is higher than Saruman in his lust-blackened sight can foresee. Rather than defeating his feared and hated adversaries, he actually saves Rohan from almost certain destruction. His commander does not continue the attack after gaining the advantage over the beleaguered Rohirrim. Though their valor was great, Saurman's forces would have likely overwhelmed them if not for this unexpected retreat. Edoras itself could have fallen before Gandalf arrived after escaping from Orthanc. Instead, the invasion of Rohan does not come for days, which allows its warriors to come later to the aid of Helm's Deep rather than be surrounded by enemy soldiers while on the way. The withdrawal also helps save Gondor, as the Rohirrim later ride to the battle of the Pelennor Fields.

After Gandalf, Aragorn, Legolas, and Gimli come to Théoden's golden hall, the king has no welcome for the visitors at first. He still withers under the crippling domination of Wormtongue. But Gandalf defeats the wicked man by using the staff Háma had allowed the wizard to retain against strict orders. Sometimes disobeying a command is the path to take, but such a situation must be carefully discerned, as Háma did and Éomer before him.

Théoden accepts healing from Gandalf and regains his freedom to act independently. The king is not another Mouth of Sauron, who has no will but that of his master. Théoden sees the world unfiltered again and realizes that he has a choice to return to the Light. He did not fall from it through his own will but from spiritual if not physical poison. The reclaiming of mastery over himself is also instrumental to the success of the war Sauron launches against Gondor. Things are still grave, but the king now vigorously defies despair rather than remaining bent under its weight.

What paralyzing anxieties do we need to free ourselves from in order to embrace our vocations and live more fully? Fear does not leave any of those who fight in the War of the Ring, but it does not keep them from acting. They move through their terror and so reach the point where they are meant to be. Let us examine our own cages and look for a way out, for there is one, if we but summon the courage to pick up the key and turn the lock. Like Rohan's king, we, too, will breathe freely again, as we exhale the poisonous fumes of doubt and fear and take in wonderful, clean air. All is not as dark as we think it is. Let us gain or regain control over ourselves rather than allow worry to rule us. Look squarely at your fears and examine them closely. They may be nothing more than phantasms conjured by our enemy to frighten us from moving, or they could be our fretting over the fear others have for us. Confront whatever makes you anxious, and tell it that you are going ahead. Like a bully suddenly confronted with an unwavering strength that proclaims that his dominion is over, the fears will lose their power, as you increasingly gain authority over them. Exercise this influence, for you have it already! No fear is greater than God, though it may *seem* greater than us. Do not be afraid to slay the roaring tigers that roam about you. You will find many of them are made only of paper. Even if they are real, there is still no excuse to avoid fighting them with all your might.

Gandalf tells Théoden that though their Enemy is immensely strong, they have the advantage over him in the secret hope that Frodo will accomplish his task. This expectation hangs by a thin thread, but it remains unconquered by the ever-present threat of doom that looms over all who contend against Sauron. Under this cloud, the wizard encourages those who struggle by saying that hope will remain if they fight to remain undefeated. We must have the same trust that Gandalf does and do our own part in the battle, while we await the One who will achieve victory for us and through us. Sauron's defeat does not come about by arms but by hearts and bodies offered up in sacrifice.

After Háma brings Wormtongue to Théoden, Gandalf acknowledges the justice of slaying the false servant, but he does not advocate this. Service to Saruman has reduced Gríma from a man to a snake, from a 'he' to an 'it.' Wizard and king know, however, that the corrupted man was not always the evil creature now before them. Théoden gives mercy in recognition of abandoned goodness, which could be reclaimed if given the time, opportunity, and will to do so.

During the bitter night-long battle of the Hornburg, Aragorn is once more the bearer of hope. Gamling speaks of the fierceness of the Orcs and the wild men and says neither will fall back before the sun. Aragorn, however, refuses to despair of victory, for he does not yet know the outcome of the battle. He advises that the defenders of the keep continue to fight by using the weapon of hope, which is the same one that Sam wields. In offering encouragement to those around him, the Ranger is the hobbit's spiritual twin. We all need to do this for those near us, who wander lost in darkness and fear. Another part of the reality of this tale is that Aragorn and Sam sometimes need to have their hope recharged. Legolas does this for his friend, just as the Star in Mordor will do it for Sam.

Another person Aragorn heartens is Théoden, who wonders how any stronghold could last against such a large number of enemies armed with violent hatred. Now that the king realizes their terrible strength, he begins to question the wisdom of Gandalf's counsel. Aragorn advises him to lay aside his doubts until the end of the battle.

In Aragorn's merciful parley with the Orcs and hillmen, he reveals another sign of the great king that he will become. He warns them that no one knows what the coming dawn will mean to any of them. He gives them a chance to escape and tells them that if they do not, they will be killed. With these words, the revelation of his royal bearing causes the hillmen to hesitate, but it does not at all impress the Orcs, who mock and reject Aragorn's overtures. They appear to have the upper hand and believe that their victory is imminent. The future king, however, strongly believes and hopes that Gandalf will return, though he does not actually know that such triumph will come. "Only faith can guarantee the blessings that we hope for, or prove the existence of the realities that at present remain unseen" (Heb 11:1). We do not know the future anymore than Aragorn or anyone else, but we can share and spread his inspiring example of trust that all will work out as it should. The wizard does indeed arrive with Erkenbrand and his men and the more unusual reinforcements of Huorns. The Orcs flee to their doom amid the trees.

After Théoden and the Rohirrim reunite with Gandalf, the king admits that in the darkness he was unsure of the wizard, but he does not wish to separate from him now. Why do we doubt so easily? Why do we believe the lies that our enemy and his servants whisper in our ears and heart rather than the words of angels and of God? We are under His care, even in the blackest night, but how deeply do we truly believe this? Do we trust in it at all, as the dark threatens to drown us and suffocate our faith and hope? As with the Nazgûl, who are mightiest during the night, our foe and his slaves are their most powerful then also, whether this be physical, mental, or spiritual. But God is also there, sending us hope, light, and strength. Sam discerns this in Mordor. We need to discover and remember it ourselves.

The hillmen Saruman tricked into fighting receive mercy after the battle is over. To their surprise, their only punishment is to fulfill Erkenbrand's orders to help restore the fortifications that they tried to destroy and then to pledge not to cross the Isen Fords while armed or to fight in any army that is opposed to men. After this, they are free to go back to their homes.

The dialogue between Gimli and Legolas, as they travel amid the wonder of the forest that sprang up literally overnight, is one rich with wisdom. The Elf longs to stay and learn about the trees, while Gimli is anxious to leave them behind. The Dwarf waxes poetic about the marvels in the caverns below the Hornburg, while Legolas says he will pay gold to avoid going in them. Beauty is indeed in the eye of the beholder! Yet Gimli agrees to go to Fangorn, and Legolas promises to see the Glittering Caves. These words give moving testimony to the strength of the loving friendship now between them. Both will gain new appreciation for what the other considers lovely because they will see it through each other's eyes.

Chapter Twelve

Non Serviam

As Gandalf and the others arrive at Isengard to talk with Saruman, the doorwardens assigned by Treebeard greet them. The glad reunion with Merry and Pippin and the teasing arguments that ensue convinces Théoden of the great devotion between the hobbits and Legolas and Gimli. Indeed, only dear friends can speak to each other thus without harm. It gives everyone, including us readers, a joyful moment in the growing darkness.

Aragorn offers an insightful comment as he confirms the rightness of Pippin's decision to let go of the Elven brooch. The man says that if one cannot part with something dear when they must, then that possession enslaves them. This point echoes throughout the tale from Isildur's inability to destroy the Ring to Frodo's will being overthrown by the Ring at the last minute.

Pippin speculates that Saruman is at heart a coward if he does not have all his Orcs and fancy machinery to back him up, like a bully who flees if not surrounded by cronies. Aragorn corrects his friend by saying that the wizard was once a great being and even now retains the dangerous power to control others. We are wise to stay away from those who may talk a good game but who are full of foulness underneath.

One of the reasons Gandalf came to Orthanc was to offer Saruman a chance at redemption. The White wizard admits to the danger and likely futility of attempting such a thing, but he knows the effort must be made. We must do the same, so that even those far gone may have the opportunity to find their way back to the Light. If they choose not to take the hand we hold out, that is their failure, not ours.

As Saruman confronts his enemies, he shows the terrible power of his voice. The history of its varying effect is briefly given. For some, it lasted only as long as the wizard focused on that individual. As soon as he turned away, his voice lost its hold, and the person watched amused as the next victim was beguiled. For others, the spell lasted much longer, and they came under the control of the demonic and obeyed its commands. Saruman holds Wormtongue so, and Sauron holds Saruman.

As others speak to us, whether aloud or in our heart and soul, we must discern what they bring us. We may rebel at first after the Holy Spirit shows us our vocation, but in the end there is peace even if fear and toil also come. We may also fight against what the adversary of our soul presents to us, but then he starts to sound much like Saruman: so seductive, reasonable, and right. If we follow such a voice, however, its wake brings confusion and despair. But if we go outside its malicious influence, we realize the folly of it and wonder why we thought it so appealing. Let us carefully watch and ponder our reactions to the voices we hear and also our responses to others who seek to guide us if we have fallen. If we believed in their wisdom before an unwholesome spell overcame us, we should continue to believe in it and not be angered by it, as our enemy would have us when he is in danger of having his hold over us thwarted.

Saruman's voice has no effect on Gimli or Éomer, who both recognize the poisonous barb the fallen Maia conceals beneath his velvety voice. Théoden proves just as wise. He tells the wizard in no uncertain terms what he thinks of him and his offer of 'peace.'

Saruman exerts all his power on Gandalf in a last attempt to seize control of the situation, but the latter breaks the spell completely merely by laughing. How our enemy and his servants also hate to have their power dismissed by something so simple. Such a sound is not heard in Hell and so is terrible to their ears.

The ensuing dialogue between Gandalf and Saruman contains a powerful refrain of one of the most important lessons in the tale. Frodo and Théoden both received Gandalf's counsel about the importance of giving mercy to their enemies in order to give them a chance for a cure. The wizard now offers his former superior the same opportunity. Saruman has a moment of doubt and anguish while his soul stands upon the knife's edge. On one side is redemption and light, which require repentance. On the other stands the dark abyss. Saruman's ability to decide in favor of the Light is greatly diluted by other choices to embrace the Dark. The fallen wizard does not have the courage or humility to admit that he made mistakes. "Pride goes before destruction, a haughty spirit before a fall" (Prov. 16:18). Saruman does not realize that he is a puppet of another haughty spirit, who is a servant of the haughtiest of them all. Rather than accepting transformation and mercy, he hardens himself against it and stubbornly continues toward perdition.

> Tolkien implies here that evil is something chosen, rather than a cosmic force that sweeps innocent people up and corrupts them. Gandalf stresses that, until recently, it was still possible for Saruman to repent his ways: 'You might still have turned away from folly and evil. . . .' Saruman might have, but he did not: he made a choice, and it was the wrong one. After that, Gandalf again emphasizes, '[Y]ou choose to stay.' Such a conception of morality as free choice is important in Tolkien's universe. (Gardner et al., *SparkNotes*, 163)

The other corrupted Maiar, such as Sauron and the Balrogs, were all made first as servants of God and the Valar, but rather than embrace this sacrificial life, they chose to rebel and follow the greatest enemy of their Creator. They all said *Non serviam* (I will not serve).

What happens after Saruman rejects redemption reveals the chief good of Gandalf's sacrifice in Moria. The Grey wizard was not strong enough to strip his erstwhile leader of staff and standing in the Istari order and in the White Council, but Gandalf the White is quite capable. He makes it clear that this is not to take the fallen wizard's place. Gandalf does not abuse the greater power that he now has, which demonstrates the stark difference between him and any who sought their own advancement rather than humbly serve God and others.

Gandalf grieves for Saruman's lost goodness, but he knows that he did what he could within the bounds set for such a confrontation. "Gandalf can force Saruman to come back to the balcony, but cannot induce him to come back to the side of right. Nor can he 'tempt' Denethor back" (Ellwood, *Good News*, 42). Good will not force itself upon a person, even to save his or her soul. Rather, God and His servants respect the gift of free will so much that they will only guide and guard and leave the decision to the individual. Saruman will receive further chances from others, but he will scorn them all and decide instead to follow "the same ruinous path down nto the Void" (Tolkien, *Silmarillion*, 19) that Sauron chose to walk after Melkor/Morgoth.

Chapter Thirteen

Pippin and the *Palantír*

*W*hile in Isengard, Pippin faces the temptation to take a peek in the *palantír* which Wormtongue threw down. The tween tries to resist, as he does not understand why he finds the desire so alluring. But rather than win his battle, he reaches a point where the desire to look becomes unbearable. He walks toward the sleeping Gandalf, retreats, then half-unwillingly moves forward again to take the globe. It is light enough for the hobbit to feel an odd relief that he may not have the Stone after all. He discovers that he does, and while he looks in it, Sauron catches him and briefly torments him.

Pippin's terrifying brush with evil provides another good description of how our enemy works, which the Ring's attempts to seduce Frodo also show. First, the foe plants a suggestion, idea, or thought that we know is or may be wrong but which still attracts us. Our conscience, if properly formed by Light and Truth, will try to warn us away, but we do not always listen. At times, we feel the same relief as Pippin that even as we are about to surrender ourselves utterly, we can still be saved from the adversary that directs our will. Other times we give in to the malevolent power seeking to ruin us and allow ourselves to be drawn in further. We fall for the lie whispered in our soul, similar to what Pippin perhaps hears just before he falls: 'You have gone this far already. You might as well go the whole way. God is not going to forgive you anyway.' As we are bent toward evil because of original sin, we find it easier to continue in the direction that our feet already face rather than to turn back. We wander then in ever deepening night as chains bind us tighter and tighter. To counter this, we must cry out for rescue during times of temptation, as Gandalf instructs Pippin to do if the hobbit gets itchy fingers and just has to look in the palantír again. If we still lose our way, we will always have a Voice calling for us to return.

Pippin's surrender could have been disastrous for the West, but instead it proves worse for Sauron. Paul H. Kocher notes, "Pippin, like every other living being, is to Sauron an impersonal 'it' to be devoured" (*Master*, 55). The thought of tormenting the hobbit in body and mind in the dungeons of Barad-dûr so enthralls the fallen Maia that he hardly spends any time with Pippin during this first discovery. If the Dark Lord was not so anxious to do worse things at a later date, he could have ripped everything from the tween right then. But he contents himself with the anticipation of the deeper delights that he assumes he will soon have.

In addition to surrendering to this lust to cause pain, evil defeats itself yet again by the false conclusions Sauron draws from the encounter and the later one with Aragorn. He does not know the globe was thrown down, so he naturally presumes Saruman still possesses it. The Enemy did not deliberately reach out to Pippin, but he latched onto him after the hobbit just happened to put the Stone in the position that made contact possible. Sauron convinces himself that the Ring-bearer is in captivity because he knows that a hobbit carries his treasure. This exposure, unforeseen by any but the Writer of the Story, is another example of a well-used chance. Aragorn's later revelation strengthens the Dark Lord's belief that his foes will use the Ring to challenge him.

Gandalf's words later about Gollum that "a traitor may betray himself and do good that he does not intend" (*LOTR*, 797) fit just as well here regarding Wormtongue's tossing down of the *palantír*. It again demonstrates God's use of even hateful acts to further His will. Even more, it shows what comes from giving mercy to one who does not deserve it. If Théoden had killed Gríma at Edoras, the ruined servant would not have been at Orthanc to cast down the treasure of his true master. If this was not done, it would not have come into Aragorn's possession. The Ranger would not be at Isengard to receive it if not for Saruman's lust for the Ring. The man makes good use of what Providence gives him to distract Sauron from where the Dark Lord's peril actually lies. If this had not happened, the Enemy would have had reason to heed the urgent reports of spies in his land, captured Frodo and Sam, and doomed the Quest. Even if the hobbits somehow escaped his nets, Sauron would not have drawn off the thousands of Orcs that stand between them and Mount Doom in order to meet Aragorn and the army of the West at the Black Gate. Another good is Gandalf's admittance that he also felt the pull to gaze into the Stone, but that Pippin freed him from this temptation.

All that comes from this one act – and from Gríma's service as a whole to Saruman, which put him near the *palantír* – has taken years to come to fruition. We should remember this while we labor under dark clouds that never seem to break. "We must never get tired of doing good because if we don't give up the struggle we shall get our harvest at the proper time" (Gal 6:9).

On the way to Minas Tirith, Pippin tells Gandalf that he was not aware of what he was doing in reaching out for the Stone. The wizard corrects him by saying the tween did indeed know. The Maia adds that even if he knew what would happen, he would not have stopped it, as it would not have lessened the hobbit's desire to look. To curb this in the future, Gandalf says it was better that Pippin learned the hard way about the perils of giving into what he knew he should not. How well this fits us. Sometimes we need to learn in our own skin what any number of verbal warnings and prohibitions cannot accomplish as well. The fire needs to burn us, so we are more respectful of it later and less tempted to get closer than we should.

Chapter Fourteen

The Pity of Frodo

Through most of the tale, Sam incarnates the baptismal grace of hope, but as he and Frodo struggle through the Emyn Muil, the Ring-bearer manifests this virtue. Sam says that they have apparently come the wrong way, then he is sure of it. Frodo is not. He is confident that because he was given the task of destroying the Ring, he will also receive a way to accomplish it. He just does not know whether good or evil will provide this. Though not speaking of the hobbit, Servant of God Fr. John Hardon sheds light on Frodo's heart and soul at this moment: "By hope we are empowered to confidently trust that all the good things promised us by God we shall obtain; that we will never be without the light and strength we need to fulfill the will of God; that no trials that God sends us will be greater than, with His grace, we can bear" ("Baptism").

Frodo wonders if Sauron is deliberately steering him wrong and doubts the goodness of his own decisions. However, he also trusts God, who has led him thus far. This combination often accompanies our own journeys. Only God sees the whole Story. We are in the deep valley of a single letter or crawling like ants across a field. Sometimes we feel lost and going in circles and share the Ring-bearer's questioning about who directs our path. Our enemy always seeks to trap and delay us, especially after he sees the forward progress we are truly making. We should be encouraged then whenever we discover obstacles and seek a way around them.

The strength of Frodo's faith is inspiring. In the depth of his soul, the hobbit intuitively understands that "nothing is impossible with God" (Luke 1:37, NRSV). He already lives what the Book of Proverbs will exhort: "Trust in the LORD with all your heart, and do not rely on your own insight. In all your ways acknowledge him, and he will make straight your paths" (3:5-6 NRSV). Fleming Rutledge notes, "The Bible is full of people who must continue on the road laid out for them. . . , trusting in God alone. The chief example is Abraham. . . . Frodo's journey is Abrahamic in more ways than one, combining as it does a strong theme of divine election with a corresponding gift of tenacious faith which persists against all contrary evidence" (*Battle*, 198-199).

Do we have this same level of belief? We must. God also asks us to surrender our will to Him, to hand over control of our life, and not to hold the reins ourselves but be led where He wills. If Frodo does this even without conscious knowledge of his Creator, why is it so difficult for us, as we have or should have a greater awareness? It should be much easier, but it is sometimes harder, for the world trains us to rely only on ourselves. We need to strip away all this ingrained and wrong-headed thinking and simply open ourselves up as Frodo does. The only thing that stands between him and God is fear. As he continually learns to move through this, he unites himself more fully to the One who made him. "We, too, then, should throw off everything that hinders us, especially the sin that clings so easily, and keep running steadily in the race we have started" (Heb 12:1). Sometimes we are as impatient as the Ring-bearer is to get things over, whether out of zeal, wishing for relief from the labor of carrying a heavy cross, or simply out of boredom and a wish to do something more exciting. But we must move at the proper speed and wait until the time is right. Other times, even though we should be moving fast, we get distracted by the pretty flowers that grow along the path and slow down to admire them. We must stay focused on what is ahead and not take detours that we should not.

As Frodo and Sam continue to travel, they hear, or imagine that they do, the sound of footsteps behind them. They also hear the sharp intake of breath, or is it just the wind? After they reach a point where they must climb down a cliff, Sam counsels that they wait until morning. Frodo, however, wishes to press on and begins his descent while Sam waits above. The dreaded shriek of a Nazgûl causes the Ring-bearer to lose his grip on the rock and slip. Lightning, or possibly the presence of the wraith, temporarily blinds him. The first thing he sees is the shimmering Elven rope that Sam lowers down. The ambiguity of what actually caused the blindness adds to the reality of this tale. Because Frodo does not know for sure, he cannot state so one way or the other. Such is often the way with us. A may have caused B but C could have also.

After Frodo is safe again, Sam says again that they should stop for the night. His master denies him once more and says he wants to leave the cliff and no longer be so exposed to the eyes he feels watching him from Mordor. The vivid imagery of this tale shows us these eyes as easily as the Ring-bearer senses them in his heart and soul. The hobbits use the rope to lower themselves down. Once they do, it comes loose seemingly on its own. Frodo teases Sam about not tying it tight enough, but the gardener's complete faith in Galadriel and all things Elven leaves him convinced that the rope came in response to his calling upon the Lady's name. Though this is a moment of grace for both hobbits, only Sam is truly aware of it. Even the stars are Elven to him, and the sight comforts him and his master.

Frodo and Sam stop after the Ring-bearer is tired enough to surrender to his guardian's third suggestion that they rest. He adds, however, that he wishes he could see the Road ahead more clearly because then he would persist until he dropped from exhaustion. We may desire the same as we scramble about rocks without much apparent progress, and our end is not obviously in sight. This may last a long time, and our energy is less when we cannot see our goal for certain. We would be much more stimulated if we could just run straight toward the finish rather than through the bogs, ditches, gullies, cliffs, and marshes that we must go through instead. But the long journey is necessary for us to gain the strength to continually walk toward what may be only a blur on the horizon and to grow in the trust of the One who called us to travel this particular path.

After Frodo and Sam spot Gollum slinking down the cliff, the creature provides the answer to the Ring-bearer's earlier wondering whether good or ill would guide him to the next part of his Road. More than anyone else, Sméagol walks in the worlds of both Dark and Light almost as much as Frodo but in opposite ways.

After Gollum slips off the wall, Sam jumps on him. Gollum attacks him, and Frodo draws Sting on their spy to save his friend's life. The gardener advocates leaving the creature tied up with the rope to die a slow death and denies him any humanity or dignity by calling him "it." Frodo says that they cannot kill him for as yet no ill had been done to them. Sam disagrees, as he was bitten in the shoulder and points out that further injury is most likely intended. Frodo does not argue. They both know that Gollum is undoubtedly up to no good. Nonetheless, the Ring-bearer bases his decision on present reality rather than on future possibility. Just because Gollum *might*, probably even *will*, harm them is simply not enough for Frodo to condemn him for a crime not yet committed.

We would be good to respond the same way. An incident during the war on terror in Afghanistan reflects this lesson well, as recounted in *Lone Survivor* by Marcus Luttrell. Four Navy SEALs captured some goat herders who had come upon their position. The warriors then had to decide what to do since they well knew their prisoners could betray them to the Taliban if released. They could kill the men before this happened, or they could wait to see what would actually take place. At the time this choice confronted them, the herders had not done them any harm even if the intent was there. The SEALs reached the same decision Bilbo and Frodo did. There was as yet no crime, so they meted out no punishment. They freed their prisoners with the full knowledge that their seemingly imprudent mercy could be abused. Such did indeed happen. A rescue helicopter was also shot down. Nineteen lives in all were lost. That preemptive action on the SEALs part could have prevented this tragedy does not make the heroically courageous choice to show mercy the wrong one. It also allowed for the grace-filled compassion of the Afghan family who cared for the seriously injured sole survivor until he could be rescued.

During Frodo's own battle between fear and mercy, he recalls Gandalf's words at Bag End about Bilbo's pity and his own lack of it. He had made it perfectly clear that he wished his uncle had killed Gollum, but Linda Greenwood observes what happens as the Ring-bearer faces the creature himself.

> As these remembered words internally ring forth, Frodo lays down his sword. His desire for justice dies and he spares Gollum's life. What is his motive? It seems to be a pure act of pity. His act is motivated by compassion.

> He acts with a mercy that demands and expects noth-
> ing in return, with the 'Divine Gift-love', which [C.S.]
> Lewis explains, enables a man 'to love what is naturally
> unlovable . . .' (*Four Loves* 128). ("Love," 179)

Frodo then speaks aloud to Gandalf, who, as far as he knows, is dead, and assures him that no harm will come to Gollum. The fear that caused the Ring-bearer to wish the wretched being dead has not left him, but what the wizard planted in the hobbit's heart months earlier now bears fruit. Frodo sees Gollum for the first time, not only with his own eyes but with those of Bilbo's and Gandalf's. Rutledge beautifully makes note of another set: "Sam and Frodo both 'see' Gollum, but only Frodo is enabled to see him as God sees him. That sort of sight, as all the Gospels make clear, can be granted only by the grace of God" (*Battle*, 198). The Ring-bearer's view of Gollum completely changes at this moment, and he wants Gandalf to know it. With such testimony, Frodo proves what Gimli said at Rivendell about the giving of one's word strengthening a trembling heart. Pity softens the Ring-bearer's former hostility, stays his hand, and enables him to give his oath. In some dim way, he realizes "There but for the grace of God go I," as St. Philip Neri will say. Like Bilbo, Frodo has no idea how momentous this decision is for himself and for all Middle-earth.

Through the sacrificial experience of carrying the Ring, Frodo gains insight into compassion for the tormented that he did not have before. The endurance of the painful presence of the demonic object, borne like a crown of thorns, makes possible the tremendous spiritual growth that the hobbit gains on the Quest. Helen Keller observed, "Character cannot be developed in ease and quiet. Only through experiences of trial and suffering can the soul be strengthened, vision cleared, ambition inspired, and success achieved." Adversity has indeed cleared Frodo's sight, which is another instance of evil doing good that it does not mean to do. Safe in the Shire, well fed, innocent, and happy, the Ring-bearer did not understand how or why pity should be shown to Gollum. Now affected and infected by the same evil that has so long ravaged Sméagol and continues to do so, Frodo understands in the growing dark what was incomprehensible in the bright sunlight. He realizes he has met a kindred spirit, where before the idea that Gollum could be anything like hobbit-kind angered and offended him. Rather than to continue to call for his enemy's blood, the younger Bearer begins to love his adversary as God instructs us all to do. In his acceptance of his role as his "brother's guardian" (Gen. 4:9), he dedicates himself to easing the agony of one whose violation by evil is much greater than his own and to guiding him back to the Light.

To Sam's surprise, Frodo tells Gollum of their intent to enter Mordor and asks for his aid. After Sméagol relieves the torture he had suffered there, Frodo says that if the creature helps him, such would also give the ruined hobbit freedom from Sauron's domination. An interesting little bit of dialogue takes place toward the end of this conversation.

> "Poor, poor Sméagol, he went away long ago. They took his Precious, and he's lost now."
> "Perhaps, we'll find him again, if you come with us," said Frodo. (*LOTR*, 602).

Indeed, Sméagol does begin to re-emerge from Gollum through Frodo's care. The younger Ring-bearer treats his brother hobbit with a dignity and compassion the tormented being has lacked for centuries. Frodo is careful to call him by his given name and, as God is the one who names, connects Sméagol once more to his Creator. Roger Sale notes, "Sméagol loves the specialness that is Frodo's care of him" ("Tolkien and Frodo Baggins," *Tolkien and the Critics*, 287). The dawning love Frodo receives in return is "the tentative unbelieving response to a caring so unlikely it seems heroic even to the Gollum" (ibid.). Even though the Ring's corruption has held sway over Sméagol for so long, a little bit of his hobbit nature remains to respond to Frodo, as a flower reacts to sunlight. Though this particular flower is horribly deformed and even pale moonlight is painful to it, it still cannot help but to turn to Frodo's light. The friendship of Frodo and Sam wonderfully exhibits many of the fruits of the Holy Spirit, which are outlined by St. Paul as "love, joy, peace, patience, kindness, goodness, trustfulness, gentleness and self-control" (Gal. 5:22-23). But this is perhaps even more moving in the "scarred and beautiful relationship" ("Baggins," 287) of Frodo and Sméagol. It is within this improbable bond that Bradley J. Birzer observes the "most telling example" (*Sanctifying Myth*, 59) of the grace that abounds in Middle-earth. Ralph C. Wood notes, "Frodo calls forth Gollum's best traits by refusing to focus on his worst ones. Tolkien thus echoes what, in his *Confessions*, St. Augustine says about God's own love for him: 'In loving me, You made me lovable'" (*Gospel*, 132). After hundreds of lonely years, Sméagol returns this care with as much strength as his atrophied goodness can. This most unusual love story also brings to light another grace of baptism. "By charity we are empowered to love others not only as much as we love ourselves. We are enabled to love others more than ourselves; to love others even as Christ has loved us, by suffering and dying on our cross out of love for others; to love others out of love for God constantly, patiently and generously beyond all human power and expectation" (Hardon, "Baptism").

Frodo first expressed this in his refusal to kill without need. He also shows it after Sméagol begs for release from the Elven rope that Sam gently tied around his ankle. The spiritual agony of evil coming into contact with goodness causes the physical pain that Gollum feels. Frodo says that he will not free him unless the creature gives him a trustworthy promise. Sméagol says that he will do what Frodo wants and insists on validating this on the Ring. The younger Bearer demonstrates another part of the discernment, wisdom, and grace that grows in him as he warns his brother hobbit about the peril of doing this. He remains in the Light even as night deepens around and in him. From this perspective, he guides his fellow Bearer and understands what is happening in both their souls. Frodo stands ever more in the same crucible as Sméagol, but he is still outside the prison that traps the latter, though his back is to the gate. Frodo asks what vow the wretched hobbit wishes to give. Sméagol promises to be good and never to let Sauron regain the Ring. Again the miserable creature says that he must swear on the Precious. Frodo refuses because they both know worse madness would result if the already ruined hobbit sees and touches the demonic object that unites and later divides them.

Frodo speaks here of the stage every addict reaches when the craving utterly possesses its victim. All Ring-bearers suffer from this affliction. Bilbo still longs for the Ring seventeen years after giving it up. After all the time that Sméagol spent searching for it, what exquisite torment it must be for him now to have it so near and still not claim it. Even though Frodo knows the dangers of the terrible thing that he has held against his heart these many months, he is becoming increasingly consumed by it as well. In some ways, only an addict understands another addict.

During this dialogue, Sam has one of the visions that grace occasionally gives him. He sees Frodo as a tall and powerful being and Gollum as a small dog. But even with these great differences, the gardener understands that the master he loves and the creature he despises are somehow alike.

Sméagol promises that he will serve the Ring's master, which he implies, but does not explicitly say, is Frodo. Gollum still intends to reclaim this title for himself, and such wording would allow him to do this and to keep his vow at the same time. Frodo accepts Sméagol's word and tells Sam to release the creature. The younger hobbit does so reluctantly. He cannot comprehend why his master is so kind, but the Ring-bearer sees more than his Sam does. Behind Gollum stands the suffering soul of Sméagol, and this is who Frodo frees.

Frodo did not write much of the mystical journey that paralleled his physical one. Perhaps it was too deep for mortal words. Nonetheless, there is enough to show that there was undoubtedly intimate union between his soul and the One who fashioned it and enlightens it during its horrible ordeal. It could not have withstood the terrible knowledge it gains from the opposite side of the spiritual spectrum as well as it did without also basking in the Light.

Out of Frodo's bond with his Creator comes the most fascinating thing said in the tale. After Sméagol chokes on the *lembas* bread, Frodo says, "I think this food would do you good, if you would try. But perhaps you can't even try, not yet anyway" (*LOTR*, 608). In the magnificent BBC Radio adaptation, his voice is sad but also hopeful that one day liberation would come to Sméagol's soul and enable him to partake of the blessed bread. What makes these words such a marvel is that they are said by someone who does not know spiritual things on a conscious level but on a deeply intuitive one. Frodo recognizes the horrific damage done to Sméagol's soul by the Ring, for he feels it happening in his own. But he also knows, perhaps again from what he feels within himself, that the Eucharistic properties of the *lembas* would have a good effect on his wretched guide if Sméagol's own spiritual journey advanced further. Gollum's rejection of the food shows how much those who live in darkness hate anything to do with God. Yet Frodo keeps hoping and trying to "find some sort of entry into [Sméagol's] imprisoned soul" (Rutledge, *Battle*, 199).

Before Frodo and Sam enter the Dead Marshes, they unintentionally sleep the day away without protection from any villainy planned by Gollum. Sam berates himself for not staying awake, but Frodo tells him not to do so. Rather than be upset at the delay, which would have bothered the Ring-bearer only shortly before, he empathizes with his friend's exhaustion and points out the good result that they are now both refreshed. Though the hobbits do not know it, this is part of God's impeccable timing for the Quest.

After Sam frets about their dwindling supply of *lembas*, Frodo shows once more the hopelessness that increasingly infects him. He tells his faithful guardian that they need not wonder about the return trip because there will not be one. The only thing they need to worry about is getting to Mount Doom. Frodo admits that he already thinks that he might not make it there. At these words, Sam takes his master's hand and weeps over it. His tears fall also in Shelob's lair and in the Tower of Cirith Ungol. Words of Washington Irving well reflect the power of such professions of devotion: "There is a sacredness in tears. They are not the mark of weakness, but of power. They speak more eloquently than ten thousand tongues. They are messengers of overwhelming grief and unspeakable love."

Another clear indication that God means to use hobbits as the instruments of the Ring's destruction is at the border of the Marshes. Frodo asks Sméagol whether they have to go into such a place. Gollum says no, not if they want to reach Sauron quickly, which Frodo and Sam likely would have if they were alone and more aware of the lay of the land. They would have bypassed the quagmire, chosen instead the seemingly better way of the hard plain of Dagorlad, and been captured. Even if they had decided to cross the Marshes, they could have gotten lost if they had not providentially met a guide, another hobbit, who knows the way. Their lighter weight also makes it less difficult for them to use such a route than it would be for anyone else.

After Frodo, Sam, and Gollum enter the nightmare that is the Marshes, they see underwater corpses who have an evil light illuminating them. There is no resolution as to whether the dead are still truly present or are "an illusion, a sending intended to do just what it does, to cause fear and demoralization" (Shippey, *Author*, 218). Whatever the case, "the right thing to do is what the hobbits do, press on regardless" (ibid.).

The vulnerability and exposure to Sauron that Frodo senses here vividly describes the terrible spiritual weight of the Ring. The hobbit's memories of the Eye looking for him in Galadriel's Mirror and the evil will that sought him on Amon Hen have shaped his perception of a malicious watchfulness focused on him alone. He feels that there is only a frail barrier keeping his Enemy's intense glare from discovering him. "An enemy who hounds me to crush me into the dust, forces me to dwell in darkness like the dead of long ago; my spirit fails me and my heart is full of fear" (Ps. 143:3-4). Gollum feels this as well. Both believe Sauron watches their every step and breath, but they are not as personally exposed as they think. They are actually quite safe, for even though Frodo feels the might of the Dark Lord beat upon him, Sauron does not know that the hobbit is the Ring-bearer. That will not come until Frodo stands upon the brink of Doom.

Sam thinks he hears Frodo call him after they follow Sméagol out the Marshes. Frodo is sound asleep, but the younger hobbit is wakened to hear Sméagol and Gollum have their tête à tête about how to get the Ring back. Out of loyalty to his new master, Sméagol valiantly resists Gollum's suggestions that he harm Frodo. In the end, however, he cannot help himself from reaching for the Ring. Sam pretends to wake just in time to interrupt the ruined creature's attempt to reclaim his Precious. Frodo rises refreshed from another moment of grace and consolation that was a peaceful dream that he does not remember but which leaves him better able to continue. One wonders if he was granted another vision of his future home in the West. Such visible signs of God's love come to us as well, as we struggle through the bleak landscapes that we must at times travel.

After Frodo, Sam, and Sméagol come to the Black Gate, the news that the present Ring-bearer intends to enter Mordor this way greatly frightens Sméagol. He begs Frodo not to and offers three alternatives: to keep the Ring, to give it back to him, or to use a more hidden path that he found long ago. After seeing the armies marching to the Gate, Frodo announces that he will trust his guide again in recognition of the fate binding them together. He warns Sméagol once more about the danger that threatens the ruined hobbit's soul. After Gollum acknowledges the peril that they all face, Frodo says that he does not refers to this but to something particularly connected with Sméagol himself. Frodo goes on to caution his brother Bearer about the choke-hold that the Ring has on the wretched creature's soul, of the futility of wishing to have the Precious back, and that lust for it may cause Sméagol's death. Frodo foretells the exact nature of this, though he is unaware that he has done so. Possessive jealousy is perhaps also in play, as he twice tells his would-be rival that the Ring will never be Sméagol's again. The younger Bearer continues to grow more spiritually attuned to the Ring himself, even as he warns Sméagol of its dangers.

While Frodo struggles to decide how best to continue his journey, he becomes aware of Gandalf's search for him and Sam. The Ring-bearer's heart perceives the truth that his dear friend lives, even though his eyes will not know this until the Quest is over. Frodo tries to remember that all the wizard told him, but he cannot think of any advice that would aid him in his dreadful decision. He thinks it unlikely that his friend ever went into Mordor but understands that he must enter himself. He does not know what he, "a simple hobbit of the quiet countryside," (*LOTR*, 630) can do if others wiser and more powerful have not dared such a way. But this simplicity is precisely why God chose him. Our vocations are no less unique. Not only does Frodo realize that his doom takes him to the Black Land, he also comprehends that he freely chose this himself. This does not, however, make his decision any easier. He wonders what the point of choosing one path over another is if both are likely lead to death. But as always, Frodo receives grace at the time he needs it to make another critical choice. In the past, Gandalf provided it, as at Amon Hen and upon meeting Gollum. This time, however, the Ring-bearer's other guardian angel, Sam, wonderfully augments such aid. The gardener's recitation of the Oliphaunt poem causes Frodo to laugh, which releases the tension inside him for a moment and allows him to make the decision to chance Sméagol's secret way.

Chapter Fifteen

Friends Unlooked For

*A*fter entering Ithilien, Sam laughs for no other reason than to ease the stress of the journey, which Frodo does as well at various times thanks to his gardener's inspiration. We all need such oases of refuge and release from the toil of fulfilling our vocations in a broken world. Sam's hope for their return journey blooms again in this fair land.

One of the more moving scenes in the tale comes while Sam watches Frodo sleep. The young hobbit observes his master's beauty and increasing glow and softly speaks of his love for him. Anne M. Pienciak notes, "This serenity and inner light is often used to characterize saints" (*Barron's Book Notes: J. R. R. Tolkien's "The Hobbit" and "The Lord of the Rings,"* 105). A Master Craftsman is carving upon Frodo's soul and is polishing it into a great gem ("Jewels of Light," *storiesofarda.com*). This is painful for the Ring-bearer much of the time because of how quickly it is done to counter the darkness that vies to twist him into something else. But sometimes, the chisel is laid aside to give him a moment of peace and to allow others to see the growing masterpiece. Of this Judith Klinger observes, "Sam's perception reveals Frodo's essential, unchanged self – marked however by the 'shaping years' that the Ring's imposed youthfulness merely disguises – and at the same time confirms the transformation Gandalf foresaw" ("Hidden Paths," 191).

Another peaceful dream gifts Frodo in this land. He wakes to Sam's treat of a hot meal of rabbit stew. The smoke that alerts the Rangers to their presence is another marvelous good cloaked as a seeming disaster. Faramir shows the same wisdom regarding strangers that Aragorn did in Fangorn Forest. He does not shoot his potential enemies on sight, but he first seeks to discover whether they are indeed foes. The timing of this meeting once again shows the guidance of Providence. If the men had not found the hobbits, the other forces massing to serve Mordor could have easily captured them. Later the Rangers also give Frodo and Sam food, which allows them to stretch out their *lembas* long enough to make it to Mount Doom.

After Faramir and most of his men disappear into the woods to fight the Southrons, two Rangers stay behind to guard Frodo and Sam. Damrod tells the hobbits that he does not doubt that doom is upon their land due to the terrible power and hatred of Sauron, but Mablung says that they will not just stand by and let Sauron have his way. The latter's words stand in marked contrast to their Steward. Unlike Denethor, they are determined to fight to the last breath. Faramir leads in this struggle. Mablung notes that his Captain's "life is charmed, or fate spares him for some other end" (*LOTR*, 645). Indeed, much awaits this young man that no one but the Writer of the Story foresees.

After the Rangers return, Faramir interrogates Frodo about why the hobbits are in Ithilien. The young man wishes to discern the danger, if any, the two pose before he automatically condemns them as prisoners-of-war. The 'sauce' as Sam perceives the Captain giving the Ring-bearer rouses the gardener's anger. He gives it right back in telling Faramir how he feels about the man's interference with the Quest and how such could play into Sauron's hands. His words are similar to those of Haldir, who spoke of division among allies only aiding the Enemy. Such tensions do arise after we meet strangers on the Road, especially during wartime when it could be dangerous to trust someone outright. But sometimes we discover these people are actually friends that we had not yet met.

Faramir is indeed one who Elrond predicted the Company may find on their Road. Frodo's growing discernment of souls bears this out, as he perceives that this jewel of a man is wiser and less vain than Boromir. Bradley J. Birzer points out several more examples of the grace that fills the Ranger: "First, Tolkien had not planned on his appearance. God had created him and inspired Tolkien to include him in the story—or so the Oxford don believed. Second, it was the healing of Faramir, along with Éowyn and Merry, that revealed the true nature and kingship of Aragorn. Third, and perhaps most important, Faramir offers one of the very few obvious allusions to religion [the Standing Silence]" (*Sanctifying Myth*, 86).

Though under orders to kill anyone who does not have permission to travel through Gondor, Faramir says that he does not slay even beasts without great necessity. This saves the Quest twice over when he does not take the lives of Frodo and Sam out of hand, and later after Anborn reports that he refrained from shooting what he thought was a black squirrel, which was actually Gollum.

Though a man, Faramir resembles the hobbits in his gentle heart and soul, as well as in his desire for peace. Even though he is a valiant soldier and respected by his men, he does not glory in the weapons he must use to defend his beloved land or fight for the joy of it. He does so only to protect his home, which is the same reason the hobbits undertake the Quest. In his love of lore, he would find a kindred spirit in Frodo and already had one in Gandalf, who had long ago recognized the young man's quiet greatness. Faramir learned wisdom and also likely pity from the wizard. In all this, Denethor judges his younger son less worthy than his martial elder one. In one way, however, Faramir is much like his father and the same time quite different. Both can read the heart of others, but such insight evokes compassion in the Ranger where the same inspires contempt in the Steward (*LOTR*, 1031).

With all these good qualities, there is the temptation to think Faramir would have made the better choice as one of the Nine Walkers than Boromir. The dream the elder brother came to Rivendell to unravel was sent first and more often to the younger. The Valar had reasoned that the milder son would be the best to join the Company, as the Ring would not find him as easy to corrupt. But would its Bearer's will have found release from the shackles of terror that held it bound if he had not so baldly seen with Boromir, as he had in Rivendell with Bilbo, how the Ring could infect a soul? If Frodo had not witnessed this change and therefore chosen the moment he did to separate from the Company, the Orcs may have captured him with his cousins. The Ring would have then come into the custody of either Saruman or Sauron.

Instead, Faramir takes Frodo and Sam to the Rangers' secret base at Henneth Annûn, where they are treated as guests. At the observation of the Standing Silence, Bruce Palmer notes, "The remnant of the Faithful here in exile had not forgotten the heavenly realm someday to be theirs, and likewise, they had not forgotten that God was still active in the world" (*Of Orc-Rags, Phials, & A Far Shore*, 23). Frodo and Sam immensely enjoy food and drink in amounts far more proper for hobbits than anything they have had in a long time.

After the meal, a few tense moments follow Sam's 'accidental' revelation that Frodo has the Ring, but it soon becomes clear that this slip is not the disaster it seems. The way of the Ring to Faramir's heart was through his desire to finally have some approval in his father's eyes, but the temptation to claim the fell object holds no attraction for him. Even before knowing exactly what Isildur's Bane was, the man had said that he would not pick it up by the side of the road. As much as he longs to see the majesty of Gondor renewed, he would rather sacrifice his beloved home if the only way to save it would be through use of the Ring. He recognizes its peril, just as Galadriel and Elrond have. "For what will it profit a man if he gains the whole world, and loses his own soul?" (Mark 8:36, NKJV). Faramir has only to look as far as his beloved brother to know how the Ring can affect men. Michael J. Brisbois notes, "Boromir is corrupted by the One Ring because of his desire for power – he believes in winning war by any means necessary. Faramir clearly does not. He is unwilling to sacrifice the virtues he is fighting for. This disregard for power and focus upon virtue is similar to Sam's focus on simple domestic pleasures – both remain largely unaffected by the Ring because neither desires power" ("The Blade Against the Burden," *Mythlore* 27, 95).

Faramir resists the Ring because he binds himself to his earlier refusal. He also has enough good judgment to realize that there are some dangers that must be avoided. If we do not give in initially to temptation, such refusal will strengthen us not to surrender another time, but it does not guarantee in itself that we will remain steadfast. The young Captain wishes the Ring away from him, so that he does not possibly fail a future test and those under him are not exposed to the demonic object's seductive allure. We must make it just as difficult for our enemy to sink his talons into us. He will not stop trying, but we must not make it easy for him, just as the Rangers do not make it so for Sauron. We need to be aware of our own strengths and weaknesses, in order to know which dangers we must avoid. Perhaps we will not discover such until they test us. Boromir had to fall before he recognized his error. Faramir is wiser. He assures Sam that the gardener's seeming blunder was meant to be and that it may even benefit Frodo. Such would be the reason that the hobbit's heart inspired his lips to speak what could have been a terrible indiscretion in the presence of anyone else.

Faramir's refusal of the Ring completely sets at rest Sam's suspicions of the man, which were already allayed by the great respect the Ranger has for Elves. The hobbit speaks of the man's inner light, which differs from Frodo's more Elvish glow. On some level, not knowing what he sees, the gardener has already discerned the angelic nature of Gandalf under the guise of a wizard. The grace that is within Faramir seems similar to Sam somehow. The young man in turn recognizes the high quality of the humble hobbit.

Chapter Sixteen

Frodo's Prayer

Faramir again shows restraint in not immediately slaying a possible adversary after the Rangers find Sméagol enjoying some fish at the Forbidden Pool. The man first seeks out Frodo, who begs for his guide's life. He says the creature is not aware of the peril he is in and is in some mysterious way connected with the great task of the Ring. Frodo asks Faramir to allow him to go down to Sméagol and offers his own life in exchange if Gollum gets away. The Ring-bearer is so essential to the Quest, yet he is willing to put himself in danger to save another who is also vital.

Richard Purtill remarks, "One of Christ's least popular commandments has always been that which tells us to 'love our enemies, do good to those who hate you' (Lk 6:27). But in Frodo's treatment of Sméagol, the hobbit who has become Gollum, the monster, we can see this commandment at work in a situation we can believe in" (*Lord of the elves and eldils*, 2nd ed., 194).

Even after Frodo's plea, he still faces the temptation to have Gollum killed after hearing his guide talking. He longs for freedom from this voice, but he fights against the desire and instead saves the wretched creature's life by the only way available. Frodo knows Sméagol's ruined mind will probably not understand this and will consider it a betrayal instead. The Ring-bearer feels miserable about this, perhaps partly because he knows how close to reality it is, not only in outward appearance but also in quashed inward wish. It grieves him to deal such a bitter blow to Sméagol's heart, which had been making tentative steps back to the Light. "[Frodo] despises using treachery even against the treacherous. . . . Even the faithless should be shown faith" (Wood, *Gospel*, 133).

After the Rangers capture Gollum and bring him before Faramir, the man says that he has so far spared him because of Frodo's plea. But he adds that he has to know for himself whether the creature is worthy of escaping with his life. The Captain continues to show the restraint that we must all have if there is a possibility of sparing a life without bloodshed, even if such could cause harm to us. Bilbo, Frodo, and Faramir all look into Gollum's soul and recognize the evil that dwells there, yet they all give mercy nonetheless. This gives the wretched hobbit further opportunity to repent and be cured.

Faramir's decision to release Gollum into Frodo's custody and declare the younger Ring-bearer free to travel throughout Gondor comes only after due deliberation. The man does not share Boromir's impulsive nature, so he does not make a hasty decision with so much at stake. He had already spoken of paths that he knew he and Frodo were fated to take. In seeking wisdom about these ways, he demonstrates that it is good to take the time to discern the will of God.

Faramir's choice to let Frodo go puts the young man in direct violation of the orders of his lord and father, just as Éomer went against a similar command in freeing the Three Hunters. Yet in both cases, the decision was the right one. The choice to free Gollum is more fraught with peril, as the Ranger not only risks his own life but those of his men if the creature ever betrayed the location of the secret base. Faramir's discernment of the ruined hobbit's soul and his trust in Frodo, however, allow him to believe that Gollum will never disclose the hiding place.

After the interrogation of Gollum ends and Rangers take him away, the ensuing dialogue between Faramir and Frodo brings home the importance of keeping one's word even if there is a possibility that it will bring harm to oneself. The Captain attempts to persuade his friend against following Gollum for the man has read Gollum's dark heart. But the Ring-bearer has fully embraced Gandalf's hope of a cure for his guide and defends him as not completely evil.

> . . . Frodo has a strange respect for Gollum. He discerns, in a deeply intuitive way, that Gollum is divinely destined to play his crucial role. . . . Far more importantly, Frodo believes that Gollum is not fixed in evil, but that he has the capacity to overcome the addictive effects of the

Ring. He wants, therefore, to extend at least minimal friendship to this miserable fellow hobbit. There is a tiny ray of light peeking into the prison cell of Gollum's life, making him long to leave his wretched isolation and to find companionship with another creature of his own kind. (Wood, *Gospel*, 131)

Frodo speaks of his promise to look after Sméagol and to travel where he goes. The Ring-bearer does not want to go back on this, even after Faramir has warned him that Gollum will betray him. After the Ring-bearer asks if the man would advise him to be false to his guide, the Ranger refrains from giving into the fear and concern which has him long to give this counsel. In their preference for an untainted spiritual life over a compromised one, both Faramir and Frodo show they value being morally upright over physical safety and prize their soul over their body.

To counter Faramir's argument against trusting Gollum's guidance, Frodo gives the man a grim picture of what would happen to Minas Tirith if the Ring was ever brought there. The grand city would die and become like the befouled Minas Morgul, which was once the shining Tower of the Moon, Minas Ithil. A barren wasteland would be between them. The Ranger does not wish to see such a fate. He gives Frodo his blessing to accompany the hobbit's attempt to forestall such a terrible doom.

Even as Faramir tells Frodo that he has no hope of seeing him again, he almost immediately speaks of this happening. While the future is unknown and indeed seems bleak, the Ranger still imagines the possibility of a bright one after the strife is over and is laughed about. He later shares his belief with Éowyn while such a thing is perhaps even more impossible to believe in than when he speaks to Frodo. This hope is another sign of the grace in the young man. He sees beyond the darkness in which his father is lost. Faramir instead beholds the dawn that he does not know for sure will come but which has already risen in anticipation in his heart. Aragorn, Gandalf, and Sam share his enduring belief of life beyond the present shadows.

At the time of departure, Faramir says that Gollum must be blind-folded to protect the location of the Rangers' cave, but he will not order the same for Frodo or Sam. But the Ring-bearer says his and Sam's eyes should be covered also to ease Gollum's anxiety that the men still plan evil for him. Fleming Rutledge notes, "The deep reserves of mercy and empathy that we see rising in [Frodo] now are new; they are not innate. They are gifts given from on high, through Gandalf. . . . Solidarity with others in mercy and sympathy is the only true and lasting antidote to the malignity represented by the Ring" (*Battle*, 225).

As Frodo, Sam, and Sméagol reach the ancient Cross-roads, they see what seems to be a cruel victory of the Orcs. They had cut off the head of a statue of one of the Gondorian kings and replaced it with a stone that had a symbol of the Eye painted upon it. The actual triumph, however, is that flowers now adorn the fallen head, which would not have happened if the statue remained intact. Moments before Frodo was full of fear of the path ahead, but the sun shines for a bit and he sees the king crowned again.

Rutledge notes that "the Power that sent Gandalf has vouchsafed a sign to give them heart in their loneliness" (*Battle*, 226). She then comments further about this special time for Frodo: "The sign given to Frodo at the Cross-roads was profoundly significant for him, because he had been resting in the bosom of the eucharistic community and now has been wrenched away, a deprivation that greatly increases the pull of the Ring. While he was in Henneth Annûn, its weight was lighter, but now he is in the orbit of the Enemy once more. Resisting temptation is infinitely more difficult for the Christian when he or she is not securely lodged in the community of faith" (ibid., 227).

What happens to Frodo at Minas Morgul prove how true these words are.

Chapter Seventeen

The Morgul Vale

*J*ust as Frodo leaves behind the light of Western lands to enter the Eastern darkness, we may feel at times that we go from life and hope to a place of death and despair. It may not necessarily be a physical location but rather a place that our soul must travel. Or perhaps, like for the hobbits, it will be or is a combination. May we pass safely through such lands and learn what we need, as we would not be brought to such desolate parts if there were not a way for us to grow.

The presence of evil at Minas Morgul has a terribly disorienting effect on Frodo. He staggers toward the tower after another power overrides his will. Such is the way with us sometimes. We do not always have the strength to overcome temptation and evil solely on our own. "I cannot understand my own behavior," St. Paul will lament. "I fail to carry out the things I want to do, and I find myself doing the very things I hate. When I act against my own will, that means I have a self that acknowledges that the Law is good, and so the thing behaving in that way is not my self but sin living in me" (Rom. 7:15-17).

God understands how weak our will is and how easily we are overwhelmed at times, so He sets others at our side. As we falter our friends are there to strengthen us and tug us back from the abyss. "Better two than one by himself, since thus their work is really profitable. If one should fall, the other helps him up; but woe to the man by himself with no one to help him up when he falls down. Again: they keep warm who sleep two together, but how can a man keep warm alone? Where one alone would be overcome, two will put up resistance; and a threefold cord is not quickly broken" (Eccles. 4:9-12).

Rutledge makes a note of this perilous time, as Sam pulls Frodo away from the brink.

> Help must come from *outside* the vicious cycle of bondage to this Power. . . . [Frodo's] tottering toward the bridge indicates his loss of mental and spiritual as well as physical balance. He has no power in and of himself to resist. . . .
> . . . The power to resist comes via other people . . . Deliverance is always a sign of God at work, whatever or whoever his agents might be. (*Battle*, 228; italics in original)

Had the Writer of the Story not arranged Sam to be at Frodo's side, either the Ring-bearer or Sméagol would have surrendered to the temptation to claim the Ring at some point and fought or even killed his companion. The forces of the Enemy would have found him then, and Sauron would have recovered his treasure. Sam's presence and words, however, allow Frodo's own will to reassert itself and to fight the compelling wish to run toward the terrible tower. Just as the gardener knew not to push his master forward at Parth Galen but to let Frodo decide on his own to continue, Sam knows here to pull backward, so as to give the Ring-bearer the same opportunity to choose his path.

We must make the same decision as Frodo does here, for the tug of others is of little avail if we do not choose to be drawn away. May we have a Sam to guide us if we too become enthralled by a way that would be ill for us to follow.

After Frodo forces his gaze away from the Tower, he feels temporarily blinded, as he had in the Emyn Muil. This gives more weight to the possibility that the presence of a Nazgûl robbed him of his sight both times.

Even after rescue by Sam, the Ring-bearer is still not out of danger. Not long after he defeats one assault, the Ring launches another. As the Witch-king comes forth with his great host and senses the Ring nearby, Frodo feels a powerful call to put it on. But this time he has no desire to do so, as he is aware it will act treacherously toward him. He then watches his hand move toward the Ring independent of his own wish.

It feels to him that all this is happening to someone else, but he reasserts his will once more and moves his hand away to hold onto Galadriel's phial instead. The compulsion to put on the Ring fades completely.

This fits all of us. Frodo resisted the first temptation because it was brutal and he could set his will against it. But the second assault, though no less violent, is also much more stealthy. This latter type of attack is the kind we must be most wary of because it comes in under the radar and evades or overcomes our vigilance and traps us even before we know that we are. We must get up as soon as we realize we have fallen because the longer we stay down, the harder it is to rise. This tug-of-war of wills drains Frodo's spiritual, mental, and physical resources but concentrates them as well, so that he can focus on the horrific battle within.

This scene shows how powerful evil is with its seemingly irresistible, unstoppable might pounding down upon us, but it also demonstrates how easily we can defeat it by deciding to do so. Frodo made this choice by deliberately seeking the Lady's phial. The song that the Elves sang to Elbereth in the Shire and the kiss that Sam will give his master near the Mountain of Fire are two other ways that defeat the Ring's compelling power. The strength of these things comes from who gave the phial and what it contains, who the song was sung to, and who will bless Frodo's hands with such tenderness. Again and again, salvation comes a moment away from disaster.

If Frodo had revealed himself to the Witch-king, events would have turned out much different. Grace, however, strengthens the hobbit, and, through it, he turns the focus of the wraith away from discovering him. The ruined man rides off with part of his master's army to counter the threat the Dark Lord saw, or thought he saw, in the Orthanc *palantír*. If the Nazgûl had instead pursued what he sensed, he would have done Sauron a much greater service, but he thinks he has more pressing matters demanding his attention. There was a Ring to be found after all.

Frodo's continuing struggles show us the battles that we have in our own life. As he watches the horrible army pass out of Minas Morgul, he suffers two more wounds to his soul, as despair deepens and pride grows. He blames himself for being too slow and thinks that the delay will cause doom to fall. His next thought is that even if he is successful, it will mean nothing because no one will be around to praise him for it. This is the opposite of why he left the Shire. He was not out for glory or gain. He was scared nearly out of his wits and would have much rather stayed home. Yet here he laments the fact that he will not receive honor. Interestingly, after he deservedly receives it later, he does not think that he should.

How hard we must fight against the infection that poisons the Ring-bearer. We should never do anything for self-aggrandizement or worldly recognition but only for the honor we have from God. This is not easy for us. We do not want our brave deeds to go unnoticed. We want valor *with* renown, not without. But rather than give into this desire, we should toil silently without calling attention to ourselves. Sam lives his life this way.

Frodo's natural humility quickly reasserts itself, as he fully wills to renew his determination to go on despite his despair and the fact that no one may ever know what he did. The desire for recognition that was so important a moment before no longer matters to him. The only thing that does is continuing as he knows he must. There is the beautiful image of the light-filled phial held against his heart to counteract the terrible darkness also laid there. The realization that he still has a vocation to fulfill clears his head. Two things cannot occupy the same place. His humility drains his pride away. His despair still nearly suffocates him, but he struggles onward. After blackness descends upon our own labors, and we feel that all our efforts are too little and too late, we should remember that new strength can come to us a few moments later.

As Gollum guides Frodo and Sam to the Stairs of Cirith Ungol, the question remains whether his role is for good or ill. Faramir tried to warn Frodo against this route, which is at the same time the least and most fearsomely guarded way. Orcs do not need to defend this area because the terror that waits in the tunnel stops anyone who dares to try to pass. All this appears to point to evil, which it is but only on the surface. The Quest would have failed without the good that also comes from the seemingly disastrous events that follow.

After Frodo and Sam climb the steep and dangerous Stairs, the Ring-bearer actually regains some hope and believes that if he could just get past the Tower, he could complete his mission. He first thinks that getting through cannot be done, but in the next moment, he is confident that he will leave behind the broken gates of the impossible and walk into the possible.

We may think at times that our own tasks are too difficult to accomplish. But if we share Frodo's faith and trust, we, too, can break through barriers that appear impassable and then turn to see their ruins from the other side. What wonders God could work in our life if we but follow the examples of all His Third Age servants!

Chapter Eighteen

The Power of Words

As Frodo and Sam rest before attempting the dread tunnel, the younger hobbit offers a powerful meditation on persevering through terrible trials with examples from stories the two loved as lads. He talks about how he formerly viewed the events in such tales, as things done out of a wish to inject some excitement into an otherwise boring life. He knows the truth now. We do not choose our tasks as much as God chooses them for us. We all have plans and dreams of what we want to do with our life, but God has plans too. Sam and Frodo both perceive that the quests undertaken in these stories are actually to fulfill vocations. Throughout the history of Middle-earth, there are times that Elves, Men, Hobbits, and Dwarves have the choice to turn around and refuse to do the job at hand. Sam is right to say that we would not know of those who did. We would not even know the gardener himself.

Archbishop Fulton J. Sheen echoes the same wisdom Sam has gleaned.

> Since man was free to love, he was free to hate; since he was free to obey, he was free to rebel. . . .
>
> . . . The world has no heroes except in those battles where every hero might have been a coward; the nation has no patriots except . . . where each patriot might have been a traitor. . . . Triumphal arches are reared only to men who succeeded, but who might have failed in the trying; . . . monuments are erected only to the memory of those who might have turned back, and yet pushed on. (*God's World and Our Place in It*, 28)

This torturous way is the true path, for through the labors of some, many gain a peaceful life they would not have otherwise. Alas for Frodo, his ordeal makes it impossible to return to such a life himself, but he does not toil for this goal. He also does not endure his ordeal just for those he loves in the present but for future generations as well. Sam's children and all Free Folk owe their lives to Frodo, Sam, and Gollum and to the One who sent them on their way.

Sam acknowledges that not all of the stories he and Frodo loved ended happily, but he makes an important distinction between what is truly sad and what only appears so. It may seem from inside a tale that there is a sorrowful ending, but the reality seen from the outside is sometimes different. The story that the two hobbits live through seems to finish like one of the unhappy ones because the deeply wounded Ring-bearer must leave behind everything and almost everyone he loves. But their journeys do not end at the same time the chronicle in the Red Book does.

The trials of Frodo and Sam reintroduce the theme that it is a good thing that we do not know ahead of time how rough the Road will become. After the gardener wonders what kind of story they are in, the Ring-bearer says that it is better not to know and indeed this is so. Certainty of victory could bring presumption and complacency. Certainty of defeat could bring despair. Either way, there is no room for hope, faith, or trust in God. It is better to discover the Road a little at a time, as we are meant to.

To answer Sam's question if tales ever have an ending, Frodo says that the stories themselves do not, just those who are in them. Darkness, hopelessness, and terror increasingly surround the Ring-bearer. For him, the Quest is life-consuming, and the end of their part means death, probably sooner than later. Sam sees beyond and hopes for a good rest, then work in the garden; in other words, a return to the life he has always known.

Frodo laughs twice after Sam imagines the telling of their tale. Rutledge notes again that gladness is "a sign of salvation and hope" (*Battle*, 161). The younger hobbit gives the Ring-bearer a moment of true joy before the terror that awaits them in Shelob's lair. The humble servant will carry his master physically only for a short while, but he holds him in his heart for the whole journey and continues to shelter him there after they return home. What a great gift this laughter is to them both. Sam notices that even the stones appear to lean closer to hear. Frodo lets himself believe that there is something other than starless night; there is also light, hope, and cheer. He sees an alternate future through his guardian's eyes, in which the Quest is over, the danger is past, and the victory is celebrated through song and story.

As much as Sam encourages Frodo, the Ring-bearer does the same here for his faithful friend by saying that when their tale is read, there will be clamor to hear more about Sam. Frodo writes his reverent tribute to answer such calls.

Just as the heroic courage in ancient tales inspire Frodo and Sam, their own inspires us. This is especially true while we think we are also trapped in the most terrible parts, just as the elder hobbit feels here. In whatever way this seems true, or actually is, we still do not know all that is to come. It should comfort and strengthen us to realize that God has already written the ending. We need only to walk along the Road, persevere in our trials, and know that their end will come if we just keep going.

Sarah Arthur notes this need to trust our Creator, as we do an author, that our story will turn out all right. We have times of suffering, doubts, and despair during which we wonder how we can possibly go on, whether there even is a God, and why He allows such horrible things if He is so good. In this darkness we need to hope, trust, and believe that our Father will come and rescue us. We will not be disappointed (*Walking with Frodo*, 160-162). We must keep our eyes focused on the light on the horizon and believe in it even when we cannot see it. This Sam has always done. At the moment, Frodo does also and falls peacefully asleep in his guardian's lap.

After Gollum arranges the betrayal of Frodo and Sam to Shelob, he return to find them resting and almost repents. Linda Greenwood notes, "One of the most beautiful and sorrowful aspects about *Lord of the Rings* is that the love and compassion that Frodo shows for Gollum are gradually reciprocated" ("Love," 179-180). In this, Frodo embodies the words of Johann Wolfgang Von Goethe: "Treat people as if they were what they ought to be, and you help them to become what they are capable of being." This painstaking care allows the slowly dawning love that the ruined hobbit has for his master to recover from the terrible blow at the Forbidden Pool. Sméagol expresses here a moment of genuine affection for the one he thinks betrayed him, but tragically Sam strangles it, though not willfully or knowingly. He wakes after he hears Frodo cry out from a nightmare and angrily and completely misinterprets Sméagol's tender caress of their joint master's knee.

Another instance when the Quest and those wrapped up in it stand poised on the knife's edge is as Sméagol's soul totters between Light and Dark. Words of St. Theophan the Recluse apply here: "The awakened one is placed by grace into the middle ground between sin and virtue. Grace draws him out of the bonds of sin, depriving sin of its authority to motivate him into action as if against his will; but it does not turn him towards the good, only allowing him to feel its superiority and joy. . . . The person now stands at the crossroads, and he has to make the final choice" ("Excerpts from 'The Path to Salvation,' *holytrinitymission.org*). Sméagol has reached this place. Even centuries after surrendering so much of himself to the Ring and to the creature that he became because of it, he still sees from the darkness of his dungeon a last bit not yet subsumed. From the time the two Ring-bearers' met, Frodo nurtured this spark in the hope it would grow stronger. After suffering banishment first from family and then surrounded by none but Orcs, Gollum, and the Precious, Sméagol had at last found someone who cared for him. He took the outstretched hand and tentatively moved toward the Light whenever he fought his enslavement to the Ring and to Gollum. But in the end he does not have the strength to hold onto Frodo. Just as Sméagol stands at the threshold of his prison, Sam's harsh words throw him back. He makes the choice to return to the night or has the decision made for him.

As also with Saruman, the more we will to choose evil, the less free we are to select good. Though Sméagol wished to return to the Light, he could not sustain his desire. Patricia Meyer Spacks observes that "the progress of evil in an individual cannot be reversed without a specific, conscious act of will, an act that Gollum, like the others characters devoted to evil, is quite incapable of performing" ("Power and Meaning in *The Lord of the Rings*," *Tolkien and the Critics*, 94). If Sméagol's hesitant return to goodness had been stronger and deeper, perhaps the fragile buds Frodo carefully cultivated could have withstood Sam's assault. Alas, they cannot. The younger hobbit's anger blazes over the tender shoots and shrivels them.

Sam is not completely at fault here, but this is the moment of death for Sméagol, of which neither Sam nor Frodo are aware. The gardener sees the return of Gollum from the wicked green light shining in the creature's eyes, but he has never truly seen Sméagol. Mistrust and ill will allow Sam only to see Slinker and Stinker, not the tormented hobbit who had been painfully crawling back to the Light.

This episode shows how careful we must be in our conversations with each other because words have meaning and ability to raise up or cast down. Sam showed this when he said future generations will call Frodo the most famous of all hobbits but named Gollum a villain and a sneak. We have greater power over others than we realize, and we abuse it too much. We should be more aware of it and use it wisely to strengthen a fragile ego rather than destroying it. Sam's loving words and support help his beloved master to continue. Sméagol's own weakness stifles his journey toward the Light, but Sam's withering words certainly also contribute. Better to use our terrible and wonderful power to ennoble and empower others rather than to trivialize and stamp them down. We never know ahead of time what consequences our words or actions will have on others. Maybe we will not know until after death that something we said or did to someone positively or negatively affected that person, who then affected others with the ripples spreading out for years. Sometimes we are hurt most deeply by those we love, but we can rise above the arrows that pierce us. At other times, we cause the wounds. We must be careful in what we choose to do and never act rashly or speak harshly. If we do, we must make what amends we can.

Frodo still addresses his fellow Ring-bearer by his given name, but Sméagol is no more. For some time the two have traveled in opposite directions: Frodo into deepening shadows and Sméagol away from them. On the Stairs they met in the twilight, but the younger Bearer was asleep and did not realize the meeting had come. They travel together now into increasing darkness.

Chapter Nineteen

Sam and the Doom of Choice

*R*ichard Purtill notes that "to taste the depths of suffering, Frodo must be betrayed by one in whom he put his trust, as Christ was betrayed by Judas" (*Myth, Morality*, 75). Even so, invisible guardians continue to protect the Ring-bearer and his faithful Sam. Michael Treschow and Mark Duckworth observe how Tom Bombadil indirectly offers aid in the great darkness and evil of Shelob's lair.

> Sam's sword does less work [than Merry's or Pippin's],
> but still helps achieve something wondrous. When Sam
> and Frodo find that Gollum has led them into the trap
> of some terrible, unknown horror . . . Sam instinctively
> reaches for the sword that Tom gave him. . . . Sam thus
> remembers Tom himself who can vanquish creatures
> of the darkness. . . . This shows . . . Sam's awareness
> that Tom is a good ally when hard beset by terror. But
> . . . at the same time it shows to Sam's mind that light
> can prevail in darkness; his memory of Tom reminds
> him of the lady's glass. . . . Such is the result of merely
> touching the hilt of the noble sword from the barrow.
> ("Bombadil's Role in *The Lord of the Rings*," *Mythlore*
> 25, 189)

The presence of another guardian is apparent as the Ring-bearer calls upon Eärendil in Quenya, which he does not know but that the voice speaking through him does. The words activate the phial that contains the reflected light of a Silmaril and empower the hobbits to challenge their fearsome enemy. Judith Klinger observes, "Overwhelming darkness stands against piercing light, oblivion against memory, suffocating silence against remembered voices and songs, death against life" ("Hidden Paths," 170).

Just as Frodo senses terrible malice beat upon him, at times we may feel almost crushed by a hatred personally directed toward us. But we also have incredible power to temporarily conquer our foe, as the Ring-bearer and Sam discover. Evil presumes to have the advantage over us and does not expect to encounter resistance to its overwhelming might. It may pause a moment in its efforts to devour us in order to enjoy our attempts to escape, but it does not believe that we can. What appears, however, as a breath from death or worse could become victory snatched into our own hands if we decide, like the hobbits, to fight instead. Rather than exulting or gloating as we cower under the assault, our adversary will find that we have strength enough to defeat him. Shelob certainly does not expect the treatment that she gets!

Shelob terrifies Frodo and Sam, but in an inspiring act of bravery, the Ring-bearer goes to challenge his enemy, brilliant phial in one hand and sword in the other, and temporarily drives her away. We should pray that such grace-filled courage fills us as well. Sam remains true to his hobbit nature as he demonstrates once more the remarkable ability to move quickly from the despair he felt before Frodo's defeat of the eyes to celebrating his master's great victory over them and wishing that he could hear the Elves sing of it. There is more than one eucatastrophe in this story, and Sam is vividly attune to them all. We need to nurture his joyful reaction in our own heart.

We must not fear our dark Roads, for God will give us all that is necessary to triumph over them, just as He provides for Frodo and Sam. Our Father gives sufficient grace to all His children, and their cooperation with it allows them to achieve the tasks before them. In his installation homily, Pope Benedict XVI thanked the faithful who helped him bear his burden, which he was well aware he could not carry by himself ("Mass for the Inauguration of the Pontificate of Pope Benedict XVI," *vatican.va*). Grace, prayers, and the support of visible and invisible guardians sustain Frodo in the same way. Without such aid, the Ring-bearer would have never made it to the Fire.

Just as Frodo's victory over Shelob is not final, the one against our own adversary will not be complete until we accept God's gift of mortality. Before then, the hatred of our enemy will always lurk, even more maliciously than does Shelob's for the hobbits. We already know that the defeat of our foe is certain at the end of time, but until then he will strive mightily to claim all the souls that he can. Let us remember never to abandon hope in our struggle against him, for we cannot see ahead for even a few seconds with any surety, and what may seem unbeatable doom may turn around in an instant. We know that there is a plot for our destruction, just as Frodo is aware that Shelob plans for his and Sam's, but nothing can so trap us that God cannot rescue us through whatever manner He wishes. There is no place on earth that He cannot reach and pull us away from our grasping enemy. We can have our own "morning of sudden hope," (*LOTR*, 707) as Frodo does after he cuts through the spider webs with Sting and flees. Even if our escape is only through death, we will defeat our adversary if we remain true to the end.

Not knowing how near Shelob is, Frodo runs out of the tunnel. Freedom from the terrible darkness gives him such great happiness that it makes him heedless of anything else. Sam, however, feels the oppressive weight of their peril so greatly that he can barely run forward. Our own enemy seeks to hinder us in a similar way, but Sam continues on and we must also. The horrible danger that the younger hobbit senses soon bursts upon them, as Gollum attacks him and the spider's sting fells Frodo.

Sam uses the strongest forces in the universe in his vicious retaliatory assault against Shelob and "begins his rise to supremely heroic stature," as Tolkien noted in a letter to Milton Waldman (quoted in *Reader's Companion*, 746). Love is far greater than any of the weapons our foe has in his vast arsenal. The strength and courage it gives does not come from us but flows into us from God. Grace aids the hobbit much here. A prayer to Elbereth springs from his lips in fluent Sindarin, which he has not learned. His unconquerable determination activates the power of Galadriel's phial, which defeats the demonic spider.

It does not matter that neither Frodo nor Sam know how to pray.

The Holy Spirit helps them to powerfully do so. "The Spirit too comes to help us in our weakness. For when we cannot choose words in order to pray properly, the Spirit himself expresses our plea in a way that could never be put into words, and God who knows everything in our hearts knows perfectly well what he means, and that the pleas of the saints expressed by the Spirit are according to the mind of God" (Rom. 8:26). Bradley J. Birzer notes Elbereth's aid here: "Thus, grace moved Frodo and Sam to call on grace; the servants of Ilúvatar aided other servants of Ilúvatar" (*Sanctifying Myth*, 62). Ralph C. Wood adds about the various times the hobbits receive the inspiration to invoke the star-queen, that she "seems to be praying through *them* as much as they are praying to *her*" (*Gospel*, 122; italics in original). God, His mother, the angels, and the saints are all willing to help us, but for much of the time they wait until we ask.

After Sam's great triumph, he plunges into the worst agony of his life when he reaches Frodo's side and cannot rouse him. At first, rage overwhelms him and then he remembers the scene in Galadriel's Mirror of his master asleep. The present reality appears much worse than what he thought he saw then. A black night of despair swallows his shattered heart. Sarah Arthur speaks of Bilbo in *The Hobbit*, but her words apply equally well to Sam.

> How tempting it is to curl up, pull our hoods over our faces, and remain where we are in the dark! And sometimes God knows we need simply to sit and grieve – and that's perfectly natural. But eventually he calls us to get up, assess the situation, and move forward. We may not be sure the direction we're headed is the right one, but we've used whatever common sense we can muster, trusting God to give us wisdom. The rest is in his hands. (*Walking with Bilbo*, 55-56)

Once the first shock of Sam's terrible loss wears off enough for the gardener to contemplate what to do next, he remembers what he said the morning after meeting Gildor about having a job to complete. The young hobbit begins to understand that this means he must leave his master and go on alone. In asking Frodo if he understands, Sam's shrewd and loving heart perceives that the Ring-bearer is still alive, even though his senses tell him otherwise.

Sam holds Frodo's hand while he decides exactly what to do after he departs. He has made many choices on the Quest involving whether to remain by his master's side or do something else. He faces the same decision here. The thoughtful debate he engages in is the same that we must have, as we weigh and discard options and gain a clearer understanding of our purpose. The hobbit is not alone in this time, and neither are we during our own deliberations. He does not pray as we do, but he receives the grace and insight that comes from such seeking of God's will. He considers pursuing vengeance against Gollum and even taking his own life, but he dismisses both as not what he is meant to do. He comes to the terrible conclusion that his task is to take the Ring to Mount Doom, as the sole remaining member of the Company.

The job that Sam saw vaguely in the Shire is now clearly shown as a vocation within a vocation. He is not only to shelter his master in his heart but to bear the Ring over it. Still he does not want to become Bearer, as he does not consider it his place to promote himself. He receives confirmation, however, that this is indeed God's will for him. "But you haven't put yourself forward; you've been put forward. And as for not being the right and proper person, why, Mr. Frodo wasn't, as you might say, nor Mr. Bilbo. They didn't choose themselves" (*LOTR*, 715).

"This passage says something to every human being," remarks Phillip Goggans. "We don't put ourselves forward; we are put forward. We don't choose ourselves for the role we have in life; we are chosen. We do not forge our destiny; we submit to it" ("*The Lord of the Rings* and the Meaning of Life," *Celebrating Middle-earth*, 104). 'God is my co-pilot' is a bumper sticker that has it backwards. God should be Pilot. 'My boss is a Jewish carpenter' is a better reflection of the order of things. We should all be servants as Gandalf, Frodo, Sam, and Aragorn are.

Verlyn Flieger makes an observation of this potent time of decision-making.

> The key words *will* and *must* follow one another now in rapid succession as Sam tells himself 'I must make up my own mind. I will make it up' (341).

Knowing the precision with which Tolkien uses words, and the weight of internal historical evidence that lies behind them, we can see that Sam is not merely lecturing himself; he is unknowingly invoking both his destiny and his free will. ("The Music and the Task," *Tolkien Studies* 6, 170; italics in original)

Sam's thinking out loud is similar to what went on interiorly with Frodo at the Council after the Holy Spirit further revealed the vocation set aside for the Ring-bearer. "Then I heard the voice of the LORD saying, 'Whom shall I send, and who will go for us?' And I said, 'Here I am; send me!'" (Isa. 6:8-9, NRSV).

Sam realizes that he is just as chosen as was Frodo, which is "the key factor in helping him make up his mind. This is called . . . 'prevenient grace,' the grace that *goes before* the human response and – even more important – is present in the response itself" (Rutledge, *Battle*, 237; italics in original). We need the same courage to step forward after we hear the call in our own heart.

Sam makes a beautiful profession of love after he kisses Frodo's brow in farewell and takes the Ring: "Forgive your Sam. He'll come back to this spot when the job's done – if he manages it. And then he'll not leave you again. . . . And if the Lady could hear me and give me one wish, I would wish to come back and find you again" (*LOTR*, 716). Judith Klinger notes how Sam's enduring hope completely changes his view of death. While facing the temptation of suicide, the gardener saw it as a void, but "death is now envisioned as a 'quiet rest' that Sam can eventually share with Frodo, and a reunion that affirms an irrevocable bond. . . . Sam overcomes death as loss and terminal separation. But his wish also manifests an intuitive comprehension of Frodo's true state, contradicting surface appearances" ("Hidden Paths," 188). This powerful embodiment of hope, now so strong that it sees beyond death to life again, is what Aragorn later tries to convey in his last words to Arwen.

After Sam first puts the chain around his neck that holds the Ring, he finds his burden quite heavy. But then the weight lessens, or he receives fresh power to bear it. "Again, images of the Cross are unmistakable, and particularly Christ's promise that those who take up their Cross to follow Him will find their burden light" (Pearce, *Man*, 114).

Before Sam leaves Frodo, he takes one last look at his master's beloved face, which, illuminated by the phial, appears beautiful even in death. The faithful servant again sees ahead, this time to after the shadows of the Quest are far behind.

As Sam moves away, doubts wrack him about whether he made the right decision. Even after the affirmation he received, he still second guesses himself, as he feels that what he is doing is completely opposed to what he knows of himself. "The battle of the will against the forces of the Enemy does not end just because one makes a decision or takes a step in the right direction" (Rutledge, *Battle*, 237). The questions Sam asks himself are natural and should be expected, even after the most carefully sought out and deeply prayed for decision. Any choice may feel uncomfortable especially in the beginning when the fears that eat away at our resolve may be their most corrosive. In an attempt to silence them, we may, like Sam, tell ourselves that our mind is made up but not truly believe that it is. Like him, we may stand still in our agony, unable to go on but go on we must. The path will become clearer the longer we walk upon it.

Sam hears Orcs coming straight toward him after he leaves Shelob's lair, and he puts the Ring on to escape them. Who or what inspires his decision at this critical moment is not made clear, which is often the case in real life. It is not Sam's own will that chooses the Ring. He obeys an unspoken command without thinking about it. This could be another effort of the fell object to announce its presence to its maker or God allowing this evil intention to defeat itself. In any case, much good comes from this, while grace shelters Sam from the grave peril that surrounds him.

The Orcs' discovery of Frodo's body resolves Sam's doubts about the correctness of his choice to leave. A servant's loyalty to his master, as opposed to the Quest, decides for him. He quiets his tortured wondering by choosing to defend Frodo's corpse until slain himself. The Quest and Middle-earth itself once again stand on the knife's edge. As the gardener throws aside his decision to bear the Ring, he enables this second part of his vocation to dovetail with his first, which is to remain at his master's side. The two intertwine so completely one could not exist without the other. Only by bearing the Ring and the Ring-bearer is the Quest fulfilled.

Sam starts to retrace his steps, but, in another instance of God's impeccable timing, he does not reach Frodo in time to stop the Orcs. They unknowingly aid the Quest as the Ring-bearer will now enter the Tower of Cirith Ungol in the only safe manner that he can: borne unconscious upon the shoulders of his enemies. The conversation between Shagrat and Gorbag reveals the providential control over this. Shagrat and his company were aware of the loud noises and strange lights in the lair, but they knew to avoid Shelob while she chased prey. This and the delay in sending out Gorbag's patrol allow Sam enough time to recover from the initial shock of his master's apparent death, to come to the decision to take the Ring, and to leave Frodo's side.

Gorbag suspects that an Elf partially cut Frodo free. If the Orcs had more accurate intelligence, they would know exactly who they found, but not even Sauron knows this. Even if he did, he would not trust his servants with such sensitive information. All Shagrat knows is that they are to search any prisoner and to keep him safe until either their master sends for him or comes himself to deal with him. Sauron issued this command so that he could personally devour any captive. But the order also guards Frodo from the peril of Orcs assaulting him any worse than they do and gives Sam enough time to rescue him. The Dark Lord again dooms himself through his own lusts, just as he had with his encounter with Pippin in the *palantír*.

After Gorbag wonders why Sauron would be interested in a corpse, Shagrat reveals to Sam's amazement that Frodo is not dead after all. The gardener realizes that his heart knew this all along, and he berates himself for making the wrong choice to depart. We may do the same thing after we think that we have made a huge mistake, but such is not necessarily true. Sam did *not* make the wrong decision; grace inspired him to make exactly the *right* one.

One of the ultimate ways evil thwarts itself is what happens because Sam carries the Ring. None of this would have occurred without Gollum's betrayal of Frodo and Sam to Shelob. Though the wicked creature does not and cannot know it, he saves his own life and the Quest itself through his hateful act. Even if Gollum had repented of his intention to turn the hobbits over to the spider, he would have had no control over her lust to have them for a meal. If somehow they avoided that, Sam would not have known the terrible grief of thinking his master dead, but he also would not have borne the Ring. Frodo would not have willingly surrendered it, and Sam would not have asked for it. Yet it remains essential that the gardener have it. As terrible as Shelob's lair and the surrounding area is, there is also a sacredness to it because of the momentous things that take place there to advance the defeat of Sauron.

This stage of Sam's journey also shows the importance of having a vital piece of information temporarily hidden, so that the best decision is made but not necessarily the one that would have been if more was known. If Sam had known that Frodo was alive, he would not have left him. The Orcs would have found and captured them both, as well as the Ring. The blessed blindness of the gardener's head to what his heart knew allowed him to take the Ring, to keep it and the Quest safe, and to prevent the fall of doom.

We, too, may only discover in stages the specific and unique reason God made us and exactly how to live it out. Just as Sam only dimly saw in the Shire that he had a job to do but did not know exactly what it was, I remember telling a friend years ago that I had a feeling Tolkien would have a profound effect on my life. I thought at the time that this meant going back to writing fantasy, which I had abandoned long before. I had no idea that I would instead begin a spiritual journey that led to this book. We must not expect to see the whole path ahead of us at once. Hopefully, we will come to a point like Sam when we are suddenly free of doubts and fears and know with clearer vision than ever that one particular path or another is definitely the one we are meant to travel. Our struggles will not end, but we will break through the first webs of darkness that our enemy weaves about us and which God allows to strengthen our faith, trust, and courage.

Evil undoes itself once more, as Gorbag tells Shagrat that he should not report anything to the Dark Tower until the more important enemy, the imagined Elf, is caught. Sam follows the Orcs part of the way but is not fast enough to rescue his master, which is another part of the timing of God's plan. Klinger makes a note of this important time: "On the very border of Mordor, the Ring-bearer is both dead and alive, accompanied by the Ring yet no longer in possession of it" ("Hidden Paths," 170-171).

Chapter Twenty

Appointed Paths

As Gandalf and Pippin come to Minas Tirith and approach the chair of Denethor, the Steward at first has nothing but mistrust and contempt for the hobbit. The tween's affronted sense of self-respect causes him to offer his service in payment for Boromir saving his life. Gandalf intuits that Pippin is "guided to do it for some higher purpose" (Rutledge, *Battle*, 247). Indeed, much good comes from this hobbit "agent of the Most High" (ibid., 251). Denethor later seeks Faramir's death, but God just as actively fights for his life, and, through the bruising of a hobbit's pride, He succeeds.

Pippin displays some of the spiritual discernment that graces his cousin, Frodo, as he sees the angelic power Gandalf that embodies but keeps hidden. After leaving Denethor, the tween also detects tremendous happiness beneath the worries of the wizard. The Maia feels this because, though dooms looms large over Minas Tirith and battle will soon begin, God is also present. Gandalf does not know exactly what is in store, but the mirth he barely restrains shows his faith that all things will go according to his Creator's plan. He perceives things with more than just his eyes, so he sees beyond the dire straits of the present moment into hope for the future. We have another wonderful example to follow, as darkness spreads in our own age.

Pippin meets Beregond, who tells him of the rumors that Denethor at times struggles with the mind of Sauron. We must not do this with our adversary lest we be caught, as Saruman and the Steward were ensnared by their Enemy. We cannot win such a confrontation with our own strength.

After Beregond asks Pippin if there is any hope that Minas Tirith will not fall, the hobbit does not answer at first. The great amount of evil already unleashed by Sauron and the cry of the Nazgûl flying above temporarily dishearten him. But then he sees the sun bright in the sky and the banners of the Citadel flapping in the wind. The long-feared night had not fallen. Frodo had felt something similar at Bag End after Gandalf first told him about the Ring. He imagined the terrible fires of Mount Doom, but then he came back to himself and saw only his own small fire; the darkness had not come. We need to see this as well. Too often we live not in the present but in the past or a feared future. If our eyes were truly open, we would see that our world is not as dark as we think it. Pippin lifts Beregond's spirits with some of the most inspirational words in the tale: "No, my heart will not yet despair. Gandalf fell and has returned and is with us. We may stand, if only on one leg, or at least be left still upon our knees" (*LOTR*, 749). Such a grace-filled response comes from his naturally cheerful and hopeful nature, which denies to adversity, real or feared, the power to defeat it. All seems dark and terrible for Minas Tirith, but the hobbit refuses to believe in the worst. If Gandalf can come back, anything is possible. What a marvelous attitude to have!

In the land of Rohan, Aragorn tells Legolas, Merry, and Gimli that he knows he is to travel to Minas Tirith, but he does not yet see by which path. He has, however, a keen sense of approaching doom and the revelation of his fate. We may know what our goal is, but not be certain how to get there, how far we will have to go, or how many perils we will have to overcome. But we do not need to know all this. All that is necessary is to trust, as Aragorn does, that God has prepared our paths long before, and that He will make sure we arrive at our destination, as long as we continue to do His will. Thomas Merton does not speak of Aragorn or Frodo, but his words are apt with regard to their trust in the One who sent them upon their Roads and who also sends us.

> My Lord God, . . . I do not see the road ahead of me. I cannot know for certain where it will end. . . . But I believe that the desire to please you does in fact please you. And I hope I have that desire in all that I am doing. I hope that I will never do anything apart from that desire. And I know that if I do this you will lead me by

the right road, though I may know nothing about it. Therefore I will trust you always though I may seem to be lost and in the shadow of death. I will not fear, for you are ever with me, and you will never leave me to face my perils alone. (*Thoughts in Solitude*, 79)

The truth of these words for Aragorn is soon borne out. The Rangers the man has long captained come to answer a summons they thought came from him. Aragorn says the only one he sent was within his own heart. The sons of Elrond also come. Elrohir tells his foster brother not to forget about the Paths of the Dead, which is the one way that Aragorn does not wish to consider. However, the chase of the Three Hunters, their meeting with Gandalf, and their travel to Rohan have all brought Aragorn close enough to take it. Hearing the man subsequently announce his intention to take this way after all frightens Théoden. Éomer speaks of his near certainty that he will not see his friend again. But Aragorn assures him that they may and so foreshadows their reunion on the Pelennor Fields.

Aragorn reveals to Legolas and Gimli that he deliberately provoked a meeting with Sauron through the Orthanc *palantír*, just as Pippin did so 'accidentally.' Tolkien noted that the man survived the terrible struggle of locking his will with the Enemy because he made a long distance call, as it were, and did not engage in a direct confrontation where only Gandalf could have triumphed (*Letters*, 332).

Aragorn's encounter with Sauron also shows how vulnerable the Dark Lord is to his own weapons of terror. The sight of Isildur's heir was a shock to him, and it filled him with fear. He launches his attack on Gondor before he is completely ready in the hope of defeating the one that he imagines is his most dangerous enemy.

What Aragorn sees in the Stone convinces him that he must use the only Path that will get him to Gondor in time to stop the approaching Corsair ships. He realizes that God gave him a sign and this spurs him into victorious action. Denethor saw the same thing, but his reaction helps drive him into suicidal despair and defeat. We can respond either way ourselves after we see danger coming toward us. After the clouds of fear and doubt part long enough for a ray of sunlight to break through and give us the assurance we need, let us make the right decision, as

Aragorn does. Though not speaking of him directly, Gracia Fay Ellwood illuminates this moment in the Ranger's life: "A purpose which we create for ourselves will never move us to the devotion of the man who knows he has been created for a purpose beyond himself" (*Good News*, 131).

After Aragorn comes to Éowyn at Dunharrow and tells her of his plans, she tries to dissuade him from such a dangerous way. In saying that he will travel a Path already laid out for him, the man gives one of the clearest signs in the tale about the guidance God continually gives His servants. Only the heir of Isildur could withstand the peril of facing the Dead, who bear the curse of remaining in the world until they fulfill the oath they broke to their king long ago. Aragorn achieves his own vocation partly through their aid, though he must wait until Frodo also succeeds.

Éowyn chomps at the bit to go into battle, as she shares the same fiery warrior spirit as her brother but has no outlet for it. Her cry that she wants to do as she pleases is the same one that we all make at times. We need strength to keep doing the same boring thing every day while we yearn for adventures and the accomplishment of our own desires rather than waiting upon others. Anger fills the young woman because her servant's role in aiding her ailing uncle has only changed direction, and she still has to tend to other duties that fall to women.

Aragorn's replies that few pursue their own whims in a respectable way. We are not put on the earth to do so. We would not have a happy life if we spent it entirely on ourselves. Instead, God places us in this time and place to succor particular people. Such service is the path He has prepared for us all, and we must walk upon it as faithfully as possible. There is honor in doing what must be done at home, as the Ranger tells the unfulfilled shieldmaiden, even if no one else knows of it or commemorates it in glorious song.

In Aragorn's insistence that he will pursue the Paths of the Dead, Éowyn sees only a reckless and unnecessary throwing away of a life that would be better used in battle. He sees the same when he refuses her plea to come with him. He has deeper sight than she does. The same Master Craftsman who carves Frodo into a jewel also shapes Aragorn. He walks into grave peril with the trust that the One who leads him in will also show him the way out, and thus he allows himself to enter the future he wishes to have.

Aragorn and the Grey Company enter "the Storm of Mordor and [are] lost to mortal sight" (*LOTR*, 773). This shows another example that Tolkien chose every word to mean something important. Even though no mortal sees where the Company travels, other Powers still track them.

Chapter Twenty-One

Courage and Hope, Pride and Despair

*A*fter Éomer counsels Théoden to return to Dunharrow once the muster of the Rohirrim is complete, the king echoes in his refusal what Treebeard told Merry and Pippin. The man knows he would be no safer in that fortress than in the midst of a battlefield, as eventually war would come to his own doorstep. He says that it would not cause him sorrow even to die if victory could still be brought about.

At Dunharrow, Théoden attempts to soothe Éowyn's grief over the departure of Aragorn by recounting the tale of Brego and Baldor, who had heard an ancient man at the Door of the Dead tell them that the path was closed until the proper time. The king thinks that perhaps this time has come, and Aragorn will pass through as no one has before. Théoden and Éomer both recognize the greatness of the man. The older man uses this to create a hope that Aragorn will survive, but the younger already grieves the loss of his friend on such a deadly road.

After Hirgon comes from Gondor with the Red Arrow that signals the grave need of Rohan's long-time ally, Théoden is hope-bearer once more. He bids the weary man to wait until morning to begin his return trip and to gain heart from the sight of the strength gathered for the defense of his land.

Sauron cannot understand why "Rohan would value loyalty to Gondor above its own safety, and thus he does not anticipate the ride of the Rohirrim" (Perry, *Untangling*, 181). Love, as shown here and throughout the tale, is the exact opposite of the Dark Lord's inward self-ishness and lust for domination. By honoring the old alliance between the two kingdoms of Men, Rohan focuses its selflessness completely outward.

After Faramir comes to report to Denethor that he had met and released Frodo, Sam, and the Ring, the Steward berates his son for such folly. He insists that Boromir would have given him the Ring. Gandalf corrects him by saying if Boromir had it, he would not have brought it for Denethor to use. Consumed by it himself, he would have returned a stranger to his father's house. The Steward is blind to this possibility. If the man could have his own way, he says that he would keep the Ring hidden away until the last possible moment. He believes that the mere knowledge he had it in his possession would be enough to release him from fear and that he could resist its seductive lure. But such words are meaningless, as Denethor has already reached the point of despairing enough to wish to use the Ring.

In one way, however, Denethor is right. The approaching army that he so dreads will destroy his City would be no match for the Ring. The fatal flaw in this view is that he sees only the fleeting military victory but not the moral destruction that would come in its wake. Frodo's prediction of Minas Tirith becoming another Minas Morgul would come true.

Gandalf bluntly tells Denethor that he does not trust the man or even himself to have custody of the Ring and keep it unused. He knows that its terrible power would overthrow even the most resistant will. The Steward does not have the wizard's wisdom or that of Faramir, who prudently chose the peril of sending the fell object away rather than the greater one of having it near. Had the Ring come to the elder man, he would have found it impossible to resist. His test would be similar to Galadriel's, but unlike her, the Steward would fail.

After Pippin and Gandalf return to their chamber, the tween asks about hope for Frodo. Trust that God knew what He was doing when He gave the Ring-bearer his task sustains the wizard's belief in the foolish hope of the Council but not in the way Denethor scorned it. The hidden Maia, nonetheless, acknowledges how startled and afraid he was and is about Faramir's news that Gollum was leading Frodo and Sam to Cirith Ungol. But he also sees this as good news because it means the Ring-bearer is not in captivity. The wizard divines that perhaps Pippin's brush with Sauron, as well as the guess that Aragorn revealed himself, has pushed the Dark Lord into action. As much as Gandalf fears Gollum will betray Frodo and Sam, he also holds onto the possibility that something beneficial may come from the creature's presence. This ability to go quickly from fear to hope comes only from one Source.

Hope, however, is beyond Denethor's reach. He has long probed the *palantír*, and through it, Sauron. The Seeing Stones show only the truth, but the Dark Lord puts his own demonic spin on what the Steward sees and poisons the man's mind with despair. But what brings Denethor to his final madness is something of which Sauron is not even aware. Like we do all too often, the man jumps to worst-case scenario with no in-between. The fact that we do not know what is ahead causes us much anxiety, but we could diminish or eliminate this dread altogether if we cultivate in our heart the same faith and hope that the heroes of the Third Age have. Such trust that God will take care of us through the worst storms is the only thing that we should rely on, for it is the one thing that will not fail. Sauron has infected Denethor's mind too long for the Steward to consider this. What he sees in the *palantír* on the thirteenth of March breaks him completely. Though not clearly stated, there are enough hints, especially from the date a dim light is seen in the Steward's chambers, that Denethor saw Frodo imprisoned in the Tower of Cirith Ungol with the Ring nowhere in sight. The man placed his hope for victory in the wrong place, and now it collapses altogether. He assumes Sauron has the Ring and the last stroke of doom will soon fall. Why should the Steward wait around for it to fall directly upon his head or Faramir's? This reveals the grave danger of assuming something is true before we know for sure. There is no way Denethor can know the truth about the Ring's disappearance. Neither can Frodo, who languishes in despair for the same reason.

Faramir lies near death because of a poisoned wound, while the terror and despair that the Nazgûl induce overwhelm the courage of many other soldiers. Yet Pippin tries to be hope-bearer to Denethor, as he was to Beregond. Part of the great strength of hobbits lies in the strong belief in this virtue, even when there seems little reason for it. We should adopt this way of thinking and living ourselves. Alas, the Steward is too far gone for the tween's efforts to have any effect.

Denethor tells Pippin to leave him and says that the only thing left for the hobbit to do is to die in whatever manner seems most appropriate. The tween counters his lord by saying that he will not consider dying until Gandalf has given up all hope. Pippin has observed the wizard's faith, and because Gandalf hopes, Pippin hopes. After accompanying the Steward and Faramir to Rath Dínen, Pippin flees the Silent Street and its houses of the dead in a desperate attempt to find his wizard friend. He becomes hope now for Faramir.

As Théoden and the Rohirrim approach Minas Tirith, the Wild Men guide the warriors to the forgotten Stonewain Valley trail, which allows them to arrive near the City two days earlier than the king's original estimate. Éomer observes the different ways evil manages to defeat itself. The terrible gloom that presses down on all their hearts also cloaks the passage of the warriors, and the hope that they can banish the darkness brings Ghân-buri-Ghân to offer his aid. The wanton destruction of the out-wall serves to aid the army, as they now ride swiftly to the aid of their beleaguered allies rather than spend many lives and much time to win through. Their enemy has done the work for them.

The Rohirrim blow their horns to announce their arrival, just as the Witch-king is about to attack Gandalf. The wraith flies off to deal with this new threat. Rutledge speaks of the perfect timing of this moment.

> Were the Rohirrim destined to come just at that moment? *Yes.* Were they free people? *Yes.* Were they more or less free because they were . . . riding . . . into their destiny? *More.* If God has prepared good works for us for walk in (Ephesians 2:10), then it is a joy and a wonder to walk in them. If God is working in us both to will and to work for his good pleasure (Philippians 2:13), then it is our delight and our fulfillment to realize that we are doing exactly what was planned for us to do all along. (*Battle*, 285; italics in original)

Théoden and his warriors come before Minas Tirith and see the devastation already wrought, which is enough for anyone to lose heart. At this time, however, Manwë shows his direct involvement in the war, as he disperses the black clouds Sauron sent forth to aid his armies. In doing so, the Vala sends a clear message to the Dark Lord that there is a power mightier than himself that is against him.

Théoden shouts a battle cry and blows so strongly on his standard-bearer's horn that he breaks it. He and his knights charge ahead to aid the City that its Steward already considers lost. They refuse to surrender to the despair that drives Denethor to immolate himself. Éowyn alone actively seeks death. In her secret ride with the Rohirrim, she does not know that she is going toward her vocation. On the Pelennor Fields, she will learn why she was made both a woman and a warrior.

The hour also draws near for the completion of another part of Merry's calling. The Witch-king prepares to slay Théoden, but the only two who can stop the wraith stand in his way to fulfill a prophecy made long ago. The Nazgûl's belief in it allows him to think himself safe from all peril, as it plainly states that no man alive can kill him and who but living men fight in battle? His downfall shows that we should be wary of interpreting such things only one way. After Dernhelm comes to the defense of Théoden, the fell lord threatens to send the warrior to the houses of lamentation. The Witch-king describes the terrors of such a place so vividly because he speaks from his own torment. He was once a man, but his flesh has been consumed and his mind left exposed to Sauron. Éowyn refuses to bow to such fears. She boldly reveals herself with a laugh and momentarily disconcerts the wraith.

Dreadful fear of the Witch-king had temporarily incapacitated Merry's will, but his astonishment after seeing Éowyn stirs his courage into flame. The hobbit knows that she may still perish, but he does his part to prevent this, just as Pippin does for Faramir. The shieldmaiden shows not only her warrior spirit but the same fire that burned within Sam in Shelob's lair. Both times a fearsome evil much stronger than themselves threatened a dear one but love inspired and strengthened them. After Éowyn kills the wraith's flying steed, the sun shines upon her.

Merry and Éowyn then strike at the Nazgûl lord and allow the prophecy to come true. No living man indeed defeats the wraith but a woman and a hobbit with a dead man's sword. God destined them all to be His agents at this time. Michael Martinez notes, "Can it be anything other than an act of divine providence that Merry just happens to be in the right place at the right time to help Éowyn defeat the Lord of the

Nazgûl? . . . As Ilúvatar could make his will known to some servants (such as Manwë) and through others (such as Aragorn), it follows that he could give Tom (whatever he is) a helping hand in choosing swords for the Hobbits" (*Understanding Middle-earth*, 439).

Great shock fills Éomer after he finds Éowyn laying on the battlefield as though dead. In a mad rage, he rushes back to the fight. At first, his enemies fall before him, but then the tide turns to favor the foe and even more reinforcements are seen. As the man watches the fleet of Corsair ships coming toward him, his reaction completely opposes Denethor's. The Steward fled in fear of a future happening, but rather than retreat from the doom that approaches, Rohan's young king has horns blown in a call to fight to the last man. He laughs in the face of despair and defiantly raises his sword to it and the arriving enemies. Great happiness then comes as they marvel at the great standard Arwen wrought for Aragorn raised on one of the ships. What enabled this triumphal entrance was another sign of the Valar's intervention in providing a sudden wind from the Sea during the night that filled the sails of the commandeered Umbar ships.

While the battle still rages, Pippin finds Gandalf and begs him to come and save Faramir. The wizard tries also to save Denethor's life and soul. Matthew Dickerson notes that the throughout the tale "what is at stake is the salvation of the Children of Ilúvatar, and therefore the moral choices of those Children are what matters" (*Following Gandalf*, 230). We are all placed as each other's "light . . . in dark places," (*LOTR*, 367) but it is up to the person we want to help to embrace or reject our aid. Gandalf tells Denethor that choosing the timing of the end of his life is not something for the man to decide. This boon, given to the Númenóreans, had allowed them to trustfully surrender their life at a moment of their own desire. This was meant as a peaceful falling asleep, but Sauron corrupted it into suicide and murder in despair. Denethor thinks he is in charge of his fate, but instead he shows that he is under the sway of the same demonic might as some of his forebears. His soul stands on the knife's edge while he watches Faramir taken away. For a moment he wavers, then he falls further into darkness.

Denethor is right that victory against Sauron is impossible in strictly military terms. He does not believe in the moral triumph that those on the side of Light still strive to make. He sees only disaster ahead. It is easy to imagine what insidious voice he listened to over long, the same one we may have heard also. 'This is bigger than you. Why bother to fight? You are only delaying the inevitable. Surrender now and save yourself a lot of trouble.' This poisonous counsel also attempts to reach Sam in Mordor. We must not listen to it. Hope rewards. Despair destroys.

Denethor fails to take into account the providence, grace, love, and mercy of God and what this could mean in his life. The man declares the basis for Gandalf's hope for victory as merely ignorance of the Corsair fleet, which the Steward has seen in the *palantír*. He has no way to know that the ships contain not enemies but allies. It would not have mattered to him in any case, for in some twisted way Sauron and Aragorn are the same to him. They are both rivals and threats to his power.

Denethor states his case against Aragorn and why he has no desire to step down to him. The Steward has forgotten that his position is that of a servant awaiting the return of the king. Anna Slack notes that Denethor "represents those who will not imitate Christ in dispensing their power" ("Slow-Kindled Courage," *Tolkien and Modernity 2*, 133-134). The man states that if he cannot live the way he wants, then he does not wish to live at all. The only future he wants is the past. His desire to remain locked in the position he and his ancestors have held for generations is so great that he deliberately stops his mortal clock while still holding this office. His final fate is not known. Those in despair could be so mentally unbalanced that they are not completely responsible for their actions.

The path that Denethor takes should not be the way with us. His lack of humility and hope causes him to flee into death to escape perceived defeat. Sam later stares death in the face and still hopes. How easy it is in hard times to see through the Steward's eyes rather than the hobbit's, but how much more rewarding and restorative it is to view life through Sam's perspective. Dickerson points out that God wishes this: "For Ilúvatar, the desire is for his Children to have hope; for Morgoth and his servant Sauron, they have already won a battle the moment they have brought about despair" (*Following*, 232). Though these words refer to Galadriel's words of hope to the Nine Walkers, such wisdom certainly also manifests itself here. Rather than running from the storm we see or think we see on the horizon, we should walk through it, not knowing ahead of time its exact nature and intensity but steadfastly enduring it as it closes around us. God remains with us always and will bring us safely through, if we do not let go of His hand. How we strain like Denethor, though, to know what is to come. Some read their horoscopes, have their palms read, or consult physics and astrologers. Not only are these avenues incapable of providing the truth about a future known only to God, demonic spirits also use them to gain power over a person. God keeps the future veiled for a reason. To seek further knowledge negates reliance on His providence. Rather than easing anxiety about the unknown, it could cause despair after the (mis) interpretation of a bleak future. "[Denethor's] despair has been brought on [partly] by his inability . . . to hold onto hope even when it looks as if there is no hope" (Greenwood, "Love," 182). There are many events in this tale that seem headed toward a terrible end. Time and time again, however, this is not so. Sometimes hope and victory are only moments away. Sam learns in Mordor that there is more than one way to view a scene, even as apparent disaster unfolds.

The defiant acts of Théoden, Éowyn, and Merry in the face of terror were the opposite of how Denethor responded. King, shieldmaiden, and hobbit actively fought their physical and spiritual battles, but the Steward surrendered to his hopelessness. Both men died on the same day but in much different ways. In Denethor's heart, defeat was certain and he fled before it came to him. Théoden, his niece, and his littlest knight stare right at it and defeat it. Though the king died after his stricken horse crushed him, he was still victorious. He did everything he could and then rested in peace with his heroic forebears after naming his beloved nephew as the next to lead Rohan. Denethor died in agitated despair after he tried to rob his son of life as well. Théoden died in graceful light after choosing the freedom to act at the head of his people in an effort to save the lives of those long allied with his own. Denethor died in disgraceful dark after refusing to act as the leader he should have.

Denethor's despair is like Frodo's, but the hobbit's reaction to it again stands in stark contrast to the Steward's. The Ring-bearer has no hope of his own but holds onto Sam's, which keeps him going even more than his own will. His despair nearly crushes him, but he refuses to give into it. Though the struggle tears him apart, he remains just as intent on saving everyone if he can as Denethor is not. Both go to fire, but while the Steward died in a darkness induced by his Enemy, the Ring-bearer's journey brings life and light free of Sauron to all.

Another great good that comes out of Boromir's attempt to save Merry and Pippin and the latter's gaze into the *palantír* is that even though Denethor lost his life, Faramir did not. Not only did God want the youngest hobbit part of the Company to help save Boromir's soul but also to aid the man's brother. If Pippin had not looked in the Stone, Gandalf would not have had to spirit him away ahead of the others, which allows for the opportunity of service to Denethor and of learning the Steward's mad plans. Pippin would not have offered himself if not inspired by Boromir's valiant efforts. Providence places the hobbit exactly where and when he needs to be. One event ties to another in ways that we cannot always see immediately, but once viewed in hindsight the intertwining of the melodies of the Great Music become apparent. We sit back in awe and listen to the symphony that we only heard snatches of before.

After the battle is won, Aragorn says that he will not enter the City until it is known which side will win the war. Éomer expects his friend to announce himself as king, but the older man refuses. He knows that his throne is not yet secure with the outcome of Frodo and Sam's struggle to Mount Doom still in question. This will determine all else, and so Aragorn says he will remain outside merely as a leader of Rangers. At Gandalf's plea, he later humbly enters as a healer. Fleming Rutledge notes, "He is willing to remain anonymous, without glory, thus offering an example of his own words to Éowyn about the need for renunciation. Like a Christian disciple, as Strider the Ranger, he has been in training for anonymous service for many years. That same self-effacing commitment to 'valor without renown' distinguished Faramir from his father Denethor" (*Battle*, 307).

In Aragorn's meek guise, he reveals his true identity as a king who cares deeply for his people. The first one who he heals is the gravely ill Faramir, whose reaction to the man is diametrically opposed to Denethor's. The young man has hoped and dreamed of the return of the king for so long that after the dream becomes flesh, he immediately gives his lord his heart and pledges himself to Aragorn's service with words "similar to those of a Christian disciple" (Chance, *Tolkien's Art*, 177). Denethor fled into death so he would not have to say such words. Faramir returns from near-death so he could. His will bends as completely to Aragorn's right to rule as the Steward's would not. Denethor saw nothing in Aragorn but the dregs of an ancient house that had long lost any worth. Faramir sees the king for which Gondor has longed. Rather than wishing to rule himself, the young man has the humility to recognize and to celebrate that the glory of his homeland will return through another man. Denethor had no belief or desire that the king would return. No one could blame him for his disbelief, as it is almost a thousand years since the last king died. But this makes Faramir's hope all the more impressive.

A newborn wind accompanies Aragorn's recall of Éowyn. He heals Merry next. With all three, the man uses *athelas*, which provides spiritual aid by lightening the hearts of all in the rooms, just as it did on Weathertop. Merry also receives the wise counsel to happily remember time spent with Théoden rather than avoid the beloved pastime of smoking because it reminds him of the king's death. We should remember Aragorn's words when the need is upon us. Visiting a favorite restaurant, park, theatre, bookstore, or just looking across at the beloved's chair can be reasons to celebrate the memories of a loved one and to absorb their *presence* and not just grieve over their absence. The loss may be too keen at first to do this, but later it will bring much healing and peace.

The next day, Legolas, Gimli, Merry, and Pippin enjoy a happy reunion while Aragorn, Gandalf, and other leaders gather to discuss the next step in their strategy to defeat Sauron. Merry wishes the war was already over, for he fears the worst is still to come. Pippin tells him not to be so downcast but rather to delight in the time that they have together. We all need to follow the tween's counsel to focus on present cheer and not on what doom we fear the future holds.

The theme of the wisdom of God veiling the future from us echoes in Gimli's words that if he had known how horrifying it would be to travel in the company of the Dead, he would not have done so. He says it was only Aragorn's will that kept him on such a terrible Path, but Legolas adds it was also out of love for the man. In the retrospective the Elf and Dwarf give of this time, they point out two more ways evil confounded itself yet again. Legolas gives a curious source of his hope for victory in that the dread power of the ghostly army grew in the darkness Sauron spread from Mordor. Gimli notes that the triumph over the Corsair pirates was through the same weapons of terror that the Dark Lord was so fond of employing himself. Michael W. Perry observes another way: "Sauron . . . seems to have assumed his allies in the south will be victorious. . . . Defeat will come because he lacks intelligence of Aragorn's journey through the Paths of the Dead, something that should have been revealed by the enormous turmoil the Dead created in their wake" (*Untangling*, 182).

During the debate that Gandalf holds with Aragorn, Éomer, and Imrahil, the wizard says that the next prudent step in countering Sauron would be to strengthen their fortresses against the Dark Lord's coming in an effort to stave off defeat as long as possible. The hidden Maia then adds that he does not recommend they act in such a manner. This may seem surprising at first, but it is not. The foundation of the entire Quest was made not on prudence but on the seemingly rash decision to send someone into the heart of Sauron's realm with the very object that would ensure his victory if he recovered it.

The Bible offers many other examples of apparent senselessness in following God's more outlandish plans. Who will think it wise to begin to prepare the sacrifice of a son through whom God promised generations would come? What good could come from marching around a town for seven days? What could a slight shepherd boy armed only with a stone in his sling do against a giant warrior? What could Gideon's army of 300 do against a foe many times larger? What good could come from a man getting out of a boat to walk upon the water in the midst of heavy winds? All of these could say to God, "No, I think not. That does not sound too prudent to me." Yet they will all do what God asks of them. Peter will only begin to sink after he doubts in the face of the wind and waves. Rather than focus on the miracle taking place, he will think, 'Hey, I can't really be doing this!' Strong trust in God will see anyone through to triumph. We need to have this, especially after we think that our 'imprudent' Creator has thought up a real doozy for us.

Gandalf has this faith. He knows that the battles we must fight against our enemy are not always physical, but they are at all times spiritual. The wizard acknowledges that military success is not possible against Sauron, but triumph could still come if the Ring-bearer completes his struggle to Mount Doom. Gandalf knows that the battle Frodo fights is the only one that truly matters. The wizard is aware that there is no lasting victory against evil in this life, but he does not use this as an excuse not to do everything to deal it as crushing a blow as possible. Our duty is not to destroy wickedness for all time, but, as Gandalf says, to do what we can to defeat it where and when we are and so aid those who will come after. With every labored step and breath to Mordor, Frodo carries his cross for this reason, as have soldiers throughout the ages down to the present day.

Another time that shows how good it is not to know the future before acting is Aragorn's confirmation of Gandalf's guess that the man revealed himself to Sauron in the Orthanc *palantír*. The soon-to-be king says that he thought it was the right time to do it, and it was why he received custody of the Stone. Wormtongue did not intend this good when he threw it down, but again one does not need to be aware to be used as one of God's instruments. Aragorn adds, however, that he may not have acted so boldly if he had known how fast Sauron would respond. The man's words that he hardly received enough time to save Minas Tirith not only show his faith in the path chosen for him but also how economical God is in His use of time. He gives us only as much as we need to accomplish the goals that He has set for us.

With the desire of strengthening Frodo's chances, Gandalf offers his 'imprudent' counsel that the army of the West go to the Black Gate to challenge Sauron and knowingly walk into an ambush of their own making. The wizard has little expectation that the horribly outnumbered force will survive, but he does not rule out hope altogether because he does not know the future. Using the same rationale for fighting that Treebeard and Théoden had, Gandalf says that those gathered at this final debate have two options. They and their soldiers can either sacrifice themselves in the hope that a new age will come in part through their efforts even if they never see it, or they can try to retreat from doom and have their cowardice ensure that they will die knowing that another age will never come for them or anyone. They firmly decide upon the former. Frodo and Sam could not have succeeded if these stouthearted warriors faltered in this somber time, but none do. Even the near certainty of death does not cause the commanders to quail at

Gandalf's counsel. Personal survival is not their goal. They are willing to go like "lambs led to the slaughter," for no other reason "other than the worthiness of their Quest" (Wood, *Gospel*, 65 and 137 respectively). "A man can have no greater love than to lay down his life for his friends" (John 15:13). Paul H. Kocher notes, "Much has been written, and justly, about the self-sacrificial courage of Frodo and Sam in the last stages of their journey through Mordor. But few or none have remarked on the equal if less solitary unselfish daring displayed by the mere seven thousand men whom Aragorn and his peers lead up to the Black Gate to challenge the ten times ten thousand inside" (*Master*, 148).

Éomer and Imrahil freely offer the gift of their lives, not only in the hope to give Frodo and Sam the time to save them all but also out of their love for Aragorn. This loyalty to the point of death brings out another aspect of Aragorn's pre-figuring of Christ. As with Jesus, the future king has a power to his personality and presence which causes others to pledge themselves to his service.

Bradley J. Birzer notes that Aragorn and Gandalf "do what is demanded of them by Providence. They willingly place themselves and their forces in a position that may prove their undoing and their death. As true servants of Ilúvatar, they are willing to sacrifice themselves for the opportunity to serve the greater good" (*Sanctifying Myth*, 83). All those who fight for the Light live out the wise words attributed to Edmund Burke that "All that is needed for evil to prevail is for good men to do nothing." They know that they fight for something more than themselves. They fix their eyes on the future in contrast to Denethor who died longing for the past. It does not matter if they are caught in the trap that they lay for themselves and for their Enemy, just as long as it catches him. Linda Greenwood remarks about this.

> In *The Return of the King*, this passion to push on even when all hope is lost is shown in Aragorn's march to Mordor. In his words, they have 'come now to the very brink, where hope and despair are akin'. . . . In this sense, they have come to the same place to which Frodo ultimately comes on his journey to Mount Doom. Tolkien explains this paradox as 'defeat inevitable yet unacknowledged' (*MC [Monsters and Critics]* 18). They

give with no thought of getting in return; they do their duty with no expectation of any reward. They give a gift that has no recompense; they give the gift of their own deaths. ("Love," 182-183)

Once Merry watches the army march away to seemingly certain doom, Bergil offers words of hope to the hobbit, just Pippin earlier gave them to the child's father. So should we comfort each other in days of leave-taking and loss.

After the soldiers endure days of marching under the dread of what is to come, and later under the shadow of the eight remaining Nazgûl, Aragorn pardons those who are overcome by the horror and desolation that surrounds the approach to the Black Gate. In assigning them another task, he allows them to retain their dignity and not to worry that they are cowards because their hearts were no longer strong enough to follow him. This gift of compassionate understanding emboldens some to continue on their hard Road, while others are glad to do something elsewhere and still help the cause.

Jane Chance observes that the coming of the army to the Black Gate is "not so much a physical attack as a spiritual defense by Gondor" (*Art*, 178). Sauron takes the bait, as he assumes the new Ringlord is there to challenge him. He has ignored the reports of spies, as he reasons that he has bigger fish to fry. Why worry about two mice when there is a lion at the gate? This "hopeless yet hopeful" ("Love," 183) situation is another instance of God's impeccable timing. It takes eight days to travel from Minas Tirith to the Black Gate. Frodo and Sam struggle in the same amount of time to reach the Sammath Naur. Aragorn, Gandalf, and the others have little idea where the hobbits are, but they draw Sauron's army away from where Frodo and Sam need to cross a road. It is a win-win situation. Perry notes, "Timing such as this is where Tolkien most often reveals the presence of the One who otherwise remains hidden" (*Untangling*, 201).

The Mouth of Sauron comes to speak to the army. This slave, who has lost his freedom so completely that he does not even possess his own name anymore, stands in contrast to the men who have come of their own free will. The Mouth considers himself superior to them all, but in reality, he is lower than any of them.

Despair stalks the army after the Mouth shows them Sam's sword and Frodo's *mithril* shirt and Elven cloak. The man tells the allies of the West that they are responsible for the fate of the prisoner and assures them that his torment will be long and terrible if they do not agree to cease their hostilities.

Gandalf refuses to have anything to do with this foolishness. He resists the hopelessness and horror the Mouth inspires. The army holds to their purpose. We must continue on our own way and not believe our adversary's lies that the suffering of others is our fault when it is not.

Pippin comes to the point Denethor had reached after an incredible host pours out of the Black Gate and the surrounding area to encompass the army. The tween joins the others who had the completely opposite reaction of the Steward. Even as the hobbit acknowledges that, as far as he knows, his death is but moments away, Frodo is doomed to unspeakable agony, and Merry will soon be dead also, he responds with compassionate insight into Denethor's heart and soul and the resolve to fight to the last breath. He saves Beregond's life by killing a troll. After its corpse fells Pippin, he calmly and even happily accepts that he is about to pass beyond the cares of the world. He knows that he has done all that he could, as opposed to Denethor who abdicated many of the responsibilities of a leader. The last thing the hobbit knows before losing consciousness is the Eagles coming to the rescue, but he does not realize that this is truly happening. He thinks he is only remembering Bilbo's adventure.

Chapter Twenty-Two

Light in the Darkness

Sam continues as an inspiration for all who journey along hard Roads. Greg Wright observes that the hobbit lives out what St. Paul will later say in Romans 5:3-4: "In fact, 'the choices of Master Samwise' perfectly demonstrate how 'suffering produces perseverance; perseverance, character; and character, hope'" (*Tolkien in Perspective*, 112). Sam knows that he must try to free Frodo, but he freely acknowledges the greater probability that he will die trying rather than achieve success. He does not allow this to deter him, however, and he immediately starts to seek a way to accomplish his seemingly impossible task. He conquers his terror and keeps moving until he returns to the place where he first saw Shagrat and the other Orcs. Here Sam's will fails for a moment. He realizes that if he takes one step more, he will pass the point of no return. Something interesting happens then. Without thinking exactly why, he puts on the Ring. It could possibly be the demonic object's will that the hobbit obeys without question, but if so, evil again defeats itself. The gardener immediately senses the Eye, but he also hears the sounds of battle. At first he thinks that this signals Orcs torturing Frodo, but this fear does not last long enough for his heart to even respond to it. Instead he concludes that his enemies are fighting among themselves. This sound, which could not have reached him without the Ring sharpening his hearing, restores his courage and hope. Love stirs his heart to boldly cry out to his master that he is coming toward him, thus proving again the truth of Gimli's words that the given word may embolden a quaking heart. Once Sam enters Mordor, he senses a warning deep inside his heart to remove the Ring. He thinks that he only does this to see better, but actually he responds to a prompting from one of the invisible guardians of the Quest.

After Sam sees the Tower of Cirith Ungol fully for the first time, he realizes to his surprise that the terrible fortress was not made to forbid entrance but to deny exit. The magnitude of his daunting task comes back to him. He thinks of how difficult it would be to pass the gate unseen, but he is not there to do that. His job is much harder, for he must get inside by himself. But this trying time for both Sam and Frodo is clearly meant to unfold as it does. Judith Klinger offers some chilling alternatives of what may have happened otherwise.

> What would have happened after all, if Frodo and Sam had left the Lair together, unharmed by Shelob? The only available road passes directly underneath the guarded walls of the tower, and later events reveal that the orcs stationed there and at Minas Morgul had been alerted to watch for trespassers. As these details are successively disclosed, it becomes impossible to envision how Frodo and Sam might have passed safely together.
>
> Trapped between the two orc-bands, surely at least one of them would have been captured, and even if the other had escaped, he would likely have done so by making use of the Ring, thus immediately revealing himself to Sauron's searching eye. ("Hidden Paths," 169-170)

During this time the terrible power of the Ring wears at Sam's mind and will, which is how our enemy operates as well. Through knowledge of our strengths, weaknesses, hopes, and fears, our foe ever seeks a way to ruin us. He cannot force us to act, but he can supply the desire to do something we ought not and pound away until our will crumbles under the assault. Or we can triumph over him for the moment and brace ourselves for the next onslaught.

The Ring presents Sam with visions of leading an army to defeat Sauron and then turning the wasteland of Gorgoroth into a beautiful garden. This enticement to use ultimate power does not sway the hobbit for long at all. Sam has grown much since the Quest began and now has "a deep capacity for discernment and reflection" (Gardner et al., *SparkNotes*, 245). He sees the truth behind the delusions of the Ring.

As Galadriel remains herself, Sam remains Sam: a heart full of love at his master's side. This saves him as much as it graces Frodo. The young hobbit has always understood his place in the world. He does not desire a garden the size of a kingdom which he could not tend himself. He just wants to be the happy gardener of Bag End. He has no wish to have people under him to order around. He wants to have someone over him to cherish. His love, humility, and common sense leave the Ring with no ability to seriously tempt him.

Let us pray that we will see through our enemy's deceptions as easily as Sam. We are all meant to serve but how much harder this is for us than for him, as he does not have the struggle that we do against pride and selfishness. We should not seek to be greater – or lesser – than our true selves. Lucifer/Melkor, Sauron, and Saruman all tried to go beyond what was theirs to grasp and failed. But if we keep our focus on the One in whom "we live and move and have our being" (Acts 17:28, NRSV) and accept the grace that He so wants to give us, we can rise to great heights and become who we are meant to be.

Sam no longer wonders what he must do. As difficult as it appears to enter the Tower, he knows that he is bound to go there. He likens the burden of his task to the despair a spring frost brings, but this does not daunt him. He would love to use the invisibility the Ring gives but refrains. He knows that such a path is no longer open to him. He shrugs his shoulders, as though to free himself of all that presses down upon him. The Ring-induced fantasy of Samwise the Strong dissipates, and he becomes Samwise the frightened hobbit once more.

Sam realizes the sound of the fighting that he heard earlier was the Orcs slaughtering each other over Frodo's *mithril* coat. This violence makes the rescue of the Ring-bearer possible, which is yet another good coming out of evil. Just as the Orcs quarreled among themselves near Fangorn, they destroy themselves in the Tower. As this is the only path open for the hobbits to use to continue on their journey, it is made easier for them.

After Sam comes to the entrance to the Tower, he cannot at first get past the Two Watchers who "barred the gateway with their hatred. For though any army might attempt to force that gate, it could not pass by strength of arms; only by a will greater than the Watchers' malice could a passage be forced" (Day, *Tolkien: The Illustrated Encyclopedia*,

228). Sam's own will fails to provide a way in, but grace inspires him to hold up Galadriel's phial. The creatures give a terrible cry after the phial temporarily breaks their power. Fear continues to grip Sam, but he still jokes about ringing the door and shouts out a challenge to any foe that could hear.

We should learn to carry ourselves as lightly as Sam and be just as open and docile to the workings of the Holy Spirit, so that we are ready to respond after the Spirit stirs our soul. Though the horror of traveling through the Tower nearly crushes the humble hobbit, his heartfelt devotion to Frodo and his cheerful nature give his terror no way to utterly overcome him. Even if we wonder how to take the next step with such evil surrounding us, we can discover the ability to do so, for "fear is driven out by perfect love" (1 John 4:18).

Sam still remains in danger from the Ring, however, even after his firm rejection of it. It knows now that it cannot seduce him into wearing it, so it works on circumventing his will altogether. After the gardener hears feet running in his direction, the fell object directs his hand to reach for it. Providence interrupts him from putting it on as an Orc comes near and looks right at him. This could have ended in disaster but for the way Snaga beholds Sam. The Orc does not see a fearful hobbit but an incarnation of Samwise the Strong holding a bright sword in one hand and some unseen and mighty threat in the other.

Snaga's flight from Sam so gratifies the gardener that it emboldens him to run after his enemy. He wonders if the terrible cry that he heard just before the Orc appeared was from Frodo. He is near to collapsing from exhaustion, but he is fed by love. He hears Snaga and Shagrat arguing about the Elf warrior who is loose. After Snaga disappears into a turret, Sam leaps at Shagrat, who stuns him with a large bundle. The hobbit runs after him but soon stops and decides to continue his search for Frodo instead. He doubts his choice is the right one, but he goes on, as we must do also amid our own uncertainties.

Sam reaches the lowest point of his long and terrifying search when he comes to an apparent dead end. He does not know, as he sits on the step and feels all his efforts were for naught, that he is just moments away from his greatest happiness. He fears Frodo forever lost, but grace touches him once more to reward his loyalty and courage and he starts to sing. His bold resistance to despair is similar Éomer's reaction as the man watched the approach of the Corsair ships. At first, Sam's songs are from his childhood or from Bilbo, but then he receives the inspiration to make his own composition drawn from his unquenchable hope. Klinger notes, "Sam's song . . . challenges the overbearing presence of darkness and death with a determined vision of spring and ultimately invokes eternal light. . . . Quite literally, this song propels Sam past a final dead end, opens the last door, and brings about a reversal from death to life" ("Hidden Paths," 192). Snaga hears Frodo's weak response and inadvertently leads Sam to the treasure that he seeks. Perhaps the loyal servant would not have found his master otherwise. The direct union that Sam's soul has with God fuels the hobbit's hope that more than once is on the brink of going out but always flares up afresh. God "does not break the crushed reed, nor quench the wavering flame" (Isa. 42:3).

Our enemy does not wish us to make any forward progress, and so he ever seeks ways to throw us off the path we have embraced to do God's will. But rather than feeling discouraged by such obstacles, we should be encouraged because we are on the verge of a breakthrough, though we do not know it. Our adversary is aware, however, which is why he is so anxious to stop us. If we refuse to give into his tactics and instead praise God for them, we will throw our foe into utter confusion, for he will have no idea how to react to this. Sam did not know what or who stirred his heart to sing, but we do. Let us press on and sing ourselves, even if we do not know how we can. Even if our voice is as small at first as Sam's was, it can grow in strength just as his did. If we feel stymied in the pursuit of our dreams, grace can still reach out to us. We should never believe solely what our eyes show us or what a heart clouded by despair tells us. We have to trust that there is so much more beyond what we see physically. Throughout the tale, and especially in Mordor, Sam shows that he believes this. He thought that he had reached the nadir of his life in Shelob's lair only to have this prove untrue. He thought so again before his grace-filled song lifted him up and out to show him that there was still life and hope beyond.

Sam and Frodo's tender reunion comes as a result of overcoming despair, seemingly irrevocable loss, and impossible odds. "Under the most adverse and improbable circumstances, surrounded by the hideous evidence of senseless slaughter, Frodo and Sam share a moment's happiness and release from the burdens of the Quest" ("Hidden Paths,"

193). This eucatastrophic liberation is necessary for them both after such a horrible time apart and gives them the chance to recharge their will to continue while "the Ring's influence is – almost miraculously – suspended or eclipsed" (ibid.). As Frodo rests peacefully in his beloved guardian's arms like a child calmed after a nightmare, Sam feels that he could joyfully hold his master forever. Ralph C. Wood quite rightly calls their blessed bond "a thing of exquisite beauty, even holiness" (*Gospel*, 135). Sam rouses his master/best friend/brother/child with a kiss to the brow and a bright voice.

Despair soon returns to Frodo, however. He laments the loss of the Ring and the inevitable triumph of Sauron. He knows that there is no way out for anyone except the Elves, though he wonders if the Dark Lord's power is great enough to reach even over the Sea. Sam assures Frodo that the Ring is not lost, but he hesitates to give it back because he now knows more about the torment involved in bearing it. It is easy to imagine what fell whispers may have attempted to seduce him into thinking that it would be better not to return the terrible thing. 'You see how ruined he is already. He is only going to get worse. You love him, do you not? If you do not him to suffer anymore, take me yourself. Stop this madness.' If temptation did come to Sam this way, it would have been perhaps worse than the first assault and more subtle as well but also just as successful.

At first, Frodo praises Sam for keeping the Ring safe, but then its malevolent influence returns with a vengeance. A terrible change comes over its Bearer and "maddened by the thing that is destroying him," Frodo demands it back (Bradley, "Men, Halflings, and Hero Worship," *Tolkien and the Critics*, 121). He angrily refuses Sam's charitable offer to help carry the burden, grabs the Ring, calls his loyal servant a thief, and glares at him with fear and hate. "This is the Ring's corruption in its most devastating mode" (Rutledge, *Battle*, 325).

Frodo's harsh words cut Sam to the heart, but the gardener continues to love without a moment's loss. After the Ring-bearer sees clearly again, he is appalled by what he said and did. The wisdom that the Enemy's best weapon is the dissension that it causes between friends echoes once more. Yet nothing truly comes between these two hobbits because they will not allow it. Frodo begs for forgiveness, and Sam immediately gives it.

Archbishop Fulton J. Sheen's observation of how Jesus loved even great sinners reflects Sam's view of Frodo: "He saw that a jewel had fallen into the mud and though encrusted with foulness that it was still a jewel" (*Fulton J. Sheen's Guide to Contentment*, 155). Words from Rabbi Julius Gordon support this as well: "Love is not blind. It sees more, not less but because it sees more, it is willing to see less." Though Sam has trouble seeing beneath others right away, he always recognizes Frodo as a being filled with light and grace, even if sometimes addiction to the Ring twists him into something else. As Sam told himself in Ithilien, he loved his master whether this light shone or not. Only such depth of devotion is strong enough to endure and even grow through their terrible trials. Again words of Archbishop Sheen are applicable: "That is why our nature is fortified by the imagination, which puts before us the thought of the beautiful, so that when earthly beauty has faded from our eyes, we might revive the ideal more beautifully still in our imagination" (*God's World*, 58). The devoted gardener remembers, adapting the words of Washington Irving, the "innocent eyes of [his] child so can never be brought to think him all unworthy. [His] love ever lives, ever forgives and while it lives, it stands with open arms and gives and gives, the strongest thing in the universe, never failing, enduring forever, always hoping." This allows Sam to actively choose to love no matter the cost or provocation not to. Sarah Arthur notes, "Love is a free gift of grace from God" (*Frodo*, 136). She does not speak of Sam, but how truly it applies to him and how blessed Frodo is by it. St. Francis de Sales said, "The measure of love is to love without measure." (Also attributed to St. Augustine.) Such love induced Gandalf to enter Moria, even while knowing his death was within, and only such love enables Frodo and Sam to struggle to the Fire.

The Ring-bearer demonstrates once more the incredible power of hobbits to recover from deep trauma. Though these are the most horrific times these sheltered beings have ever had to endure, Frodo still teases Sam about finding out about inns between the Tower and Mount Doom. This is their secret to surviving almost unbelievable torment. We may have to battle with despair like the hobbits do, but we should also fight to emulate their wonderful ability to rebound after the immediate danger is past. We must not be in denial of what happened, but we cannot let the pain of our trials poison the well of our soul. Alas, the harm done to Frodo by the end cannot be so easily repaired, but how marvelous to see him jest even now.

Frodo gives an insightful answer after Sam asks whether Orcs drink and eat. The Ring-bearer recognizes that evil cannot create things with its own will and power but can only manipulate and wreck things already made. He feels this happening within himself. Such twisting of the true nature of a being also explains the hatred Orcs have of anything Elven. This includes the *lembas* crumbs that Frodo gathers from the floor to feed his famished friend. Hateful acts had slashed the Ring-bearer's water bottle and stolen the food from Faramir. The same enmity leaves the best food trampled but still edible for Sam's benefit.

After the Watchers stop Frodo and Sam from escaping the Tower, the Ring-bearer nearly faints from this and the torments of his captivity. But Sam remains certain that they will get away. He holds up Galadriel's phial and responds to the inspiration to invoke Elbereth in Sindarin. Frodo calls out in Quenya. This not only checks the malevolent will of the Tower's guardians but also brings down part of the gateway. The hobbits break free just as a Nazgûl dives from above to answer the Watchers' cries.

Sam shows twice more the reverence and faith in which he holds all things Elven. The loyal servant gives his master his gray cloak to replace the orc-mail shirt Frodo discards after it becomes too heavy for him to bear with the weight of the Ring already wearing him down. Sam also invokes Galadriel in his pleas for light and water. He does not know any higher power to pray to and is not even aware that he is praying. Likely the Valar grant both petitions, which shows that not just evil keeps watch over the Black Land.

Light comes first. We can receive the same in our own struggles. After we learn that there are angels guarding us, it renews our strength for the battle. Sam and Frodo feel a wind drive back the dark clouds and bring a faint light. This immediately heartens the gardener, but he does not know what it means. He asks Frodo if he has regained some hope, but the burden of the Ring leaves its Bearer with little ability to appreciate this moment of grace. The wheel of fire that burns in the elder hobbit's mind and eats at his soul has already begun to steal his memories and replace them with itself. Any good that is happening is too far away to make a difference to him. In an effort to give Frodo the strength to hope, Sam offers him some *lembas*.

After Frodo and Sam next miraculously come across water, the younger hobbit says he wants to drink first. He reasons that if it is poisoned it would be better that he die rather than his master. But Frodo says that they will drink together, as the water could possibly be "our blessing" (*LOTR*, 900) instead. The Ring-bearer once more shows faith in his invisible guardians. At any other time, it would have been meaningless for water to fall into the dust of Mordor, but Tom Shippey beautifully speaks of this particular grace-filled moment. "'Fruitless' . . . ? The water seemed so, but turns out not to be. By refreshing the Ring-bearer it does the best that any water could. The 'streamlet', in its apparent failure and eventual success, becomes a kind of analogue to Frodo's pity for Gollum, say, to all appearances useless, in the end decisive" (*Road*, 219). The Biblical story of Elijah's long Road to Mount Horeb will echo such gifts as this and the *lembas* bread. Before the prophet leaves, he will receive a baked scone and a jar of water to drink, so he is not overcome by the rigors of his journey (1 Kings 19:6-7).

As much as Frodo needs and receives consolations, Sam needs them as well to continue as his master's light and hope. Indeed, one of the greatest blessings comes to the gardener alone while Frodo sleeps. Just as the Ring-bearer's spiritual batteries were earlier recharged by pleasant dreams, Sam's are renewed as he gazes upon Gil-Estel, the Star of High Hope, which is the Silmaril that shines from the brow of Eärendil. Elbereth had long ago set him aboard his ship to give hope to those struggling against Morgoth. Watching this light shine far above him, Sam realizes that evil will not last forever. There are things that it can never touch, mar, or destroy. Jane Chance observes that

> [Sam's] sensitivity to spiritual reality is expressed by his understanding of the beauty beneath the appearance of waste, of light beyond darkness, of hope beyond despair.
> This insight is triggered by the appearance of a star above, an instance of divine grace that illumines understanding and bolsters hope. (*Art*, 180)

Sam realizes that "the world is in abler hands than his" (Kocher, *Master*, 45). He has put all his love and energy into devoting himself to his Frodo, but now he receives the comfort that there is care for him also. The burden of looking after his master does not rest completely on his own shoulders. The sight of goodness in the heavens re-fills the sails of his flagging hope. The wonder of it releases the young hobbit for a blessed while from fear of his and Frodo's fate, worry over betrayal by Gollum, capture by Orcs or Nazgûl, or anything else. Darkness cannot eclipse this light, and only the black night makes it possible for him to see it. Fortified by the peace and assurance of this sign, Sam sleeps easily under the light and shelter of the Star, even this deep into enemy territory and at the same time Frodo does. Brian Rosebury notes that this is

> at once a necessary reaction to accumulated stress and an act of quasi-religious faith.
> . . . [It is] a moment of grace, release and self-abandonment. (*Tolkien: A Cultural Phenomenon*, 62)

It would be an easy delusion for Frodo and Sam to think that they toil alone and that they and Sauron are the only ones left in the world. But those who watch over the hobbits remind Sam of the truth. The same consolation can reach us whenever the weight of our burdens drive us earthward. After we find the strength to lift our head, we should follow the wise advice to "look to the east right before dawn or the west after dusk. With any luck, you'll catch sight of Eärendil's Star of Hope – the blended light of the Two Trees of Wisdom and Mercy, the brightest of the messengers sent over Middle-earth, and its light will help guide you on your way" (Harvey, *The Origins of Tolkien's Middle-earth for Dummies*, 232).

If we live right, this is how God and others also perceive us, as lights shining in the darkness, candles in the night. Sometimes we glow brightly and steadily. Other times troubles toss us about and we flicker. Even if we think that we have given all that we can and the last spark is about to die out, God lights us anew. Nothing will ever conquer us if we hold fast to Him. This insight has the power to completely change our outlook. Darkness is at times necessary for us to shine the way for others and to give them hope in their trials. Far more than Galadriel's phial, Sam is Frodo's light in the dark places that the Ring-bearer's soul treads. Indeed, the two are living phials for each other.

Chapter Twenty-Three

The Power of Sacrificial Love

As Frodo and Sam look upon the great Orc host that stands between them and their goal, they both acknowledge the apparent impossibility of crossing such enemy-infested territory unnoticed. The Ring-bearer plainly speaks of his lack of hope but also of his unbending resolution to continue on and elude capture as long as he can. We must struggle forward as he does despite whatever our enemy flings at us from his vast arsenal in his attempts to suffocate our soul.

If Sam were not by his master's side, Frodo's despair could easily have become Denethor's. The grace-filled combination of the gardener's sturdy will and the Ring-bearer's battered and bleeding one is what gets them to the Fire. Frodo's will alone, though completely committed to the Quest, would not have survived the Ring's increasingly brutal assaults if not for Sam's constant support. The elder hobbit would not have even made it out of the Shire without his guardian's presence beside him. A great part of Sam's vocation is that of being Hope-bearer for the Ring-bearer. If the gardener had given into despair as well, the Quest would have failed. Peter Kreeft notes, "Frodo . . . loses hope in his task, but he still has hope in *Sam*. Sam never did have much hope for the task; the object of his deep hope is *Frodo*, and that hope is not disappointed" (*Philosophy*, 202; italics in original).

Frodo and Sam soon receive more signs of the invisible protection that guards them after they overhear the Orcs who pursue them. The creatures do not know who they are chasing. Gollum found the mail-shirt Frodo discarded, threw the tracker off the scent of the Ring-bearer and his companion, and muddled any footprints they left. The shirt also saved Gollum's life by deflecting an arrow shot at him. There is no way Frodo could have known what a great gift he left behind for his brother Bearer and betrayer or for himself and all of Middle-earth. Once more he has saved Gollum's life and with it the Quest. Such ripples spread out from our thoughts, choices, and actions as well. Even the tiniest may have a great effect.

As Frodo continues to deteriorate under the horrible physical and spiritual agony of the Ring, Sam takes on more responsibility to ensure the completion of their mission. The depiction of Sauron as the Eye is telling, for the 'I' is all that he is aware of in his lust to become ruler over all. But there is no 'I' in Sam. There is only 'you.' Marion Zimmer Bradley notes that "every thought and movement of Sam's reaches an almost religious devotion and tenderness toward easing Frodo's path, even though he cannot share his torment or even his burden" ("Men," 121). Rolland Hein notes that Sam "epitomizes the ideal of servanthood, which, in Christian terms, is the epitome of heroism" (*Mythmakers*, 207). As the gardener dies to himself in service to his master, he provides us a wondrous example to follow. His myriad acts of love are all freely made choices, as is his enduring hope. Rather than have these sacrifices weaken him, they strengthen him. Grace gives him this gift. In renouncing much of his own need for food and water, Sam is like a mother who feeds her dying child rather than herself.

But nourishment is much more than just food. Sam provides Frodo with his cloak for a pillow, his arms for a bed, and his hand for holding. Gandalf tried to bring light to Denethor, but the Steward refused to heed it. Frodo, in contrast, clings to it in the form of Sam's hope and love. These give the Ring-bearer the strength to endure another day with its tortured doubts and anguished beliefs of what doom awaits them at the Fire. Sam is strength in his master's weakness, peace in his turbulence, solace in his grief, warmth in his coldness, and sweetness in his bitterness.

Fr. Patrick Hannon does not speak of Frodo and Sam, but his words reveal much about them: "And I remember once again that love – fierce and mighty and unrelenting – has no rival. It gives us permission to face unimaginable suffering unafraid" (*The Geography of God's Mercy*, 47). Frodo and Sam are not without fear, but they are there for each other. In fact, Richard Purtill observes that "their self-sacrificing love rises to such heights as to be comparable to the greatest love the world has known" (*Myth, Morality*, 77). This love never abandons Frodo, for it involves not only Sam's but God's and his own love of all those for whom he bears such torment. Pope Benedict XVI states, "In the end . . . love alone enables us to live, and love is always suffering: it matures in suffering and provides the strength to suffer for good without taking oneself into account at the actual moment" (*Benedictus*, 208). This is what keeps all four hobbits on their Road. Ralph C. Wood notes, "To be a servant is to be liberated from self-concern. It is to be so fully devoted to the common good that one hardly thinks of one's own wants and needs at all" (*Gospel*, 163).

As Frodo and Sam continue their perilous journey, they see torches coming right toward them. The Ring-bearer is sure that there is no escape. Sam allows for this possibility, but he also leaves the door open that it is not the unmitigated disaster that it appears. He is right to do so because by no other means than the forced march that the hobbits endure can they safely travel this part of the Black Land.

Evil defeats itself in two other ways during this time. The darkness Sauron spreads keeps Frodo and Sam from discovery. Without the speed that the Orc leaders unknowingly press upon them, there is also no way, considering the Ring-bearer's worsening condition, that they could have reached the Fire in time to save the army of the West at the Black Gate. The hobbits know nothing of this. St. Leo noted, "On the road you will have to face fatigue and exhaustion, the clouds of sadness, and the storms of fear" (quoted in *Joyful Soul*, 102). The only thing that Frodo sees ahead is the torments of the Tower repeated upon him or something worse, and he has no choice but to drag himself toward this doom. But the outcome of this and the other apparent disasters in the tale should convince us that we should never be afraid. Even if God brings us to the point where we see no way forward without calamity, this is not the only possible fate. Sam sees and hopes farther than his master. After their band comes to a cross-roads just in time to meet up with another company, the gardener takes advantage of the animosity among Orcs to get himself and Frodo away just before the Ring-bearer's faltering strength fails altogether. The timing of everything that happens to us is down to the second for our blessing and redemption, just as for the hobbits. We need to be aware of this and be ready to act, as Sam is without even knowing it.

Within this terrible land Sam again wrestles with despair, but he never lets it conquer him. The gardener does not have the malevolent power of the Ring clutched at his heart like a viper that bites again and again as does Frodo, who must endure its poison. The Bearer fights this with all his strength, but he knows he is weakening. He relies on Sam's hope and strength to fuel him after his own iron will begins to bend under the weight of his burden. Sam shields him as best he can. One of the most touching things about the BBC Radio adaptation is the many times that Sam tells his master, "It's all right," when it most definitely is not, but at the same time, somehow it is because he says so. The humble gardener would agree with Blessed Julian of Norwich, who lived during the Black Death but could still say, "All shall be well, and all shall be well and all manner of thing shall be well."

Sam embraces this approach to life so completely that it does not frighten him that the job he has to do may involve dying beside Frodo after the completion of their task. "At the inner core of any life well lived, moreover, is the love of others, not love as an emotion so much as love understood as a commitment so deep that it seeks the good of the other even to death" (Rutledge, *Battle*, 323). Yet even as the younger hobbit accepts this possibility, he immediately expresses a wish to see Rosie and his family. He realizes that he may not, but rather than have this fill him with despair, he feels strengthened against it. "If" dying is part of the job, he is willing to do it. Later he thinks "if" there is a way back home, it lies beyond the Fire. The two times Sam uses this word are significant. He knows that he must complete his mission first, but as he does not know whether death is all that awaits him and his master, he retains hope for survival. Gandalf aptly names him *Harthad Uluithiad*, Hope Unquenchable (Tolkien, *Sauron Defeated*, 62). Nothing less could have got both hobbits to the Mountain, and nothing else could hope for life beyond it even after it appears there will be none.

After Sam decides, in an effort to conserve Frodo's rapidly dwindling strength, to take the main road again rather than crawling and stooping around, he does not know the risk he takes. This again shows the goodness of not knowing the future, for it could paralyze us from doing what is essential. Children are fearless because they have not been taught to fear. Some lessons in this must be learned, of course, but many others are not necessary and could even cripple us from moving forward if we do not unlearn them. Sam's ignorance of the dangers of this road allows him to make the necessary decision to take it. The hobbits would not have otherwise found water in a muddy cistern that helps sustain them.

Aragorn's description of his struggle with Sauron in the *palantír* as bitter just as aptly describes the Ring-bearer's much more drawn out battle. Tolkien noted in a letter that "the most important part of the whole work [is] the journey through Mordor and the martyrdom of Frodo" (quoted in *Reader's Companion*, 615). Sam sees his master raise his hand to protect himself from being beaten and to hide from Sauron's devouring Eye. These are either from hallucinatory memories of the torment in the Tower or an external reaction to the violation the Ring-bearer feels inside. As the hobbits continue to pass through the Dark Country, not only physically but spiritually, Frodo shows that one of the greater signs of increasing sanctity is that the temptations that seek to destroy us become fiercer and more frequent. Sam watches his master's hand creep at times toward the Ring and then slowly move away as Frodo regains authority.

Though Patricia O'Brien does not speak of Frodo, she still sheds light on the state of his soul in her description of the three stages of the spiritual life on the way to sainthood. "In the purgative, one is being purified and cleansed from sin; in the illuminative one is enlightened and inspired; and in the unitive one is united with the holy will of God so as to say: 'not my will but yours be done.' At the beginning, God shows Himself. During the whole progression, He gives more and more grace and strength while withdrawing sensible consolations and spiritual sweetness, leaving only darkness and aridity" ("God's Silence," *Challenge*, October 2007, 25).

Frodo received solace through grace-filled dreams and visions, but then nightmares began to invade. More and more he suffers the deprivation of adequate sleep, warmth, food, and water. The Ring creates within its Bearer a sense of isolation and loneliness that cuts him off even from his memories. Its weight is an increasingly unbearable burden. The closer the hobbit gets to the Fire, the more the Ring tries to coerce his will. After it can no longer seduce him, it attempts to bypass his will altogether and force itself upon him, which in the end it does. It is no stretch to say that Frodo is a victim of brutal and repeated rapes, not physically but in how such attacks violate the free will choices of the one harmed.

After Sam offers to carry the Ring again, Frodo nearly assaults his faithful guardian in another demonstration of the terrible power of the fell object. The Bearer tells his Sam that he is nearly completely under its control and movingly describes the depth of his agony in the most mystical speech in the tale: "No taste of food, no feel of water, no sound of wind, no memory of tree or grass or flower, no image of moon or star are left to me. I am naked in the dark, Sam, and there is no veil between me and the wheel of fire" (*LOTR*, 916). Frodo is facing the ultimate vulnerability. His ordeal has stripped away every bit of himself and leaves him feeling completely exposed to his Enemy. He has no way to know when the next full-scale attack will come, only that it will and that he cannot hide or protect himself from it.

Yet even in Frodo's darkness, with the fiery Ring as the only illumination he senses, there is still deep union between him and God. Evil continually forces its way into the hobbit's soul, but God is already there to strengthen him in his struggle to keep the demonic power from overwhelming him completely. As Frodo burns upon the kindled wheel, he becomes a candle set alight by both Light and Dark, a figure "clothed in flame" (*LOTR*, 890), as Sam saw by the red light in the Tower chamber. The combination of this torment, God's love for him, and his own love for his world consume him in "a holy sacrifice, truly pleasing to God" (Rom. 12:1).

Words of Fr. Jacques Phillipe easily fit the Ring-bearer at this time.

> Every Christian must be throughly convinced that his spiritual life . . . must be viewed as the scene of a constant and sometimes painful battle, which will not end until death – a struggle against evil, temptation and the sin that is in him. This combat is inevitable, but is to be understood as an extremely positive reality, because, as Saint Catherine of Siena says, 'without war there is no peace'; without combat there is no victory.

And this combat is, correctly viewed, the place of our purification, of our spiritual growth, where we learn to know ourselves in our weakness and to know God in His infinite mercy. This combat is the definitive place of our transfiguration and glorification. (*Searching*, 9)

Colin Gunton notes, "Again and again we are reminded of biblical texts about the way the power of God works not through the great forces of history but through the cross" ("A Far-Off Gleam of the Gospel," *Tolkien: A Celebration*, 133). Frodo carries his on a chain around his neck, just as Jesus travels later toward even deeper evil with His on His shoulders. Joseph Pearce remarks about this as well. "The parallels with Christ's carrying of the Cross are obvious. Furthermore, such is the potency of the prose and the nature of Tolkien's mysticism that the parable of Frodo's burden may even lead the reader to a greater understanding of Christ's burden. All of a sudden one sees that it was not so much the weight of the Cross that caused Christ to stumble but the weight of evil" (*Man*, 112).

Pope Benedict XVI's meditation on the meaning of "Lead us not into temptation" has relevance for Frodo's battle too.

But should it not put us in mind of the fact that God has placed a particularly heavy burden of temptation on the shoulders of those individuals who were especially close to him. . . . Even more, they enjoy a very special communion with Jesus Christ, who suffered our temptations to the bitter end. They are called to withstand the temptations of a particular time in their own skin, as it were, in their own souls. They are called to bear them through to the end for us ordinary souls and to help us persist on our way to the One who took upon himself the burden of us all. (*Jesus of Nazareth*, 164)

Frodo's willing suffering for the "ordinary souls" of Middle-earth is also a channel of grace for any of us who have benefited from his tremendous example of perseverance and endurance through horrific conflict. His death to himself gives us a challenging and inspiring example of what service to God means. Sean McGrath makes note of this.

> And here, in Frodo's agonizing pilgrimage to Mordor and the cracks of Doom the depth of our sacrifice is at last adequately portrayed. For when God asks us to transcend our present state of being he is asking us to break and spend ourselves as relentlessly as Frodo gives his entire being to the quest. . . . Kazantzakis in *St. Francis* [speaks of] the explosive emotions involved in surrendering to transformation: . . .
>
> . . . He who never once said to poor unfortunate mankind "Enough!"
>
> "Not enough," that is what he screamed at me.
>
> "I can't go further," whines miserable man.
>
> "You can!" the Lord replies.
>
> "I shall break in two," man whines again.
>
> "Break!" ("Passion," 177-178)

Jentezen Franklin comments as well about the cost of giving ourselves completely to God. If we apply his words to Frodo's increasing inner light even as the hobbit's torment grows, they give more weight to the insight that Gandalf had in Rivendell.

> Gideon led his puny army into battle with 300 men against 250,000, and all they had were a trumpet and breakable pitchers that held a candle of fire. When Gideon said, 'Break the jars,' those torches flared up. (See Judges 7:19). . . .
>
> You see, the breaking of the glass pitchers represents a willingness to be broken so that God's light can shine forth. (*Believe*, 63)

The Book of Job gives another example of horrific affliction from our enemy, God's ultimate victory, and the reward that we will receive if we remain true to Him. Job will lose everything bit by bit, just as the deprivations of Frodo build. But God will rebuild Job's life, family, and livelihood to be greater than ever because of His child's faithfulness through terrible trials. He allows Frodo to go West to restore life and joy for the same reason.

Things we think we cannot live without surround us, but one day only the true essentials will remain. We may be required to hand over something or someone well loved but never anything or anyone we truly need to achieve our goal and salvation. Frodo is right that he and Sam will not need anything physical at the end of their Road.

Frodo and Sam set their faces toward the Mountain, just as Jesus later sets His to Jerusalem, even while knowing what will come of His journey there. St. Paul, at the end of his missionary travels, will continue to Rome, with the full knowledge that his death will come as a result. None choose the easy way out but embrace their own Passion and Cross and walk the path laid out before them. If they had not, as Sam already noted of other heroes, their stories would not be known. Instead, they run the race, they fight the good fight, they keep the faith (2 Tim. 4:7).

Near the last stage of Frodo and Sam's ordeal, the demonic makes one last attempt to seduce the younger hobbit into despair and abandonment of the Quest. It tells him that death or something even worse is all that awaits, so he might as well just give up now. It uses Sam's own voice, but the humble gardener recognizes it for what it truly is. He tells it in no uncertain terms that he will have nothing to do with it. St. Francis de Sales will note that our enemy does not care how much good we do, just as long as we do not complete any of it. After Sam soundly defeats the voice, he hears a rumble in the earth, "as if some outside power had recognized and resented his decision" (Shippey, *Author*, 140). This voice will come after us also. We must send it away with the same firm answer that Sam does.

Sam's success against the voice refreshes him. Throughout the Quest, he wrestles every despairing thought to the ground and uses every hopeful thought as a shield. "[E]very thought is [taken] prisoner, captured to be brought into obedience" (2 Cor 10:6). Margaret Sinex observes that this "final fixed resistance to despair . . . is explicitly described as a conscious act of will: 'no more debates disturbed his mind. He knew all the arguments of despair and would not listen to them. His will was set, and only death would break it'" ("'Tricksy Lights,' *Tolkien Studies* 2, 108). She contrasts this with the hopelessness of Denethor, who lost his battle because he desired only one future and that was the past. "Sam does not presume to set the terms of his future in Middle-earth and he succeeds where Denethor fails in withstanding the temptation of despair through a heroic act of will" (ibid., 109).

Though Tom Shippey does not speak of Sam specifically, his words still offer illumination regarding this victory: "What one can be absolutely sure about is that giving up does the other side's work for them, and ruins all your own possible futures and other people's as well" (*Road*, 165).

Frodo and Sam are without water for the last two days of their journey and too parched to eat what little *lembas* they have left. They fall many times because they are dizzy from dehydration and breathing the terrible air. But they always set their wills to rise again and so highlight the idea of free cooperation with God's will and grace amid great suffering.

> In their hunger and thirst and drastic deprivation, and especially in their virtual abandonment of all hope, the two hobbits traverse something akin to Christ's own *via dolorosa*, his final path of sorrow to Golgotha. Sam becomes almost a Christopher, a Christ-bearer in his portage of Frodo up the mountain. Having abandoned their mechanical defenses against evil, they also experience a virtual *noche oscura*, the black night of the soul described by the sixteenth-century Spanish mystic, St. John of the Cross. The dark night comes when, stripped of all earthly and human supports, one experiences the bracing strength of reliance on absolutely nothing other than God. . . . Frodo and Sam experience something akin to the Christian mystery of finding their power in their utter weakness. (Wood, *Gospel*, 110-111)

The night before the Quest ends, Sam takes his master into his arms, and they sleep at the foot of the Mountain. Marion Zimmer Bradley observes, "This growth in intensity, this closing the distance between the two, each change documented and studied, is surely one of the most compelling analyses of heroic friendship" ("Men," 122).

Throughout the grueling trek to the Fire, but particularly in its last stages as exhaustion reduces Frodo and Sam to crawling, the hobbits live out the words of Louis L'Amour that "Victory is won, not in miles, but in inches." Sam had already sworn that he would carry his master if need be, and so he does. He expects to find the combination of Frodo and the Ring a terrible weight that he wonders how he will ever carry. But instead his burden is light. The Bearer has been burned away as Gandalf the Grey was. Richard Mathews remarks, "At the time when they are at their furthest extreme from hobbit-hole comfort, when their strength is not sufficient to their cause, a final lightening of their load comes as an unexpected blessing. When strength and will have stood their test in the face of the hopeless defeat (the Northern courage), Tolkien allows a final gift of grace which makes that strength suffice" (*Lightning*, 52). Sam carries Frodo halfway up the Mountain and then begins to crawl. "We are not at our best when we are perched at the summit. We are at our best when climbing – even when the way is steep" (Anon.). Though not speaking of the hobbits, words of Dag Hammarskjöld are applicable to them: "When the morning's freshness has been replaced by the weariness of midday, when the leg muscles quiver under the strain, the climb seems endless, and suddenly, nothing will go quite as you wish – it is then that you must not hesitate" (*Markings*, 105). Sam goes as far as he can before his will and strength are, for the moment, unable to advance further.

After Frodo and Sam stop, the gardener sees that the Road going from Sauron's Tower to the Sammath Naur is in good repair. Again evil thwarts itself, for the hobbits use this to carry the Dark Lord's doom to him. The sight of it renews Sam's hope that they will succeed in their task. While they rest, grace touches them again, as they hear and heed a call in the heart to continue. Even though they do not understand its urgency, they still obey. This essential trust and faith is what we need to have also if we are to accomplish what God wishes us to do. The Ring-bearer responds with the dying embers of his will and strength and crawls to the path with his faithful companion.

Once Frodo and Sam reach the Road, the elder hobbit responds to a coercive urge to face the East. For a moment he sees the top of the Tower of Barad-dûr and glimpses the Eye. His will to resist the call of the Ring remains, but it is no longer strong enough to succeed on its own. Sam responds to Frodo's soft plea for help by gently holding his master's hands as one would in prayer and blessing them with a kiss. Tolkien's careful choice of words again conveys an important message. The detail of exactly how the gardener holds Frodo's hands show that "Sam redeems Frodo in a spiritual sense" (Gardner et al., *SparkNotes*, 231). The devoted servant seeks to protect the Ring-bearer's soul, just as much as the Ring attempts to devour it. That only a tender grasp is necessary to completely stop what a moment before was an irresistible compulsion proves the greater force of love.

Frodo's struggle and Sam's blessed aid demonstrate once more that our will alone is not always enough to resist the temptation before us. We need others to reinforce our flagging strength and build a wall between us and the thing that seeks to destroy us. Whenever we feel we are about to go under, we need to grab onto whatever lifeline there is and cry out to a friend or to God. This moment in Frodo's life also shows what may be uncontrollably alluring to one person has no power over another. All sin and addiction work this way. Alcohol, nicotine, drugs, pornography, or gambling may hold no attraction for some but have complete power over others.

Even though Sam now fears that Sauron has seen him and Frodo and capture is not far off, he still refuses to despair. He takes his master onto his back again, and they continue up the Mountain. Before they can enter the Ring's nefarious birthplace, however, Gollum attacks them. But even Frodo's own lust for the Ring serves a good purpose, as it revives the last flickers of his will and enables him to break free. He makes another prophetic declaration of the manner in which Gollum will meet his death.

In a vision, Sam sees his master's shining soul shorn of the veils of flesh that surround it. Even though the Ring has tried to destroy this, God has preserved it in all its glory. At the same time, Sam also sees the wheel of fire, which has slowly burned itself into Frodo's being. This double image of a pure figure but also one unreachable through pity shows how close the Ring-bearer is to falling off the edge other white-robed figures have or could have. On one side is Saruman, whose lust for the Ring's power conquered him. On the other is Gandalf the White, who remains angelically good and able to withstand such temptation while completely aware he would be overcome if his will did not remain strong. Galadriel stands by Gandalf, having endured her test. Close to them, but still far enough apart to be alone, is Frodo, his soul on the knife's edge. Sam's vision gives him an exterior image of the terrible inner battle that has torn the Ring-bearer apart for months. The gardener sees the brightness of his master's light but also the terrible power at Frodo's fingertips while the Ring rests against his heart. After this transfiguration, Sam's normal sight beholds the Bearer as a spent figure gasping for breath and consumed by both Light and Dark.

After Frodo walks wearily but upright toward the fulfillment of his vocation, Sam is left alone with Gollum. Here the thread upon which doom hangs is thinnest. Whether it snaps altogether depends upon the actions of an angry hobbit, who has longed for the opportunity before him. As it seemed for Bilbo in that dark tunnel, to kill such an evil creature appears the only prudent thing to do. But something keeps Sam's wrath in check, just as something kept Bilbo's fear from overwhelming him—the same something actually. After pity can no longer stir Frodo's heart, it reaches Sam's because the gardener held the Ring himself and felt a small degree of the agony that each Bearer endures. This tremendous moment of growth for Sam bears within it the final good fruit coming from the torment that the young hobbit felt after his master's apparent death. He does not hate Gollum any less, but he spares him out of newborn compassion and freely wills to let him live. The extension of mercy at this critical moment is the pinnacle of all that Sam has done for Frodo and the culmination of all that was given previously by Bilbo, the Mirkwood Elves, Frodo, and Faramir. Had just one of these not performed their own act, Sam would not have had his opportunity to choose to do the same. The pity of Bilbo does indeed rule the fate of many, but ultimately the pity of Sam rules the fate of all. All of his myriad other sacrifices have brought him and Frodo this far, but another one is necessary to fulfill the Quest. If Sam had not given up his desire for Gollum's death, everything else he and Frodo did could have proved vain. But Sam does not act from any of this anymore than Bilbo did in his own equally momentous decision. Only the Writer of the Story knows the consequences of both choices and the others that have come in between. This is why we should also give mercy to an enemy if at all possible because we do not know the future and how such compassion, or the lack of it, will impact us or those we love.

Chapter Twenty-Four

The Edge of the Abyss

"**M**an always travels along precipices," Blessed Pope John Paul II said. "His truest obligation is to keep his balance." Frodo loses his at the Sammath Naur after enduring a months-long demonic siege of his body, mind, heart, and soul. Bit by bit, the Ring has eroded his self away, but his torment is also his glory. Gunnar Urang notes that "the world is saved, ultimately, not just by grace as overwhelming presence and power but by grace as humble redemptive suffering" (*Shadows of Heaven*, 117). Kreeft observes that "the self is saved only when it is lost, found only when really given away in sacrifice. True freedom comes only when you bind yourself to your duty" ("Wisdom," 46). This the Ring-bearer has done to the utmost. At the end of his task, he drinks the last dregs of a bitter cup and has no strength left to endure the Ring's most horrific assault.

While men are willingly fighting and dying at the Black Gate in the blind hope that they can give Frodo and Sam the time that they need, and Éowyn speaks of feeling as though she stands upon the edge of an abyss, Frodo truly does in body and soul. He passes beyond the point where his mortal flesh and will can withstand the Ring's malevolent power. "The cords of death encompassed me; the torrents of perdition assailed me" (Ps. 18:4, NRSV).

As the Ring consumes its Bearer, Sam hears terrible words come from his master: "I have come. . . . But I do not choose now to do what I came to do. I will not do this deed. The Ring is mine!" (*LOTR*, 924). Does this pronouncement, however, truly convey what seems a free renunciation of the Quest, or does it instead demonstrate a reality that is the opposite? It must be noted again that every word in this tale was deliberately chosen to convey something in particular. Some of the most respected Tolkien scholars, including Tom Shippey and Verlyn Flieger, not to mention Tolkien himself, consider the words "I do not choose" to mean literally this. Frodo does not claim the Ring; it claims him. He is not perpetrator but perpetrated upon.

Shippey remarks, "It is . . . interesting that Frodo does not say, 'I choose not to do', but 'I do not choose to do'. Maybe (and Tolkien was a professor of language) the choice of words is absolutely accurate. Frodo does not choose; the choice is made for him" (*Author*, 140). Flieger observes, "His use of *choose* and *will* makes it clear that he believes he is acting freely. But the negative, the repeated *not* is telling evidence that his will has been perverted and his choice preempted" (*Splintered Light*, 153-154; italics in original). Tolkien noted, "At the last moment the pressure of the Ring would reach its maximum – impossible . . . for any one to resist" (*Letters*, 326).

Frodo's will is the least free at this time than at any other. He felt the Ring's compelling power many times throughout the Quest and already knew he could not surrender it. The fell object has seduced, enslaved, obsessed, and increasingly attempted to possess him for months. Now through the most brutal of the rapes Frodo has had to endure, it overrules what little is left of his own will, coerces him to betray the Quest and to briefly become another Mouth of Sauron.

But though Sauron rules in Mordor, his authority is not absolute. Even at the black heart of his strength, where even a phial containing the captured light of a Silmaril cannot shine brightly, there is still one Power that he cannot crush. As Frodo, small, spent, and mortal, stands defenseless and exposed to his Enemy, he is also just as visible to God, who had set the hobbit aside as His Ring-bearer. His. In spite of what the Ring twisted Frodo into, he remains a holy vessel, who was given a sacred task that no other could perform, for no other was made to do so.

Only *after* Frodo fulfills his vocation does his will fail at last. "The Other Power then took over: the Writer of the Story (by which I do not mean myself)" (Tolkien, *Letters*, 253). Even if Ring-bearer and Ring-destroyer were thought to be one and the same, they were always two different missions in God's mind. He knew it would be too much for one person to bear. None of us could carry such a terrible cross and not crumble under it.

In requesting that Frodo become Bearer, God asked for everything that His child had to give. Months of demonic torment wore the hobbit down to the point of becoming the Ring's puppet, but he also spent this time in grace-filled service to his Creator. At the nadir of Frodo's strength and the height of the Ring's, God turns the no that comes from His child's broken will into the yes foreseen from all eternity. Wilfrid Stinissen observes, "In God's hands, our very enemies are the ones who benefit us most" (*Into Your Hands, Father*, 29). Though these words were not written about Gollum, they easily apply to him. Marion Zimmer Bradley notes that the miserable creature's fall into the Fire "is more, far more, than accidental. . . . In 'saving' his 'precious' from destruction, he *genuinely* saves Frodo, whom he loves as much as he hates, from destruction too" ("Men," 123; italics in original). As Gollum completes the Quest and fulfills his own vocation, Frodo's soul passes beyond the moment of its greatest peril. He receives the same mercy and compassion that he originally gave to his brother Bearer, who was a child of God just like himself. "Happy the merciful: they shall have mercy shown them" (Matt. 5:7).

By working through Gollum's lust, God shows that He can accomplish His will through whatever instrument He chooses. Sean McGrath notes that Gollum's "hate is channeled into obedience to a higher plan and becomes the catalyst of transformation. Gollum serves Frodo until the bitter end much as Judas remains in Jesus' company; because his hate, his violence, plays a crucial role in the outcome" ("Passion," 181).

St. Paul will say God "had especially chosen me while I was still in my mother's womb," (Gal. 1:15). Sméagol was also. Sometimes God chooses the most unclean vessels to achieve some of His most significant work. Saul violently opposed the Church and sought to destroy it before he became one of its most fervent promoters and was renamed Paul. St. Augustine and St. Mary of Egypt were great sinners before they became great saints. Gollum was long in the Enemy's possession, but God uses him to achieve Sauron's defeat.

That God waits to claim victory until it appears that evil has won is completely in keeping with the way He works. He allows the Ring to overcome Frodo, just as later death claims Jesus. After demonic victory seems assured both times, God reclaims what is His to demonstrate no one is stronger than Him.

C. Baillie speaks beautifully of this.

> Love watched [Frodo] all the way through Mordor. "You can do this and you must do this, or I will demand a reckoning of you," Love said. Then Frodo came to the brink of utter damnation and fell, and Love said, "This is beyond your strength, what I am allowing to happen. Therefore I will not demand reckoning of you. I will save you."
>
> In that instant, when [Frodo's] soul hung imperiled between life and eternal night, he became no longer responsible. The trial had become too much.
>
> So, no, I don't think Frodo failed, not morally. Because nothing he could give could save him, only something given to him.
>
> Only Love. ("Frodo and Grace," *entropyhouse.com*)

We would have cause for despair if we had only ourselves to depend upon while everything appears to fall into ruin around us. Fortunately, we can also rely on the power of God. He will carry us through every difficulty if we allow Him. "I know the plans I have in mind for you . . . plans for peace, not disaster, reserving a future full of hope for you" (Jer. 29:11). Such is the love God weaves about all His children. We must trust that He will take care of us, just as Frodo, Gandalf, Aragorn, Faramir, and Sam do.

After Sam carries Frodo out of the Sammath Naur, the Ring-bearer demonstrates once more the growth in grace that came from his fearful but willing embrace of his calling. He recalls Gandalf's words that Gollum would have a special role. The Ring-bearer is intimately aware of the ability of evil to twist one, so his last words about his wretched guide, brother, and betrayer contain a plea for forgiveness. This he does from his heart despite the treacheries that were mysteriously a necessary part of his journey.

Frodo then gently tells his beloved Sam that there is no hope left for them. There is no place that they can go, no other thing to do but to die. But the gardener stubbornly refuses to surrender to despair, even in the face of imminent death. "This is the nature of the 'hope against hope'; it continues when human possibility is at an end" (Rutledge, *Battle*, 136). Though these words do not refer to this moment, they are still relevant to it. Sam coaxes his master further away from the Cracks of Doom. Frodo has shown docility to the guidance of others the entire Quest, and so he allows his guardian to lead him to where the Eagles come to rescue them. Neither hobbit have any idea this will happen, but it shows another instance of Sam's soul in such union with the action and will of God that even on an unconscious level he obeys. The hobbits stand in a small area that is not yet overwhelmed by the lava streaming toward them. Their last strength is spent but not Sam's last hope. His heart still hopes because it still beats. As he caresses Frodo's bleeding hand, he allows room for miracles and speaks of his desire to listen to someone tell the story of the Ring and its Bearer. This moment is "the pinnacle of the two hobbits' friendship" (Gardner et al., *SparkNotes*, 246).

Sam accepts that there is a near certainty his physical eyes will not see the golden dawn that he has long gazed upon with the eyes of his heart. But just as Gandalf was mirthful as the storm of battle was set to break upon Minas Tirith, the hobbit perceives more than what his senses tell is in front of him. He still hopes for a bright future, even if he and Frodo do not survive to see it.

Sam receives his reward after he wakes in Ithilien and sees Frodo sleeping contentedly beside him. To his utter amazement, he also sees Gandalf alive and well. The elder Ring-bearer soon wakes and joy and laughter refresh the souls of both hobbits. They come before Aragorn, who fulfills another of the gardener's dearest wishes by treating them to a song of their Quest. The minstrel introduces it in almost the same way Sam had speculated bards would when he told Frodo at the Mountain how he imagined their story would be told. Reunions with Merry, Pippin, Legolas, and Gimli follow.

Chapter Twenty-Five

Gifts

The days stretch slowly by in Minas Tirith after the men leave for the Black Gate. As no word comes back of their virtually certain doom, the suspense of those left behind grows ever more intolerable. Yet there is still life and hope for those open to embracing it.

Faramir proves as much Hope Unquenchable as Sam. He sees life through a different lens than Denethor, who was Despair Unquenchable. If doom is indeed about to fall, the new Steward tells Éowyn that he hopes to meet it with a unshakable heart, which is again the opposite of his father.

The greatest manifestation of Faramir's hope comes as the world seems poised upon absolute ruin. He and Éowyn suddenly witness in the far distance what may be the end of their world, but the young man is not at all convinced of this. He says that it appears that such has come, but he immediately remarks upon the wisdom of his heart, which denies this and rejoices instead.

Faramir speaks at the same time that Sam and Frodo are in the midst of the cataclysmic destruction of Mount Doom. The Ring-bearer's reason had told him they were at the end, just as Faramir's does, but Sam's heart, just as the man's, was full of joy and not about to give up hope. The fulfillment of Pippin's vocation to save Faramir's life comes as the young man frees Éowyn from the despair that still held her prisoner after Aragorn called them both back from the Shadow. She had thought death in battle was the only way she could gain the peace she desires. But Faramir's gentle courting shows her another path and allows her to have a joy-filled life at last.

By the time Aragorn, Gandalf, and the four hobbits come to Minas Tirith, the tale of Frodo of the Nine Fingers has already grown into a legend. Ioreth tells a cousin that one of the brave little creatures had gone into the Black Land with only his servant and fought Sauron personally. Frodo has indeed struggled long against his Enemy but not in the way the wise-woman means.

The contrary reactions to Aragorn of Denethor and Faramir are again seen as the young man kneels in front of his king and asks for permission to give up his position as Steward. Such humility had long deserted Denethor, but Aragorn allows Faramir to retain his title and promises that the line of Stewards will continue.

Aragorn fully and humbly acknowledges that he is king primarily through the valiant efforts of others. All his own toil would have been meaningless if the Ring had not been destroyed. The man asks Frodo to take the crown and Gandalf to place it upon his head, for he is aware of the great debt that he owes them. "All three heroes converge at the crowning, as the past and present make their gift to the future" (Ellwood, *Good News*, 141).

Aragorn's heart is not yet at rest, however, as he still looks for an indication that his reign shall be blessed. He also yearns for the fulfillment of his long-held desire to wed Arwen. Gandalf takes him away from the City to the abandoned hallow on Mindolluin, where the ancient kings once gave God praise and thanks. There the cloaked Maia shows the man a young tree growing. The sprouting of this sapling is the grace-filled sign that the king was hoping to find. He brings it back to replace the dead tree in the Court of the Fountain. Arwen and her father soon follow from Rivendell for the long-awaited wedding.

Frodo's words upon Arwen's arrival contain a hint that not all is well with him. He once enjoyed traveling at night, but now he carries physical and psychological scars from assaults that occurred in the dark. But the sight of the Evenstar restores his love of the night and removes his fear of it.

Arwen clearly perceives the internal wounds that Frodo bears from his bitter battle against Sauron. The damage she sees in the hobbit's soul is perhaps similar to her mother's, who was so deeply hurt centuries earlier by the slaves of the Enemy that she fled West to seek healing there. The queen now gives the Ring-bearer, a mortal being, the rarest of all possible graces: the same opportunity and hope. She also gives Frodo a gem to help him combat the terrifying memories of his nightmare journey.

Many others receive presents as well. Representatives of all the races who dwell in the Light grace the funeral of Théoden. Faramir receives Éowyn's hand, which is a gift from Boromir through Pippin and Merry. Éowyn gives Merry the horn of Eorl the Young, which he will put to good use later in rousing his fellows in the Shire to oust the ruffians.

On the way back to Rivendell, the Fellowship of the Ring and their Elven guests stop at Orthanc, where they meet Treebeard. The shepherd of the trees reveals that Ents destroyed many Orcs in the Wold. If they had not aided the men of Rohan in this way, the warriors would not have gone far or had any place left to come home. Here Aragorn, Legolas, and Gimli part company with the others.

As the dwindling group continues, they meet Saruman and Wormtongue upon whom they bestow more gifts. Gandalf once more offers his aid to his former superior, but the ruined Maia rudely rejects it. He is certain that Galadriel chose this particular route to smugly enjoy his misfortune. She replies that it was instead lucky that they met, for the wizard now has a final possibility of redeeming himself. Through His children, God offers the fallen Maia many opportunities to save his soul, but Saruman stubbornly chooses to remain in his sin. Our Father will not abandon His quest to bring us back either if we stray. Nonetheless, He makes it our choice to take or refuse the hands that He extends through the efforts of His servants. In slapping away every chance that mercy and compassion give Saruman, the wizard rejects the offered rope and prefers to drown. After Gandalf gives Wormtongue a chance to part from Saruman, the wretched man chooses fear over freedom in his refusal to embrace this longed-for desire and remains instead with his abuser.

A joyous reunion with Bilbo in Rivendell is another gift given and received by the hobbits. Yet mixed with this happiness is Frodo's longing for the Sea and release from the heavy burden he still carries. Before the four hobbits return home, Bilbo gives them some material presents as well.

Barliman Butterbur also receives the blessing of the hobbits' company and news from them and Gandalf that sets his mind at ease. Sam reunites with his beloved pony, Bill. As they depart, the Breelanders see a glimpse of the great light that Gandalf holds within himself. The wizard anticipates the gift of a rest from his labors and a long talk with Tom Bombadil.

Chapter Twenty-Six

Mercies Given

$\mathcal{F}$rodo, Sam, Merry, and Pippin have suffered through more than they ever thought that they could bear, but they come back stronger and wiser because of it. Their trails have taught them much that they could not have learned otherwise. Barliman had noticed how much they had changed and said he had no worries that they could handle whatever trouble was rumored to be in the Shire. Gandalf goes so far as to say their ordeals were to equip them to take care of such things.

As the hobbits come home, they are quite vocal in their views about the ridiculous new rules and rulers that have appeared since they left. What made the terrible privations Frodo suffered on the Quest bearable was the thought that he was taking the danger farther away from his beloved home. For the already deeply traumatized Ring-bearer to come back and find it violated is another stab to his heart.

Yet Gandalf's words about the hobbits' growth still ring true. Frodo shows how much he has matured in compassion because of his wounds in expressing his desire to rescue even his despised cousin, Lotho, from the ruffians. This scandalizes Pippin, but the tween's soul has not been torn as badly as the Ring-bearer's, so he does not know all that his elder cousin does. His terrifying brush with Sauron in the *palantír* was soon over and forgotten. But Frodo's endurance of constant demonic assault for months has given him a viewpoint that no untouched hobbit could possibly imagine or understand. As with Gollum before, it gives him a grieved realization for the damage done to Lotho.

In insisting that there be no killing if at all possible, Frodo does not want the peaceful nature of hobbits to change. They know how to defend themselves, but they do not glory in battle like the Rohirrim. They know archery and have great aim with a slingshot in order to bring down animals for food, but they do not kill wantonly like the slaves of Sauron do. The Ring-bearer has not given so much to remove such evil only to see it spring up again in his homeland. He has also become aware that the real battlefield is in the soul. He used every spiritual, mental, and emotional weapon that he could bring to bear just to keep himself together long enough to get to the Fire. He knows, because of the violence done to his own soul, what hatred, anger, and vengeance would do to the souls of his fellow hobbits.

The rebellion that repels the ruffians is a physical one, but it begins as a spiritual one. The invaders had mistreated and jailed any hobbits who had resisted them, which frightened others from acting. Merry's blowing of the horn of Eorl the Young wakes them from their dispiritedness. Once they release themselves from the invisible chains that bound them, they rise up to fight.

Rosie Cotton somehow knows of the victory at the Fire, though she does not know what she knows. She says she was waiting for Sam to return since spring, which is the time the Ring was destroyed. Grace touched her with some sign that her Sam lived still.

Frodo, Sam, Merry, and Pippin move on to Bag End, where the Chief of the ruffians had taken up residence. The Ring-bearer does not take Merry's advice to be ungentle with this leader, who turns out to be none other than Saruman. If Frodo did act on his cousin's counsel, he could not teach his most powerful lesson about pity and mercy after the wizard murderously assaults him. Sam is hot for retribution, but Frodo says that no matter what he does not want any aggressive action taken. Rather than respond with like violence, the Ring-bearer forgives his attacker without anger or hate and as quickly as Sam has forgiven him his own trespasses. Frodo has learned much about the power of this during the Quest. His active but peaceful resistance to Saruman's violence is as effective a barrier to harming him as the *mithril* coat. Even if the wizard was successful and Frodo's lifeblood poured out, his radical words of forgiveness and forbiddance of revenge would have been the same. Clyde Kilby remarks that this compassion "surpasses the norm of ordinary morality. It has the quality of mercy such as Portia calls 'an attribute of God himself'" ("Mythic and Christian Elements in

Tolkien," *Myth Allegory and Gospel*, 137). Only grace could have given the Ring-bearer this and the strength to extend it.

Frodo also does not want his Sam's soul damaged by hate or anger. It would not solve anything but only leave more bleeding wounds. The gardener already learned this lesson in Shelob's lair after he discarded the idea of going after Gollum in order to avenge the wretched creature's betrayal. He practiced such wisdom again in sparing Gollum's life near the Fire, but he needs a reminder of it here.

Once more Frodo displays his gift for spiritual discernment, as he recognizes the goodness that had once been in Saruman before pride and lust for power overwhelmed it. The Ring-bearer wishes for the wizard to receive the same opportunity to find a cure for his afflicted soul that the hobbit had tried to bring about in Sméagol. In fact, Frodo saves Saruman's life twice over because the defeat of Sauron means the wizard will not be sought and punished for being a traitor to the cause of Mordor.

Saruman does not realize this. He believes that his life is in ruins. He no longer comprehends mercy and pity because he has forsaken them. Upon seeing the terrible wounds in Frodo's soul, he realizes that such agony has not turned the hobbit to darkness, but instead it has caused a growth in grace and light that the corrupt wizard had long abandoned himself. He is so lost that rather than accept Frodo's loving gift, the offer enrages him. Those who do evil do not like reminders that they are no longer who they should be and that what they are doing is wrong. They would rather dwell in their darkness so their deeds are not exposed. Saruman refuses the antidote to what poisons his soul with his most venomous hatred yet.

We should respond as Frodo does after we see the torment of others reflected in their eyes, words, and actions. Compassion moves us to pray for them or to guide them, so that they can find the Light. As gentle love and sorrow for the state of their soul confronts them, they may react as bitterly as Saruman but perhaps only in the beginning. What they see and feel from us can also bring healing, peace, and hope, if their heart is open enough to run, stumble, or crawl toward it. Wormtongue begins to wish to do this in response to Frodo's kind words to him. Saruman's soul unfortunately continues to spiral down into the abyss. His violent death, so sudden and unexpected, comes as a result of the abuse he heaped upon Wormtongue for years. The miserable man's own equally quick death follows shortly after. We must be prepared for our end at any moment because we do not know when it will come.

After Saruman's death, his soul rises from his body and is seen for a moment facing the West. He seeks at last to repent and to seek forgiveness, but he has slammed the door each time mercy offered aid before. The way is now shut forever, and he shut it himself. His realization of this fact comes too late, for no decision can be changed after death. The myriad choices he made to rebel and the chances of redemption he rejected now solidify and become permanent.

While we are alive, our choices are fluid, and there is always a chance that we can find our way back if we stray. Beyond our own decisions that determine whether heaven or hell is our final home, there is also God's mercy and love, which we depend upon to make it into heaven at all. He understands that our will is less free at times to make choices for the good, and that the more we delve into darkness, the more imprisoned we become. But if we are at all open to the grace God wishes to give us to help us make it back home, He will take us there. We can also rebel and not come to Him. God does not force heaven upon anyone if they have plainly chosen another route. He respects our decision even if it means that we are lost to Him forever. The Valar reject Saruman, as he rejected them earlier.

The last lesson in compassion that Frodo teaches is rescuing Lobelia Sackville-Baggins from the lockholes. The bad blood between them would not have healed if the Ring-bearer had not gone on the Quest and learned so much. Much good comes from this mended relationship, as Lobelia restores Bag End to Frodo and leaves money for homeless hobbits in her will.

In a way, Sam's Ring-induced fantasy of becoming a gardener of a realm comes true after he takes advantage of the dust Galadriel gave him from her orchard and uses it throughout the Shire to repair the damage done. This does not take away the hobbit's humility as use of the Ring would have in replacing the waste of Gorgoroth. He knows the power to heal the Shire of its lost trees does not reside with him but in the Elven gift he received.

A baby boom results as the hobbits celebrate their freedom from the ruffians and treasure the peace and blessings that they always had but took for granted. Such gifts are sweeter now in the reclaiming of what was lost.

Though Sam "longs to stay with Frodo forever," (Bradley, "Men," 124) he also wants to be with Rosie. Frodo grants both wishes after Sam accepts the invitation to live with his master after the wedding. With both sides of his heart beside him to cherish, he has another wish come true. Yet Sam's heart aches that Frodo does not receive the honor that is due him for all that he did for his fellow hobbits. They see and laud the efforts of Merry, Pippin, and Sam in restoring the Shire, but they have no interest in deeds done outside the borders of their land. Frodo's combat was done within his heart and soul, unseen by any but for the glimpses that Sam had.

Sam and Rosie's first child is born on the second anniversary of the destruction of the Ring, which is a fitting reward for the sacrifices made by both Ring-bearers'. With the proud father at a loss for a proper name, Frodo suggests Elanor. She is the only child he is there to welcome. The ordeal of the Quest has left horrific marks on his soul, and there is no peace for him.

Arwen, Galadriel, and Gandalf had already noted that the Straight Road to the West would be necessary for Frodo, but none pressured him to accept the blessing. Both paths, to stay or to leave, were deliberately left open to him. He could have chosen to live with chronic pain, but he also had a chance to relieve his suffering through a virtually unheard-of boon. Either way would require sacrifice. He receives the time to reconcile himself to the fact that leaving is a terrible necessity if he has any hope of healing. By the time Elanor is born, there are only six months left before he leaves his home forever.

Elrond had told Frodo to look for Bilbo in the Shire during the autumn, but the Elf-lord did not give the exact time or location. Still somehow the Ring-bearer knows. Perhaps the Vala Irmo had sent it through another prescient dream, or there was a communication from Rivendell kept secret from Sam, or a prompting in Frodo's heart. The timing of his departure from Bag End with Sam is significant, as it begins a day before his and Bilbo's birthday, just as the original Quest began the day after. The journeys of both Bagginses will now continue far beyond the bounds of their home. There is another battle that they must fight. This time it is to cleanse their souls from the damage caused by the Ring, and this can no longer be done in Middle-earth.

In Frodo's embrace of the grace that the Valar gave him, the seemingly powerless hobbit gains by sacrifice the home that Saruman forsook out of lust for power. The Ring-bearer leaves Middle-earth and nearly all he loves with nothing but the clothes on his back. Yet he still takes everything that he needs, for he has the same spiritual goods that he carried on the Quest. He has Sam's love, trust that he will be taken care of, humility to accept another difficult task which he will do his best to accomplish, and detachment as ever more is taken from him. Looked at through this lens, we realize what riches he has and what he teaches us about the journeys we may be called to take far away from everything that is familiar.

Change is inevitable and sometimes painful, but it also allows us to emerge as the glorious being we are meant to become. God did not choose Frodo and then leave him without a chance to live with joy again. Our Father does not wish us to remain shattered either. The Ring-bearer went East, but broken by the darkness there, he travels West to be re-made. Even before he left his home the first time, he understood that the life of any child of God is sacrifice. He was willing to give up everything to save those he loved. He makes another sacrifice now to save himself. Kurt Bruner and Jim Ware movingly observe what this means to Frodo.

> Great sacrifice was necessary to defeat evil. Frodo had been chosen to carry a load none other could bear and fulfill a task none other could endure. Though Frodo was only one of many who had given up something for the greater good, none had suffered such direct confrontation with darkness or remained as faithful when tormented by the terrifying, possessing power of wickedness. Such was his role, to lose that others might gain. And so, by completing his scene in the story, Frodo Baggins also performed its most heroic part. . . .
>
> . . . From soldiers storming the beaches of Normandy to free Europe from tyranny to a frightened hobbit willing to destroy the Ring of Doom, every heroic

act is a reflection of the ultimate hero of history, Jesus Christ. . . . He faced death to give life, endured sorrow to restore joy, confronted hate to show love. He humbled himself to the point of death on a cross to pay for our redemption. He was chosen for a burden none other could bear and a task none other could endure. (*God in "LOTR,"* 105, 106)

Frodo's last sacrifice is one that Sam makes also. Clearly the elder hobbit does not want to part from his beloved guardian a moment sooner than absolutely necessary. He tells Sam that, as a fellow Ring-bearer, the same opportunity to travel West is open to him. This hope that they may see each other again helps give them the strength to part. Frodo further announces that Sam is now his heir and presciently names several more of his friend's children, who he has been blessed with the consolation of knowing will come. He also notes that Sam will be Mayor. With all this foreknowledge, Frodo knows that the brother of his heart will be happy and fulfilled.

Gimli's earlier lament to Legolas about parting from Galadriel echoes here. Sam would also crave more than memories and wish to have Frodo at his side to watch over and nurture. But both dwarf and hobbit let go of the one they love. Frodo and Sam's separation is freely made in sorrowful recognition that the most powerful human force in the elder Ring-bearer's life, his Sam's love, was not enough to cure him. This alone shows the terrible depth of his torment.

The Ring gutted Frodo, but his story does not end there. Sam surrenders his master to the arms of the Vala Ulmo, but he has his Rose to hold. Frodo's new life could be his own rose, though he must reach through the thorns of loss to gain it. The rest of his journey is veiled to us, but we hope that Sam came West to see that his beloved master had indeed become the glass completely filled with light that Gandalf foresaw in Rivendell. The Ring-bearer could not have achieved this without first going through the flames. Patti Benson notes beautifully, "Evil found him, and for a brief, terrifying time it took him; but it could not keep him. His light still shone out of the darkness, despite it all" (*Mallorn*, August 2008, 5).

Such light awaits us as well if we remain true.

A Parting Note

Le hannon for taking this journey with me! I hope you will continue down the Road with me in my next book, which will continue to explore the rich spirituality of Middle-earth at the end of the Third Age.

I am also planning another book, which will detail the myriad ways these tales and peoples have changed lives in our own Age. Many have kept on their own dark Roads because of Frodo's inspiring example or drawn strength, guidance, and hope from the other shining heroes throughout the tales. I would be eager for any stories you wish to provide! You can reach me at annemarie@annemariegazzolo.com. God bless!

Bibliography

Agan, Cami. "Song as Mythic Conduit in *The Fellowship of the Ring*." *Mythlore* 26, no. 3/4 Issue 101/102 (Spring/Summer 2008): 41-63.

Arthur, Sarah. *Walking with Bilbo*. Wheaton, IL: Tyndale, 2005.

———. *Walking with Frodo*. Wheaton, IL: Tyndale, 2003.

Auden, W. H. "At the End of the Quest, Victory." Published January 22, 1956. http://www.nytimes.com/1956/01/22/books/tolkien-king.html.

Baillie, C. "Frodo and Grace." Accessed January 7, 2012. http://entropyhouse.com/baillie/candme/essays/frodoandgrace.html.

Benedict XVI. *Jesus of Nazareth: From the Baptism in the Jordan to the Transfiguration*. Translated by Adrian J. Walker. New York: Doubleday, 2007.

———. "Mass for the Inauguration of the Pontificate of Pope Benedict XVI." Published April 24, 2005. http://www.vatican.va/holy_father/benedict_xvi/homilies/documents/hf_ben-xvi_hom_20050424_inizio-pontificato_en.html.

Benson, Patti. Letter to the editor. *Mallorn: The Journal of the Tolkien Society*, August 2008.

Birzer, Bradley J. *J. R. R. Tolkien's Sanctifying Myth: Understanding Middle-earth*. Wilmington, DE: ISI Books, 2003.

Bradley, Marion Zimmer. "Men, Halflings, and Hero Worship." In Isaacs and Zimbardo, *Tolkien and the Critics*, 109-127.

Brisbois, Michael J. "The Blade Against the Burden: The Iconography of the Sword in *The Lord of the Rings*." *Mythlore* 27, no. 1/2 Issue 103/104 (Fall/Winter 2008): 93-103.

Broadway, Cliff, Erica Challis, Cynthia L. McNew, Dave Smith, and Michael Urban. *More People's Guide to J. R. R. Tolkien*. Cold Spring Harbor, NY: Cold Spring Press, 2005.

Bruner, Kurt and Jim Ware, *Finding God in "The Lord of the Rings."* Wheaton, IL: Tyndale, 2001.

Buffi, Giacomo. *The Man Christ Jesus: How the Lord Looked, Acted, Prayed and Loved.* Translated by Charlotte J. Fasi. Manchester, NH: Sophia Institute Press, 2008.

Cameron, Peter John, O. P., ed. *Benedictus: Day by Day with Pope Benedict XVI.* Yonkers, NY: Ignatius/Magnificat, 2006.

Chance, Jane. *Tolkien's Art: A Mythology for England.* Rev ed. Lexington, KY: The University Press of Kentucky, 2001.

Crabbe, Katharyn. "The Nature of Heroism in a Comic World." In *Readings on J. R. R. Tolkien,* edited by Katie de Koster, 54-60. San Diego: Greenhaven Press, 2000.

———. *J. R. R. Tolkien.* New York: Frederick Ungar, 1981.

Croft, Janet Brennan. *War and the Works of J. R. R. Tolkien.* Westport, CT: Praeger, 2004.

Day, David. *Tolkien: The Illustrated Encyclopedia.* New York: Fireside/Simon and Schuster, 1991.

Dickerson, Matthew. *Following Gandalf: Epic Battles and Moral Victory in "The Lord of the Rings."* Grand Rapids, MI: Brazos Press, 2003.

Ellwood, Gracia Fay. *Good News from Tolkien's Middle Earth: Two Essays on the 'Applicability' of "The Lord of the Rings."* Grand Rapids, MI: Eerdmans, 1970.

Finseth, Claudia Riiff. "Tolkien in Winter." Published October 21, 2008. http://www.theonering.net/torwp/2008/10/21/30345-essay-tolkien-in-winter/.

Flieger, Verlyn. *A Question of Time: J. R. R. Tolkien's Road to Faërie.* Kent, OH: Kent State University Press, 1997.

———. "The Music and the Task: Fate and Free Will in Middle-earth," *Tolkien Studies* 6 (2009): 151-181.

———. *Splintered Light: Logos and Language in Tolkien's World.* Rev. ed. Kent, OH: Kent State University Press, 2002.

Forbes, Cheryl. "Frodo Decides - Or Does He?" *Christianity Today,* December 19, 1975, 10-13.

Forest-Hill, Lynn. "Boromir, Byrhtnoth, and Bayard: Finding Language for Grief in J.R.R. Tolkien's *The Lord of the Rings.*" *Tolkien Studies* 5 (2008): 73-97.

Franklin, Jentezen. *Believe That You Can*. Lake Mary, FL: Charisma House, 2008.

Fuller, Edmund. "The Lord of the Hobbits: J. R. R. Tolkien." In Isaacs and Zimbardo, *Tolkien and the Critics*, 17-39.

Gardner, Patrick, Drake Bennett, John Henriksen, and Joel Dobson. *SparkNotes: "The Lord of the Rings."* New York: Spark Publishing, 2002.

Goggans, Phillip. "*The Lord of the Rings* and the Meaning of Life." In West, *Celebrating Middle-earth*, 103-107.

Gordon, Barry. "Kingship, Priesthood and Prophecy in *The Lord of the Rings*." Published May 13, 2009. http://uoncc.wordpress. com/2009/05/13/kingship-priesthood-and-prophecy-in-the-lord-of-the-rings/.

Greenwood, Linda. "Love: 'The Gift of Death'." *Tolkien Studies* 2 (2005): 171-195.

Gutton, Colin. "A Far-Off Gleam of the Gospel: Salvation in Tolkien's *The Lord of the Rings*." In Pearce, *Tolkien: A Celebration*, 124-140.

Hammarskjöld, Dag. *Markings*. Translated by Leif Sjöberg and W.H. Auden. New York: Alfred A. Knopf, 1964.

Hammond, Wayne G., and Christina Scull. *"The Lord of the Rings": A Reader's Companion*. Boston: Houghton Mifflin, 2005.

Hannon, Patrick. *The Geography of God's Mercy: Stories of Compassion and Forgiveness*. Chicago: ACTA Publications, 2007.

Hardon, John A., S.J. "Baptism, the Sacrament of Regeneration and the Supernatural Life." Accessed December 31, 2011. http://www. therealpresence.org/archives/Sacraments/Sacraments_008.htm

Harvey, Greg. *The Origins of Tolkien's Middle-earth for Dummies*. Hoboken, NJ: Wiley Publishing, 2003.

Head, Hayden. "Imitative Desire in Tolkien's Mythology: A Girardian Perspective," *Mythlore* 26, no. 1/2 Issue 99/100 (Fall/Winter 2007): 137-148.

Hein, Rolland. *Christian Mythmakers*. 2nd ed. Chicago: Cornerstone Press Chicago, 2002.

Honegger, Thomas and Frank Weinreich, eds. *Tolkien and Modernity 2*. Zollikofen, Switzerland: Walking Tree Publishers, 2006.

Isaacs, Neil D., and Rose A. Zimbardo, eds. *Tolkien and the Critics: Essays on J. R. R. Tolkien's "The Lord of the Rings,"* Notre Dame, IN: University of Notre Dame Press, 1968.

John XXIII. *A Joyful Soul: Messages from a Saint of Our Times.* Edited by Jerome M. Vereb, C.P. Kansas City, MO: Andrews McMeel, 2000.

Kilby, Clyde S. "Mythic and Christian Elements in Tolkien." In *Myth, Allegory and Gospel: An Interpretation of J. R. R. Tolkien/C.S. Lewis/G.K. Chesterton/Charles Williams,* edited by John Warwick Montgomery, 119-143. Minneapolis, MN: Bethany Fellowship, 1974.

———. *Tolkien and "The Silmarillion."* Wheaton, IL: Harold Shaw, 1976.

Klinger, Judith. "Hidden Paths of Time: March 13th and the Riddles of Shelob's Lair." In Honegger and Weinreich, *Tolkien and Modernity 2,* 143-209.

Kocher, Paul H. *Master of Middle-earth: The Fiction of J. R. R. Tolkien.* New York: Ballantine Books, 1977.

Kreeft, Peter. *Making Sense Out of Suffering.* Cincinnati, OH: Servant Books, 1986.

———. *The Philosophy of Tolkien: The Worldview Behind "The Lord of the Rings."* San Francisco: Ignatius, 2005.

———. "Wartime Wisdom: Ten Uncommon Insights About Evil in *The Lord of the Rings.*" In West, *Celebrating Middle-earth,* 31-52.

Larner. "Moments in Time Chapter 35: Jewels of Light." Accessed August 5, 2012. http://www.storiesofarda.com/chapterview. asp?sid=3966&cid=23158.

Luttrell, Marcus with Patrick Robinson. *Lone Survivor: The Eyewitness Account of Operation Redwing and the Lost Heroes of SEAL Team 10.* New York: Little, Brown, 2007.

McGrath, Sean. "The Passion According to Tolkien." In Pearce, *Tolkien: A Celebration,* 172-182.

Mathews, Richard. *Lightning from a Clear Sky.* San Bernardino, CA: Borgo Press, 1978.

Martinez, Michael. *Understanding Middle-earth.* Poughkeepsie, NY: ViviSphere Publishing, 2003.

Merton, Thomas. *Thoughts in Solitude*. New York: Farrar, Straus and Giroux, 1998.

O'Brien, Patricia. "God's Silence." *Challenge*, October 2007, 25.

Palmer, Bruce. *Of Orc-Rags, Phials, & A Far Shore: Visions of Paradise in "The Lord of the Rings."* n.p.: Bran's Head, 1981.

Pearce, Joseph, ed. *Tolkien: A Celebration*. San Francisco: Ignatius Press, 2001.

Pearce, Joseph. *Tolkien: Man and Myth*. San Francisco: Ignatius, 1998.

———. "True Myth: The Catholicism of *The Lord of the Rings*." In West, *Celebrating Middle-earth*, 83-94.

Perry, Michael W. *Untangling Tolkien: A Chronology and Commentary for "The Lord of the Rings."* Seattle, WA: Inkling Books, 2003.

Petty, Anne C. *One Ring to Bind Them All: Tolkien's Mythology*. 2nd ed. Tuscaloosa, AL: The University of Alabama Press, 2002.

Philippe, Jacques. *Searching for and Maintaining Peace: A Small Treatise on Peace of Heart*. Translated by George and Jannic Driscoll. Staten Island, NY: St. Pauls/Alba House, 2002.

Pienciak, Anne M. *Barron's Book Notes: J. R. R. Tolkien's "The Hobbit" and "The Lord of the Rings."* Woodbury, NY: Barron's Educational Series, 1986.

Purtill, Richard. *Lord of the elves and eldils*. 2nd edition. San Francisco: Ignatius, 2006.

———. *J. R. R. Tolkien: Myth, Morality, and Religion*. San Francisco: Ignatius, 2003.

Rateliff, John D. *The History of "The Hobbit" Part One: Mr. Baggins*. Boston: Houghton Mifflin, 2007.

Rosebury, Brian. *Tolkien: A Cultural Phenomenon*. New York: Palgrave Macmillan, 2003.

Rutledge, Fleming. *The Battle for Middle-earth: Tolkien's Divine Design in "The Lord of the Rings."* Grand Rapids, MI: Eerdmans, 2004.

Sale, Roger. "Tolkien and Frodo Baggins." In Isaacs and Zimbardo, *Tolkien and the Critics*, 247-288.

Sheen, Fulton J. *Fulton J. Sheen's Guide to Contentment*. New York: Simon & Schuster, 1967.

———. *God's World and Our Place in It*. Manchester, NH: Sophia Institute, 2003.

Shippey, Tom. *J. R. R. Tolkien: Author of the Century*. Boston: Houghton Mifflin, 2001.

———. *The Road to Middle-earth: How J. R. R. Tolkien Created a New Mythology*. Revised and expanded ed. Boston: Houghton Mifflin, 2003.

Sinex, Margaret. "'Tricksy Lights': Literary and Folkloric Elements in Tolkien's Passage of the Dead Marshes." In *Tolkien Studies* 2 (2005): 93-112.

Slack, Anna. "Slow-Kindled Courage: A Study of Heroes in the Works of J. R. R. Tolkien." In Honegger and Weinreich, *Tolkien and Modernity 2*, 115-141.

Spacks, Patricia Meyer. "Power and Meaning in *The Lord of the Rings*." In Isaacs and Zimbardo, *Tolkien and the Critics*, 81-99.

Stinissen, Wilfrid, trans. *Into Your Hands, Father*. San Francisco: Ignatius, 2011.

Taylor, Taryne Jade. "Investigating the Role and Origin of Goldberry in Tolkien's Mythology." *Mythlore* 27, no. 1/2 Issue 103/104 (Fall/Winter 2008): 147-156.

Theophan the Recluse. "Excerpts from 'The Path to Salvation' A Manual of Spiritual Transformation by Theofan [*sic*] the Recluse." Accessed December 31, 2011. http://www.holytrinitymission. org/books/english/salvation_theofan.htm.

Timco, Amy L. "Weavers, Witches, and Warriors: The Women of *The Lord of the Rings*." *Silver Leaves ... from the White Tree of Hope* (White Tree Fund, Toronto, Ontario, Canada) 1 (2007): 39-45.

Tolkien, J. R. R. *The Hobbit*. Boston: Houghton Mifflin, 2007.

———. *The Letters of J. R. R. Tolkien*. Edited by Humphrey Carpenter. Boston: Houghton Mifflin, 2000.

———. *The Lord of the Rings*. 2nd edition. Boston: Houghton Mifflin, 1965-66.

———. *Sauron Defeated: The History of "The Lord of the Rings," Part 4*. Edited by Christopher Tolkien. Boston: Houghton Mifflin, 1992.

———. *The Silmarillion*. Edited by Christopher Tolkien. Illustrated by Ted Nasmith. Boston: Houghton Mifflin, 2004.

————. *Unfinished Tales of Númenor and Middle-earth*. Edited by Christopher Tolkien. Boston: Houghton Mifflin, 1980.

Treschow, Michael and Mark Duckworth. "Bombadil's Role in *The Lord of the Rings*." *Mythlore* 25, no. 1/2 Issue 95/96 (Fall/Winter 2006): 175-195.

United States Catholic Conference. *Catechism of the Catholic Church*. Liguori, MO: Liguori Publications, 1994.

Urang, Gunnar. *Shadows of Heaven: Religion and Fantasy in the Writing of C. S. Lewis, Charles Williams and J. R. R. Tolkien*. Philadelphia: Pilgrim Press, 1971.

Ware, Jim. *Finding God in "The Hobbit."* [Colorado Springs, CO?]: SaltRiver, 2006.

West, John G., Jr., ed. *Celebrating Middle-earth: "The Lord of the Rings" as a Defense of Western Civilization*. Seattle: Inkling Books, 2002.

Wright, Greg. *Tolkien in Perspective: Sifting the Gold from the Glitter; A Look at the Unsettling Power of Tolkien's Mythology*. Sisters, OR: VMI Publishers, 2003.

Wood, Ralph C. *The Gospel According to Tolkien: Visions of the Kingdom in Middle-earth*. Louisville, KY: Knox, 2003.

Zimbardo, Rose A. "Moral Vision in *The Lord of the Rings*." In Isaacs and Zimbardo, *Tolkien and the Critics*, 100-108.

52620993R00135

Made in the USA
Lexington, KY
04 June 2016